To Live Within

To Live Within

Lizelle Reymond
and Sŕi Anirvân

Introduction by Jacob Needleman

Translated from the French by Nancy Pearson and Stanley Spiegleberg

Morning Light Press

323 North First, Suite 203
Sandpoint, ID 83864

Published by Morning Light Press 2007

Printed in Canada on Acid-free Recycled Paper

ISBN-13: 978-1-59675-016-6
ISBN-10: 1-59675-016-2

MORNING LIGHT PRESS

Morning Light Press
323 North First, Suite 203
Sandpoint, ID 83864

morninglightpress.com

Table of Contents

INTRODUCTION

There exist certain books that quietly appear in the world and quietly live apart from the world, where their inner force moves the hearts and minds of all who chance to find them. Such a book is *To Live Within* by Lizelle Reymond. Originally published in Switzerland in 1969 and in America in 1972, it unfolds both the practical and the metaphysical aspects of the ancient Samkhya tradition of India. As presented to Mme. Reymond by her guide and teacher, Sŕi Anirvân, it may be seen as a source teaching previously unknown in the West, universally relevant regardless of one's tradition or cultural background. As such, this teaching points us to a primordial science that may lie at the source of all spiritual traditions in their presently known forms.

By now, the religions of India and the East have communicated to the West their central idea that the ultimate source of truth and meaning is the Universal Self within ourselves. Philosophically, this is one of the world's most fecund great ideas. And once one begins to study what it really means, this idea can be detected in different articulations and contexts at the heart of all the world's great spiritual philosophies and religious traditions, including the religions of the West in their mystical or esoteric expressions. And as such, as an idea, it has lately become in our culture a source of hope for increasing numbers of men and women yearning for a sense of the sacred in their lives—

something they have found neither in secular humanism, which does not recognize that there are higher levels of conscious identity calling to us within ourselves, nor in the prevailing institutional religious forms of our time, which explain the aim of human life by reference to an external God who to many seems powerless to effect the Good in the great sweep of human history and in the day-to-day experience of one's own personal life.

But the idea of the Self that is our real self is not meant to remain only an idea. It is meant to call us to an entirely new kind of life within the everyday life we are now living. It is a representation in words referring to an actual force that occupies a very central place within the scale of forces in the universe itself. The idea tells us that a human being is meant to live in conscious, palpable relationship to this force—not to settle only for thinking about it, or feeling great interest in it or a sense of wonder about it. In such a case, our socially conditioned sense of self, what we call the ego, would remain with its illusions intact, having absorbed a great idea into itself, while imagining it had transcended itself.

Although the present book often refers parenthetically—and lucidly—to traditional Sanskrit terms and doctrines from the ancient scriptures of India, the knowledge that it offers us is given mainly in scientific and psychological language. And in that language, which has also become the language of the modern era, we are presented with indications, as precise as they are astonishing, of what takes place within a man or woman when there exists a sustained conscious relationship to the energy of the Self. Along with this we are given glimpses of the work on oneself that is necessary in order to touch and then establish within ourselves this transforming conscious relationship.

Of course, no written work by itself can ultimately liberate us from the self-deceptions of our mental and emotional automatism. But the ideas in this book and the form in which they are given by Sŕi Anirvân are a lamp that illuminates the immensity of the question of who I am and what I am meant to be. Part of the book's benevolence is that it must be read slowly. But it cannot be read casually. Attention, seriousness, awareness of need and a willingness to be sincere with oneself: these qualities are essential in order to approach this text and to benefit from the voice of a great spiritual teacher through whom, by means of a process that is as mysterious as it is no doubt lawful, the vast wisdom of India may be reborn in a form attuned to the subjectivity of contemporary man in his contemporary world.

•

In Part One of this book, Mme. Reymond illustrates the process by which her own extensive understanding and acquaintance with Indian culture gave way to the awareness of an entirely different kind of wish in herself. In a previous book she had written how after years of visiting various ashrams and meeting renowned spiritual teachers, and in the midst of the exceptional experience of living in the bosom of a priestly Brahmin family, she was invited by her host to accompany him to meet a certain *sādhu* passing by in a nearby village, a scholar engaged in translating the Vedas. This was to be her first encounter with Sŕi Anirvân. "He has a childlike simplicity," she was told, "and he lives a long way away, up in the mountains." [*My Life With a Brahmin Family,* p. 135]

The meeting took place in the early evening on a veranda. She waited for the man who had brought her to initiate a conversation, but he said nothing. "A strange silence fell upon us," she writes, "enveloping us completely." And the silence persisted, soon becoming heavy and oppressive. "I no longer knew what I was doing. I yearned to escape. My back and neck grew numb ..." and soon she was wondering if she could bear it much longer.

The time seemed without end. But then "the atmosphere seemed to lighten and, at the same time, there came a relaxation of mind and muscles, a slackening of tension in the plants and trees, in the very air itself. My breathing became almost imperceptible, my body felt supple, as light as a feather; I thought that it was filled with a new consciousness that came from the heart."

Two or three hours passed. Night came with the stars and the sounds of crickets. And at a certain moment, her host quietly rose, bowed before

Sŕi Anirvân, as did she, nodding farewell, and both left without breaking the silence.

This was Lizelle Reymond's first inwardly received experience of the conditions created by a master that support what she calls the 'meeting with myself.' "There was nothing left of the emotional impulses that I had known in some spiritual disciplines—impulses of devotion, of self-abandonment, of submission, of a sudden understanding of what was beyond me, of gratitude to those on my path who had opened my heart and mind."

She continues: "This time I felt alone and laid bare in my inner life. And his look held me to the awareness of the moment without any possibility of escape."

This taste of the truth of herself led her, months later, to ask Sŕi Anirvân if she could work with him "under any conditions whatsoever and no matter where." The whole of Part One in this book shows us her years living in the powerful special conditions created by him in his remote Himalayan hermitage. As India itself with its ancient atmosphere of spiritual intensity has seeded the arising of countless spiritually developed men and women, so the "atmosphere" of Sŕi Anirvân's *being* empowers his vast knowledge of both the traditions of India and the nature of the human heart, enabling Mme. Reymond to reach a stage of her inner life where her teacher sends her away to continue her search in the midst of her life in Europe. "I knew," she writes, "that the time lived close to a Master is a period of initiation into all the requirements of life as a whole and that the true discipline would begin for me only when I went back into the world."

Of special interest—among many, many other things—is the light this section of the book throws on the meaning of what is often misleadingly spoken of as the "oral tradition" in the religions of the world. It is not simply a question of words spoken, rather than written down. The oral tradition may here be seen to be the entire web of often invisible psychological, social and physical conditions created by a master, not the least of which is the specific, often silent intensity of the atmosphere created by the being of the teacher and the community of pupils. It is an indispensable aspect of all spiritual transmission. Thus, Lizelle Reymond is sent back, seemingly paradoxically, to work in her life both alone and fully engaged in the companionship of others who are working towards the same aim of inner freedom and the power to love.

A few days before they part, Sŕi Anirvân brings her a recently published book which had been sent to him from Allahabad. He had read it through in one sitting. "Read this carefully," he said. "It contains ideas that are very dear to us and that have been your food in these past years. Look for the people who are working in this direction; they are living for a conscious reality. You will find among them men and women who are capable of carrying an idea." The book was P. D. Ouspensky's introductory lectures on the Gurdjieff teaching, *The Psychology of Man's Possible Evolution*. Lizelle Reymond's subsequent life-long engagement in the Gurdjieff Work is discussed at the end of this book in the account of her life, written by her pupils and companions in the Work. We need only mention here the penetrating light Sŕi Anirvân's teaching throws on some of the deepest levels of the Gurdjieff teaching.

•

Lizelle Reymond and Sŕi Anirvân maintained their intimate spiritual bond through an extensive, extraordinarily dynamic correspondence, and through her periodic visits to him in India. Excerpts from his letters to her, along with other writings and notes by Sŕi Anirvân, constitute the major portions of *To Live Within* including the sections entitled "Facing Reality" and "Rambling Thoughts," which were added in the 1984 edition of the book published by The Coombe Springs Press. The present edition contains all the material from Sŕi Anirvân's letters and from conversations with him contained in both editions.

From the very first pages of the Anirvân material, one becomes aware of a unique concentration and purity of thought—like water drawn from a very deep well. The water is not only clear, but crystalline, and tastes of an energy unlike any other—except perhaps the water one drinks when desperately thirsty. Or, to put it another way, the all-encompassing ideas of Sŕi Anirvân—as they are generously poured out from a boundless cornucopia—are permeated by silence, the silence that may be a reflection of what so deeply affected Lizelle Reymond in her teacher's presence. This concentrated purity of silence helped her to be nourished by what she saw in herself both of the closeness to her of the Self within and, equally strongly, of how great her distance from it was. Recognizing in our own selves, at some level, how difficult it is for us too to accept both what we know we are meant to be and what we actually are, we shall be better prepared for the hard work of understanding the main portions of this book.

Repeated readings of this material bring one to the realization that, in a very real sense, the whole teaching is contained in every part of the book—in every chapter, on every page—even, one may say, in every paragraph and sentence. In this the text itself reflects, on the plane of the written word, the essential idea that the Self permeates all of reality, all of human life, all of nature and all of the cosmic world.

Sŕi Anirvân makes powerful new empirical—and, in a deep sense, verifiable—observations with respect to the details of both the world of nature and the world of human experience—so much so that one begins to understand that this teaching really is a science. Just as the Self, when it is accepted by the human body, reveals and brings true order and light into every cell, tissue, impulse and thought within oneself, so the awakening conscious mind continuously discovers real and new connections between all the phenomena of matter and the human soul. This is science of a kind not only that sees and discovers connections "horizontally" on the plane of ordinary sense-based and logically ordered experience, but science also that sees and discovers "vertical" connections between levels of reality unknown to and unknowable by modern science. The ultimate reality is the great Self, but the energy of this great Self pours into everything and illuminates it in all its facthood and complexity. Call this teaching, if you wish, the "higher empiricism." In this, it can be sharply distinguished from some more familiar forms of what is termed "mysticism," which turn away from the infinitely rich world of nature and the sometimes terrifying forces of human society and human history. In the teachings of Sŕi Anirvân the reader will find a longed-for understanding of one's own intimate and problematic life—just as it is, and yet at the same time illuminated by and referred to another level of conscious unity.

To be sure, the book is arranged in a certain sequence, with chapter headings reflecting various aspects of the teaching—"spiritual discipline," "observation of oneself," "emotions," etc. But as one reads the book, one sees that this is neither more nor less than a literary convention and convenience. Every chapter and nearly every sentence is a world in itself and refers the reader to his or her own experience as well as to the whole of the book and beyond. In short, the book is a kind of hologram in which the whole is sensed everywhere. The reader, therefore, is well warned against any premature attempts at systematization. More importantly, perhaps, the reader is not warned, but well-advised, simply to read and let oneself be stopped inwardly again and again as both the heart and the head are simultaneously touched. It is in this direction that the sacred appears in conscious literature or in a work of great art or in the observations of a true scientist.

•

Perhaps more widely than ever in human history, the world, the very earth itself, is yearning for the unity of mankind. The startling advances of modern technology, combined with the accelerating disappearance of traditional knowledge and the customs that support inner human development, are amplifying the lonely human ego and its tendencies toward resentment, suggestibility, fear and violence. All over the world, the lonely ego grasps for relationship in shared superficial slogans and crusades, in systems of belief, in thin electronic communication, in the secondhand life of media, journalism and consumerism. At the same time, there exists the growing intuition that we human beings are on earth under some unknown sacred obligation—that we are not here for ourselves alone, that we are here to serve something greater than ourselves. The desperation of our culture lies in this direction. There is such an undercurrent of disappointment, such a sense of the immeasurable wasting of human life, not only in the horrendous mass crimes of insane hatred and illusory power, but in all the countless hours and years, all the incalculable human life-energy spent on endlessly trying to satisfy all desires except the need to be able to love, and vainly struggling to protect oneself from all dangers except the danger of sleeping one's life away. And now, it seems, the planet itself, the Angel known as Earth, is crying for mankind at last to take its predestined place in the scheme of creation, sending out its cries in the language of the land, the oceans, the air—everything that lives and breathes and waits for man to "move up."

"The day will come," Sŕi Anirvân writes to Lizelle Reymond, "when the principles of *Samkhya* will deliver the European mind from its present dreams and psychoreligious nightmares." Looking at the world around us, one may well wonder, however, if it is not already too late; one may well wonder if there is still time. As one may well wonder if our own "all-powerful" lonely human ego can ever recognize where the real meaning of our life lies, the real relationship we yearn for. Is there still time for you and me?

One principal message we can draw from this teaching is surely that we do not know the laws of the energy of the Self. For years Lizelle Reymond searched and searched and in one brief encounter with the silence of Truth her whole life began slowly and lawfully to turn towards a new inner order. Then what can we say of the great teachers of our era who, with uncompromising impersonal love, have been doing all in their power to transmit the knowledge of the Self? If in one human life, one moment of relationship to the higher can trump all the laws of ordinary time, is it possible that these teachings which live apart from the noise of the world have already begun to turn the heart and mind of our world? In order for that to be so, it is certain that the essence of such teachings, in order to radiate their influence, need to be received even by a small handful of "thirsty" men and women. Do such people exist? What would it mean for us to work to receive the help that is already here begging to come to us? That is quite a different question, holding a much greater force of hope, than asking about the whole entire world as it is now.

—*Jacob Needleman*

Preface

This book consists chiefly of letters from Sŕi Anirvân to me and of recorded conversations that took place during our numerous meetings, in Almora, in Assam and Bengal. A few of Sŕi Anirvân's essays have been added, as well as 'Rambling Thoughts'[1] shared with his devoted students.

Before his death he read the present text carefully and revised it by shortening certain things or adding what he felt was needed to express better his own ideas. In his lifetime he neither taught nor wrote about his ideas in a dogmatic way but spoke very directly to seekers or passers-by who came to him with their problems, which filled their minds and hearts full of anxiety.

Sŕi Anirvân was a Bâül, a solitary man with no ashram surrounding him, who received in exactly the same way a cloth merchant from the near-by hamlet and a Member of Parliament residing in the District. His approach was very simple. He wanted no sign of veneration. He knew how to listen without haste, even when his available time was limited. One felt in him a widely cultured man, and this impression was heightened by his attitude of respect toward his visitors.

He always spoke with reference to the Science of Samkhya, not the philosophical Samkhya as taught by Vijnana Bhikshu in the 15th century, but that Samkhya which is the essence of life—like a pure Voice coming from the Vedas and the Upanishads, revealing a gnostic wisdom concerning the Fullness of Great Nature and the order of the Cosmic Laws. He made immediately clear to his visitors that to live in accordance with the Cosmic Laws, which are all-powerful, involves following a long course of inner discipline aimed at cultivating mental concentration and giving a right direction to the will. This wisdom is in fact a mystical approach which derives from the primal substance.

Sŕi Anirvân was a Bengali, born the eldest son of Sŕi Raj Chandra Dhar, in 1896 at Mymensing, in the Eastern part of the country. At the age of thirteen he already wanted to follow his father, who had joined the vast Ashram of Swami Nigamananda in Assam; but the Guru of that Ashram decided that he should have a university career in order to be able to serve the Saraswat Sangha to the best of his ability.

Accordingly he went from Dacca, where he first studied, to Calcutta University and there, in 1918, he received the title of Kavyatirtha, the highest degree in Vedic and Panini Grammars. His return to the Saraswat Sangha was a festive day for all the disciples. During each vacation that he spent at the Ashram, he had been for them 'the beloved poet' illuminating the talks of the Guru, and making the work on themselves seem like labouring on the land to bring forth a garden of fruits and flowers.

In time he became Swami Nirvanananda Saraswati and served his Guru faithfully. But after a number of years, one night—with the blessing of his Guru who knew that he would never bow to any other *darsána*—he left the Ashram with only his staff in hand.

As a Bâül, he took the name of Anirvân. It was no doubt Nirvacaniya becoming, with a privative 'a', a-nir-vac-aniya, which corresponds syllable by syllable to in-ex-plic-able in English, the root meaning being clear in the former and figurative in the latter. In general, people called him 'Maharaj', and those who know him: 'servant of the *ṛṣis*.'

Although he never spoke of his past, through his letters we learn of some striking incidents in his life. As a Bâül he simply disappeared, becoming a traditional wanderer through the Himalayas. He lived for some years in a cave at the foot of the Kamakhya Hill in Assam. Later he was discovered apparently as an anonymous 'man walking through the market place'. This was in Delhi where, while working as a tutor, he was translating the books of Rama Tirtha because he thought that the Bengali needed to listen to his voice. He was reputed to have become a consultant on many difficult philosophical problems posed by scriptures ranging from the Bhagavad Gita to the *Gathas* of the old Iranian Prophets.

Still later, some people from Ranchi called on him for help. They wanted to have a few chapters of *The Life Divine* of Sŕi Aurobindo translated into Bengali. This huge work had been written originally in English. Fascinated as he was by the text, Sŕi Anirvân accepted on condition that their Guru, Sŕi Aurobindo, would agree. The result was that Sŕi Anirvân retired for four years to Almora in order to give his whole time to translating the entire work.

Against his will, many people, including refugees, knocked at his door. They harassed him so much that a very simple kind of life was organized around him to protect him; it was devoid of encouragements to stay!

When, in due course, Sŕi Anirvân came to translate the *Third Mandala of the Vedas*, his work became even more intense. He needed more helpers as well as complete isolation. It was at this point that I, among a few others, came into his circle.

At first I felt completely disoriented. We lived near his dwelling in small houses near the forest. In complete solitude the importance of each action was evaluated and accepted as a model of inner discipline on a wider scale. The previous kind of work I had done had equipped me so all I had to do was simply to conform.

To meet him, to work with him, and to attend our gathering every evening to prepare the work of the next day, was an invaluable teaching in itself. At night, we sat around a bowl of rice and a cup of milk. Very little was said. But a real spiritual atmosphere was created. No formal teaching was given but an awareness within oneself became a definite part of one's being.

This stage of life, however, was not to last. We knew that one day he was going to say: 'The work is over. I shall be gone in less than three days.' And so it happened.

As a Bâül he was a completely free man. All that remains are his letters, which contain the kind of advice a Bâül can give:

> *The days that you were here appear so soft through the fading light of the past. We can always flit away to the Infinite through the door of the inner being. Can the march over hills and dales ever end? Remember the expansion is not doing anything, it is only being and becoming. The Spirit is and the manifestation does. It grows from the centre outwards just like the sprouting of a seed, quiescent, and yet the initiator of all movement. Remember that you are both Spirit and manifestation in yourself. That is why I am repeating: Be yourself.*

Endnote

1. *The title 'Rambling Thoughts' was given by Śrí Anirvân to these talks.*

Part One

Life in a Himalayan Hermitage

Chapter 1

Opening the Notebooks

A few months ago I reopened the notebooks filled day by day during the years I lived in the Himalayas. These notes tell the story, as a Hindu would put it, of how I served a Master and of how I came under a spiritual discipline based on the Samkhya teaching.

I did not publish them sooner because I was obeying a rule that was often stated in my presence. It applied to me just as much as to the others who were following the same teaching:

> *Let twelve years go by before speaking about your life here, before forming an evaluation on any subject whatsoever. What will have ripened in you, what will have taken root in your life on all levels will belong to you. Nothing else. Everything you hear has been said thousands of times over thousands of years, and in many different ways. But who is there to listen to it, to understand it, to live it? The living spirituality of India is made up of the sum of the experiences of those who have walked the way before us. In the name of what would you harvest the fruit of another's sacrifice before having paid the price yourself?*

I asked the Master, 'May I mention your name?' He thought awhile and then answered:

Yes, if you like, but I hope you will use it very simply, like a peg on which very ancient thoughts have been hung that are not of my making, nor of yours. But don't be in a hurry to write about all this. Remember that our understanding of life progresses at the speed of a bullock cart. The impatient man runs, greedy for conquest. Our mind has wings and can soar over difficulties, but we have a fine pair of feet to keep in touch with Mother Earth. We have to plow through it and often stumble over roots and stones. Then comes the time for sowing. Our feet dance in joy and this spontaneous joy is the daughter of our soul. Remember that all the real things in life are in accord with a very slow rhythm like the changing of seasons and the coursing of stars. This work in depth is done in darkness, without sound.

Seated around Sŕi Anirvân on one day or another were Hindus, Buddhists, Christians, Muslims—believers or unbelievers—each one carried by his own discipline, his own effort, his own ideal; each one receiving the food he was in need of. We were learning, day after day, how to live within.

Chapter 2

Meeting With Myself

I first heard of Sŕi Anirvân when I was living at Narayan Tewari Dewal, near Almora. I was working on the translation of a book. When I had finished my task, I began to look for sacred texts to send to my publisher. A wandering *sādhu*—little knowing the role he was to play in my life—told me about Sŕi Anirvân, an independent monk, very learned, who lived in a distant village, and who was translating the *Third Mandala of the Vedas* into Bengali. This monk received no one.

I decided to write to him to ask for Vedic texts to be published in France. I doubted whether he would answer. However, a month later a reply came: a refusal. But one sentence in the letter attracted my attention. I decided to write again—this time, without mentioning texts for translation. I spoke from myself asking a question about spiritual discipline.

Two weeks passed. A letter arrived that, with the directness that had already impressed me, gave a date for an appointment two months later after the rainy season. Sŕi Anirvân lived in a valley at right angles to the one where I was living, some sixty miles from Almora. In order to get there across the hill-tops, I would have to hire a guide and a porter and count on a four-day march. I answered, accepting the appointment suggested and undertaking to arrive on the day and at the hour stated.

I have a rather confused memory of the three days I spent in Sŕi Anirvân's Lohaghat hermitage as I was neither prepared for the welcome I was given nor capable of understanding it. The travel notes from that year show that my only preoccupation was to miss nothing of what was said in front of me, to take in everything that happened and engrave it on my memory so as to be able later to recapture the same current of thought.

Nothing was as I had expected. Sŕi Anirvân was neither a Master of *yoga*, nor of spiritual discipline, nor of traditional philosophy; as a result, having spent years in India searching for just these various paths of knowledge, I felt suddenly at a loss. I was consciously aware of a feeling that everything to which I had been most attached was fading away. In Sŕi Anirvân's room no altar was to be seen, no pictures of the gods, just a vista of blue mountains through the french windows.

Sŕi Anirvân appeared frail. He was shy. He wore a long white robe and had a black beard. He had interrupted his work to receive me and had prepared the tea himself. A local cloth merchant who had done some travelling had advised him to serve it to me in a porcelain cup, which had been brought for the purpose. His eyes laughed at my confusion at being shown so much attention, and also with his own pleasure in being able to offer me freshly cracked nuts. He explained that a friend had brought food prepared especially for me and that the same thing would be done the next day. I gathered that he lived on offerings and that everyone around him knew about my visit.

Although I scarcely remember the words that were exchanged, I retain, nevertheless, a deep impression of the hours of silence passed on the terrace of his house where, seated before him, I found myself for the first time 'alone in front of myself'. There was nothing left of the emotional impulses that I had known in some spiritual disciplines—impulses of devotion, of self-abandonment, of submission, of a sudden understanding of what was beyond me, of gratitude to those on my path who had opened my heart and mind; this time I felt alone and laid bare in my own inner life. And his look held me to the awareness of the moment without any possibility of escape.

On the third day I left without knowing whether we would ever see each other again. I went to Calcutta. There, during the winter, Sŕi Anirvân came to see me.

I was at a crossroads in my personal life, in a strange kind of freedom that had cost much suffering. I was facing a choice. But to know the direction rested entirely on one question: 'What is my place in the universe?' I no longer know whether I said those words aloud, but he answered them: 'There I think I can be useful to you, but the road is stony. …'

On hearing these words, I came to an immediate decision: to work with Sŕi Anirvân, if he would allow me that privilege, under any conditions whatsoever and no matter where. He suggested that I should come to him at the hermitage that I already knew, but not until six months later. Nothing was said about the 'gap in time' that was to pass between the moment of my decision and the time of my departure for the Himalayas—a period during which, as it happened, all the opposing currents were unleashed to hinder me from following my way.

Sŕi Anirvân asked me to bring some kerosene, a lamp with two spare globes, and a minimum of personal things. Apart from that, for as long as he would keep me with him, I was to live, according to tradition, entirely under the discipline of his School, on what he would give me, and without being allowed on my side to give anything at all. I was to receive everything from him: food for my body, his teaching and the instruction necessary to enable me to assimilate it on my level of understanding. I was going to discover an aim in every hour of the day, to live as a direct experience, however humble at the heart of life. In Sŕi Anirvân, I had chosen a Master whose gentleness was equalled only by his firmness.

By letter he established our future relationship:

> *I shall be free for you twice a day, the first time after five o'clock, before one of my friends arrives – when he is here, he sits down without disturbing me, sometimes asks a question, and meditates. The second time will be after the evening meal. I know there will be many questions we shall have to discuss together, but if we do it regularly and methodically, we shall say a lot in one hour. The rest of the time, night and day, the house will be plunged in the silence of the Void, so that you will not be able even to feel that somebody is living there beside you.*

Having protected himself in this way from invasion, he failed to add that his kindness and comprehension would follow me step by step. I had a room facing west, with eucalyptus trees, yuccas and ferns outside my french window—a table and a chair in addition to the writing board placed on the floor in the customary way. Some fruit, some sweetmeats were sent to me whenever he received any. And between one conversation and the next my solitude was filled by my vigilant effort to discover myself. I guessed that I was being put to the test. And the test lasted several months without respite.

A young servant used to come for two hours every day, bringing water and milk and to peel and cut up vegetables. I used to make myself a cup of tea early in the morning. The happy surprise for me was the chief meal of the day at eleven o'clock, which Sŕi Anirvân himself prepared. We ate sitting on the floor, side by side, absorbed in the thought of our work. Occasionally, he would speak to me very openly, helping me to catch the trend of his thinking. When this happened, the hours that followed would be filled with cheerful pictures!

In the afternoon I used to take a walk alone in the forest, rather fearfully at first, for as soon as dusk fell one would hear the call of wild beasts. This long period of solitude taught me to be very simple in my movements, my attitudes, my words; to find what was essential in my relationship with Sŕi Anirvân—a deep accord.

Then came the monsoon. Enormous black clouds climbed up the mountains and burst with a crash; the whole of nature was impregnated with mist and it penetrated into the rooms. The high grass was covered with leeches. I no longer went out. This was a time meant for study, for retreat.

The walls of my room and those of Sŕi Anirvân's room were lined with books—a library classified by subjects, some four thousand volumes on the esoterics of Eastern traditions. I had taken down a few books from the shelves, haphazardly, in order to escape from my own thoughts rather than to study. Sŕi Anirvân made no comment. Without interfering, he watched me live.

In the obscurity of my search, when I came to realize that there was only *myself* setting out to discover *I am*, something became disjointed. Did

I accept being helpless and being aware of it? I had become afraid, with an instinctive fear of losing something precious, whereas the right move would have been to hold onto the slender thread which I guessed was the link between *me* and *I am*. If I was able for a few seconds to experience this as a certainty, the pursuit came to a stop, only to start up again very soon and with greater intensty. Then Sŕi Anirvân came forth with a suggestion: 'Try to see that relaxation is nothing but the transformation of something rigid into something supple, if to it you add a notion of expansion.'

I tried it, as hour after hour I attempted to follow the path of my thought. The very question, 'Who am I?' had a snare in it that I tried to avoid. There was a risk that I would become attached to the question like a miser to his gold and lose sight of my real aim in a new kind of slavery. This aim was a light shining through the fog. I sensed its warmth in me, which was all I could perceive of the consciousness towards which I was groping my way.

I had arrived at the Lohaghat hermitage defeated by life, having given up everything I had believed to be a possible answer, according to Hinduism, to the 'Why?' of life. Hindu philosophy, I knew, was divided into watertight compartments, learnedly expounded by intelligent monks in order to capture the attention of the West: yogas of asceticism, of knowledge, of action, of love, which in India formed a solid whole. Rites owing allegiance to many faiths and a wide variety of customs flowed out from these in a materiality enfolding all possible concepts of life. By then I had given up looking into all these philosophical teachings and instead had plunged into everyday life as it is lived amongst the people of the cities and villages, among the refugees who, at that time, were pouring in from Pakistan stripped of all their possessions. This had brought me to understand why the vision of the Lord Krishna dancing to the sound of his flutes enchants the Hindu in his poverty and why we of the West, enjoying a profusion of everything, worship the Man-God dying on His Cross.

Sŕi Anirvân smiled at my outbursts. In a practical way I had dicovered why any discipline, whatever it may be, can be pictured as a wheel whose rim exerts constant pressure inwards, in the direction of the hub, where the *Iṣṭadevatā*, or chosen image of the Divine, stands, but I did not yet know that to be attached to an Iṣṭadevatā is just as precarious as to be attached to some human love. Adolescent love stands up neither to the pressure of facts nor to the hazards of life.

Cracks in my outer shell were opening one after another, each time exposing some new zone of darkness in my understanding. At the moment I am speaking of, all inner feeling being rejected, an extraordinarily dry period ensues, during which the Master's hand is indispensable. Discrimination gives rise to contradictions, in the midst of which one struggles; one lives without love, without patience. The vital attachment one had felt with those around one and the tasks undertaken lose their meaning; the aim, hitherto considered indispensable, becomes blurred. The imaginary ideal is broken. This is a cruel moment, but a necessary one, until there arises from the depths of one's being a new, more contained, though still eager, impulse.

Since every Master sees the influences that govern the pupils who come to him, I had admitted to myself that since Sŕi Anirvân was keeping me near him, it meant that a certain inner work was possible under his direction. There was not the least sentimentality in our relationship, but an expression perhaps of deep respect and commitment to a mutual responsibility. Our life was like a harmonic chord with exactly known intervals.

For my part, I knew that if Sŕi Anirvân had given me a place, one day, in the same way, he would send me away. With a touch of disguised effrontery, I had asked him, 'When will you send me away from here?' He answered seriously, looking at me quietly, 'When you have found your place in life, you will have nothing more to do here.'

One evening, after the usual meditation hour, Sŕi Anirvân told me of his plans for leaving Lohaghat. As it happened, our hermitage, hanging as it did on a mountainside, was too precarious a place in which to remain the whole year and to receive the pupils who were asking to come from Bengal and Assam. The road was dangerous in the rainy season. At that time it was really only a track that was washed away and disappeared in some of the river beds. One had to go through a jungle where tigers, leopards, and wild elephants were coming into their own again. Nobody willingly ventured into it. The mails were rare, the postman making the ascent only once a week.

Of course, the monks in the Mayavati monastery that perched on a hill opposite were only too glad to spend their winters in that isolated retreat created by Swami Vivekananda, but our plans made it necessary to remain in touch with life. It was up to us to find a less trying and more accessible environment.

It was decided that I should go ahead to Almora, which I already knew from having stayed there twice for long periods.[1]

My journey across the mountains was uneventful. The Joshi family was waiting for me. Bepin, a young lawyer, put himself at my disposal for they were all anxious for Sŕi Anirvân to come and settle in Almora.

The very next day Bepin took me to look at three houses. The first two were too spacious for us and the rent too high. The third one, four miles outside the town, was built on the edge of the forest. It faced south, and its deserted terraces and solidly constructed outbuildings had disappeared behind the overgrown mimosas.

Forewarned, the owner was waiting for us on the spot. As I went forward to meet this paunchy lawyer who was twirling a silver-knobbed walking stick, he began in a Shŕill voice to boast about his house as though it had been a palace. In actual fact, every windowpane had been replaced by planks. Moss and cactus were growing between the cracks in the paving. A few worm-eaten pieces were all that represented furniture in the house itself. The roof was leaking. The owner's arrogance and his comical arguments were irritating, but the place was suitable. I decided to take it at all costs. After lengthy discussion, a lease was signed.

I was thrilled and still full of joy when I went that evening to pay a courtesy visit to the late Pandit Joshi's uncle. This austere Brahmin always made me shy, although I knew he liked me. I would need his support in order to be accepted in the closed society of Almora and in my future dealings with the inhabitants of the small village near the new house.

He received me seated on a woven grass mat, the Bhagavad Gita open in front of him. In a niche hollowed out in the wall, incense and an oil lamp were burning before the picture of the Lord Krishna, his Iṣṭadevatā. Uncle Biren knew that since I had neither old parents to care for nor children to bring up, it was incumbent on me freely to find my own direction towards the inner disciplines. From his point of view, logically and clearly, I was entering the third *ashrama* of my life.[2] 'But how would you know the Divine if you do not know yourself?' he asked me. 'What dwelling place would you be able to offer Him? It takes a long time to prepare the heart for the inflow of the divine Name, like a wave pouring into the hollow of a rock.'

Through his nephew, Uncle Biren knew about the work of translating sacred writings of India with which I had been associated in Europe. He knew that I had sat at the feet of Masters who had given me their grace so that I might have access to the 'sensitive heart'. But the real work was only now beginning, in direct experience, lived under control. He was glad to know that I had decided to stay at Almora as long as might be necessary in order to distill and put into practice what I was receiving.

'On the esoteric level your decision is justified,' said Uncle Biren. 'One has to taste and to recognize what one receives, and learn to find it again, day after day, for this taste fades easily. Often nothing remains but the memory of it. Just as with a plant, one has to let it grow and develop without fear of apparent frustrations. Then alone does the inner flowering become possible – on our level, it goes without saying. The resistance comes from the hardened covering, but this conceals the kernel of palpitating life. Have confidence; obey without asking questions. In this way the being will come to have priority over the ego. Be blessed in your effort.'

On the following day I returned to Lohaghat with the signed lease in my bag. In time with the rhythm of my footsteps, I was already organizing the new house in my thought, putting a nail in here and there, painting the shelves, pulling out an odd bush, planting hollyhock, arranging trellises around the windows. By the time I arrived at the hermitage, our future house in Almora was practically restored!

Srî Anirvân, as always, was writing on the veranda. He barely raised his head. His look was calm and full of peace. Face to face with him, I suddenly felt how false my inner attitude was and how difficult it is, in words that are simple and right, to give account of an assignment one has carried out. He listened attentively, then said, 'Well, I shall live in the little outbuilding at the bottom of the garden from where one can see the river. The men will live in the building on the lower level and you in the big house with the women.'

'So you know this house?'

'No, I have only seen it through your eyes,' he answered. 'May this house be open to the spirit, to life. For now, let go of it, the better to hold onto it.'

And he began to recite a poem:

... and one day the Bâüls
came into the house.
They sang, danced and drank
and then they went away
and the house remained empty. ...

Sŕi Anirvân sat still. My arrival had interrupted him in the middle of a sentence he was writing and now, with his pen raised, he was waiting for me to go away before continuing.

There was a long pause without any movement. Standing, ill at ease, I felt the tears running down my cheeks. I put the lease down in front of him and went away.

This house at Almora had invaded my thought. It was driving me out of myself, preventing me from working. Sŕi Anirvân did not speak of it, nor did I. How were we ever going to move all those books, without crates, without servants, without money? I lived with a deep sense of shame. Then, in order to tame the rebellious mind, I began to learn a Sanskrit hymn by heart and recited it in the forest to the trees and the mountains.

One evening, Sŕi Anirvân suggested, 'In the future house it will be good if we study some hymns of praise to the great forces of nature. They will be chosen from the Vedas. What do you say? Starting tomorrow morning we will begin to pack the books. Punetha has brought up some canvas for that purpose.'

Endnotes

1. My Life With a Brahmin Family *(London: Rider & Co., 1958; New York: Roy Publishers, 1960).*
2. Vanaprastha, *the stage of spiritual search.*

Chapter 3

Haimavati

We left in December. There was already hoarfrost on the ground and the mountains glistened with fresh snow. A small truck followed us with the books; the rest mattered little. Sŕi Anirvân left immediately for Delhi where his disciples awaited him. Ahead of him were three months of wandering from town to town as far as Bengal and Assam.

My own task was to open the house in Almora and prepare myself for the life that would come to fill it. When we parted, Sŕi Anirvân had said:

> *It is good that you are going to the new house by yourself and will live there quietly, in retreat. Certainly you can absorb new ideas and make them your own, but later you will have to create freely your own way of expressing them. That is the work of the active power* (śhakti). *And it can only be done in silence. I can help you to find your own power, suggest a way, a means, for you to approach it, but nothing more. I never impose any thing; I love freedom too much, and so do you! I am not expecting anything in particular and have no preconceived or stereotyped idea about you. I shall only be glad if you open your petals and you, yourself, find yourself.*

I arrived at Almora the next day, late in the afternoon, and was happy to find Bepin Joshi at the entrance to the town. He was there to warn me that the road up the hill was blocked by a landslide. The bales of books had been unloaded by the roadside. I was somewhat alarmed when I saw a horde of Nepalese coolies rushing at me and asking to be hired as porters. Bepin finally chose about fifteen men, as well as some torchbearers for the trip through the forest. What a procession! Bent double under the heavy bales of books hanging in leather straps, the men kept shouting at each other—a violent rhythm that punctuated the march.

I was exhausted by their efforts, ashamed because of their sweat, their fatigue, their tatters, their gaunt legs—all this so that our 'knowledge' should shortly be arranged on the shelves that the carpenter had just finished. And I was imagining in advance the uproar there would be when the men scrambled for their shares of the few rupees that I was going to give them.

That first night I made acquaintance with the forest, the wind rustling in the pines, the yapping of the jackals together with the furious barking of the dogs, and then, early in the morning, the notes of a skillfully played pipe, repeated over and over like a prayer.

Sŕi Anirvân had suggested that this house on a hill in the forest be called 'Haimavati.' In the *Kena Upanishad*[1] Haimavati is the immaterial whiteness, the daughter of the sky who incarnates the principle of expansion on the terrestrial plane. As snow she falls lightly, piles up, is transformed into ice so that torrents may flow from her energy. In silence, she is a blessing from the sky to the earth.

The hill stretches to the rock of Kasardevi, a natural hollow, like a matrix of the world, where human sacrifices were undoubtedly offered up in the old days. A vast landscape extends to the horizon—valleys and mountain ranges, on the summits of which dwell goddesses in tiny white temples. Almora, however full of light, nevertheless remains a land of dissolution (*pralaya*), its beauty lying in the bareness of its mountainsides and the play of light on stones.

Below the house the road winds from terrace to terrace down to the bank of the River Koshi where the dead are burned. The green of rice or wheat alternates, according to the season, with the russet shade of the earth.

From a distance Sŕi Anirvân followed what I was doing; I kept him informed. A month after my arrival he wrote me:

I am so glad to learn that the toil and moil of putting the house in order is over, and that you have settled down again to your personal work in a quiet rhythm. I know you will not mind if my letter is short since I have nothing to say. Only one thing is important; become an adult! You are responsible for the first atmosphere of Haimavati. May this house resound with the call of the Vedic sages: 'Live, and move about in the atmosphere of the Vast!'[2] *Let all our friends come soon, may they hasten to visit Haimavati. For her alone, the force which is the child of the Void! Let no one come for you or for me! Let everybody throw off all poses, all trammels, and stand nude in the silence ready to bathe in its light until his soul is drenched by it. Discover yourself, identify yourself with the profound dumb power of the earth which silently fashions the dark clay into a spray of sun-kissed blossoms. You have this power in you, but you do not yet know it. It is the power of the dark night holding its breath in order to give birth to the new dawn.*

A few days later he wrote again:

I could not bear Haimavati to become a rendezvous. It must be a deep pool of life wherein one must plunge to live in death. And the work. *This work is not a pretext to be taken lightly. It is a deep inner work in the rhythm of the heart of life. It is creation. For the moment, you can do but one thing—create in yourself respect for your own work, for your own effort, in silence, and with the discipline you are approaching.*

I was impatient, and at the same time I had an unacknowledged fear of what was going to take place. I came and went in the empty whitewashed rooms of the house, which were waiting for life to fill them. Rope beds had been made on the spot as well as stools and a low table for the refectory.

Speaking of his pupils, Sŕi Anirvân wrote:

A great period of interiorization has taken hold of them. I have planted a seed in their hearts and done my part of the work. I have only to wait, but without desire, without expectation. I may see a mighty oak grow or the seed may rot… My days are so full that I cannot snatch even half an hour to write letters. So I give up! The people who come to see me are so kind, so quiet and so free. They are cultivating their soil. I give them all my time. About your own work, do not force yourself. There is no hurry about anything. Remember the Bâül's song:

O stubborn one, by your cruel impatience,
by your merciless insistence,
by the fire do you really wish
to force tight buds to open, flowers to bloom
and fill the air with their perfume?

So, let Haimavati grow and let these things find their own place while calmly observing their movement. To be a tangent that touches the circle of energy at one point only without twining oneself round it—that is the whole secret of life!

Sŕi Anirvân arrived a few days before his pupils. News travels quickly in India among the elite. The idea of establishing a Cultural Center where Hinduism and Islam would be studied side by side, where seekers would be received who would dedicate a part or the whole of their lives to collecting and translating texts hitherto unknown and having them published by Indian universities, resulted in an offer from patrons in Delhi, Allahabad, and the South to follow our work and bring us substantial help. The first to arrive was a Muslim from the South who was translating texts from the Upanishads into Arabic.

Sŕi Anirvân's dream was taking shape, or so I was only too ready to imagine, since my enthusiasm created conditions favorable to this train of thought. In addition to my personal work, I felt myself free to carry a big share of the responsibility for the practical organization of our Cultural Center. Sŕi Anirvân was much more cautious, knowing how, in India, although the mind may be free and discussion open, custom shackles and crushes those who do not obey the caste laws.

Three Hindu pupils arrived together, two women and a man. I welcomed them from the top of the terrace steps with open arms; they greeted me with respect. Our entire relationship had to be built from nothing since everything separated us except the idea of serving the same aim—language, manners, foods, all sorts of habits associated since childhood with attitudes toward the sacred.

Of course I had set up a plan for running the house and Sŕi Anirvân had watched me doing it. Bepin had chosen a high-caste servant for me so that everyone should feel at ease, and indeed everyone was except I, for I could no longer go into the kitchen! A Buddhist writer who arrived at this point used to eat in his room, coming to join us only for the study groups. I understood that the more I effaced myself, the less I would disturb everybody's movements. Seeing my embarrassment, Sŕi Anirvân had remarked, 'In this house you will be the eye which sees nothing. One can inspire another by one's way of living, allowing each one the freedom to search for himself and set up his own way of life.'

One morning, one of the two women, a widow, came to see me. She was small, unusually energetic. She was a barrister in a big eastern city and spoke English fluently. She brought me a poem to translate from the Hindi. She sat on the floor and began to recite the verse, clapping the rhythm with her hands. Then by an ingenious word-for-word process, we passed into English and then into French. While the words slipped from one to the other, something else came to life between us and made it possible for us to share the same experience. In the evening, during the study hour, we sat side by side, each with one hand open and stretched out toward the other to make sure of the other's approval. Nandini called me 'Mother' because I was the older. Years later, with the same heartfelt tenderness, she brought her married children to me so that I should know them.

Living so completely removed from any accustomed mode of thinking made my meetings with Sŕi Anirvân stand out in an extraordinary way; he saw what a struggle I was having with myself. The wish to concentrate every observation into very short sentences, to put an end intentionally to the outward expression of the inner nature in revolt, necessitated intense work on oneself in which the least reaction became the size of a mountain. In my immediate surroundings I had the same impression of being stranded. Had I not been living in the house of a sādhu, I would certainly have incurred the suspicion of the people of the neighboring village. The fact that I was not English intrigued them. They showed me great respect.

When Sŕi Anirvân passed by, the village people called him Maharaj (Lord). In the close circle of his pupils we called him, '*Ṛṣida*'. *Da* is an abbreviation for *Dada*, which means 'elder brother'. Sŕi Anirvân liked this form of address, which created amongst us a certain intimacy and brotherhood. The word '*Ṛṣi*', of course, calls up the picture of a very old sage absorbed in the study of the revealed writings. While a monk is expected to live in retirement from the world, a Ṛṣi has a more independent life; with a Ṛṣi at the centre of a hermitage, pupils and whole families come to live around him.

The Upanishads were born from such communities, from their austere search for pure thought. Sŕi Anirvân wrote unceasingly. Several philosophical treatises, published in India by institutes for traditional studies, bear his name. At the time when he was living in his Guru's ashram his writings were anonymous. Only writings for laymen circulating from hand to hand are signed with his pseudonym, 'Satyakama.'

In fact, no one knew very much about his life or about the sources of his teaching, which was so direct and practical. Everyone had his own opinion about this and thought he knew better than the other. It was often the subject between us when we were reading newspapers and letters after meals. If someone asked Sŕi Anirvân a question about his life, he would answer precisely, giving atmosphere and background as a framework for the events he was relating; but if he felt the question came from the wish to establish a chronology of his pilgrimage and the periods he had spent in various ashrams or brotherhoods, immediately places and dates were intentionally mixed up. Long periods of his life remained unknown. For him, time was of no account except in the relation that exists between the inner life and life in the world. And years lived in a one-pointed search had taught him the art of silence in which time loses its importance. Fifteen years later he himself told me of the first part of his life, perhaps so that I should understand that he had paid a high price for his luminous freedom.

Endnotes

1. *3.12.*
2. *Vasa brahmacaryam (*Chandogya Up. *6.1.1.)*

Chapter 4

A BÂÜL

Sŕi Anirvân was born in a little town in the east of Bengal like all the other towns in the region: houses with thatched roofs jutting out over circular verandas, beaten earth steps, brass utensils drying in the sun. Everywhere on the outskirts are banana and palm trees and hedges of flowering creepers dividing one garden from the next.

This exuberance flows down to the many ponds covered with lotuses and reeds. Beyond these, the rice fields and pastures stretch to the horizon. Many birds abide there—among them kingfishers and white cranes. Over it all is the sun which burns up everything or the rains which turn the earth to mud. It is all excessive, violent, and at the same time full of tenderness, for the sun's rays play with the dust and with the evening mist.

His father was a doctor. At the age of eleven, like all the little boys of his caste, he said the ritual prayers in the morning. Every day he recited a chapter of the Bhagavad Gita, and on some days Panini's treatise,[1] scanning the rhythm and marking the long syllables. At school he was a good pupil, anxious to learn because this is why ones goes to school and because it is a privilege. One day the teacher who was taking the class, in commenting on a poem, said: 'Everything we see is unreal. This is the basis of Vedanta.'[2]

With the rest of the class, the child repeated the lesson word for word, but when it came to saying: 'All that we see is unreal,' he was looking at a rosebud that was opening on a bush close to where the pupils were sitting. He saw the birth of his independent thought. 'If I am seeing this rose blossoming in front of me, how can I say that it does not exist? Am I seeing this rose? Do I exist? Do I see this rose?' In recitation the next day, he found it impossible to repeat the theme. While hearing it chanted in chorus by the pupils, he was saying to himself: 'I, I am alone… I don't think like the others. What is going to happen to me? It hurts…'

This became a burning question: 'When I look at something, does that thing exist?' He felt that behind the question there was no answer. One cannot argue with the schoolmaster any more than with one's father. He felt insolent in his thought and in his heart, and yet his question was alive. Who was going to be able to answer him? He wondered to himself, 'And so all I see around me does not exist? But *no*, it is not true!'

From that time on, a secret life took root in him, based on a nagging doubt. Everything around him seemed mechanical, having nothing to do with his living question. The rites and customs methodically determining what was to be done at every hour of the day lost their content. Yet all the members of the family—brother, sister, mother, grandmother, even his father—conformed to them. Why? He himself continued to submit, out of obedience, to all these requirements, but what was the sense, he wondered, 'if nothing exists,' of all these rules of life? He looked around him as for the first time, observing what went on, noticing what each person did. Twenty years later, he still remembered things said by every member of his family. Everything seemed to him to be an unreal play without beginning or end.

Several of his father's friends were Muslims. He took refuge with them because they spoke another language. One of them, the head of a large family, was a Sufi. Hindus from the neighborhood liked to visit him because they considered him a pure diamond, full of a caustic wisdom that made them laugh heartily. Sometimes one would hear him wildly lamenting: 'Ah, divine freedom, true gift of God, where are you? What are you doing to me? Just look at me, here among my own'—and he would point to his wife, his children, his grandchildren—'I am bothered with so many little worries. If I did not undergo them, I would not know that you exist. So where are you hiding? Why do you not come to me?' And he would begin to sing, making big gestures, his hands opened towards heaven, sometimes weeping, and those who heard him would beat time to the rhythm of his chant. The schoolboy listened eagerly. Where was this divine freedom known to the Sufi? Was it real or unreal? But the child was afraid of a rebuff and did not ask questions. He thought, 'I shall find it by myself, I shall go off and search for it.'

He began to go to the bank of the Brahmaputra very early in the morning, where Hindus and Muslims used to bathe. He would thread his way between them and pass unnoticed—just one more youngster among those who were shouting and playing around. He used to make his way cautiously towards a pandit who was highly respected by the people around him for his saintly life as well as for his free thinking. The pandit was accustomed to meet on the bank with a Sufi from a neighboring village. After greeting each other, the two men used to chant, each in his own fashion, the one hundred and eight or the ninety-nine Divine Names. Then, while the Sufi repeated tirelessly '*la illaha ilallāh*' the Brahmin, up to the waist in water, proceeded with the rites of his purification, loudly invoking the mystical fire of heaven: '*Marudbhir agna ā gahi*'. As soon as he came out of the water, the Sufi stopped praying. Before taking leave of one another, they embraced warmly at length, not caring for the taboos that should have divided them. Some days they would sit down on the stones and, while the bathers made a circle around them, they would tell stories, each in turn. Could the orthodox of the Shariyat and the Brahmin priests from the temple prevent these accolades and the freedom of expression of these two men?

One day, coming out of school, the Hindu boy went with a Muslim schoolfellow down to the riverbank to play. They had a great time jumping into puddles and playing ducks and drakes with carefully selected stones! The sun was high and after a while, worn out, the two youngsters threw themselves on the ground in the shade of a bush. They were hungry. The young Muslim said, 'I have something to eat with me; come on, let's share it!' He took a little parcel wrapped in a banana leaf out of his bag, opened it, and held out half of it to his companion. The children began to eat while teasing the tadpoles with their toes.

All of a sudden, the Muslim boy said slyly, 'Do you know you have lost caste by eating forbidden things with me? I will tell and everybody will speak of you!' 'No, you are wrong,' replied his Hindu comrade, surprised. 'I am free like Kikirchand.[3] I can eat anything I like, for I am a Bâül and I am above castes.' As he spoke, he stood up, for when one says a thing like that, one calls on the sun as a witness. The freedom that was ripening in him burst out. 'I am a Bâül seeking for divine freedom and nothing will hold me back.' But at the same time it was clear to him that he would have to submit to the classical traditional disciplines—no matter which—if he wished to go towards the freedom he longed for and towards the expansion of the self. He had already understood that one can only grow starting from the seed that one is and that a sure road is a necessity. At that very instant, he knew that his search had begun.

Carried away by the idea of becoming a sādhu in quest of the supreme freedom, he found that nothing else counted any more. He meekly accepted all rules, all fasts, telling himself that they were milestones on the road. He began to read all he could find about the lives of saints and masters.

Now at this time his father, who was very devout, came by chance on a book of instruction in yoga that contained a portrait of the author. Fascinated by the expression of his face, he decided to find this man and invite him to his house. He wrote his intention to his son, who was spending a few weeks' holiday with an uncle in the north of the province.

When the boy received the letter, it was a shock. He left immediately, and in order to get home quickly, he walked even during the hottest hours of the day, repeating over and over like a prayer: 'I am on the way to meet my *Thakur*,[4] a man who has reached the goal! He is my Thakur!' But on reaching home, he was disappointed to learn that the monk would not arrive for another three months. He waited for him with the same song of enthusiasm in his heart. His ideal created in advance the food of which he was in need. He was tormented by the idea of God. One night, the vision of a long road reaching to the horizon, and of himself making his way on it, reassured him as to his destiny.

When the monk finally appeared,[5] the boy knew as soon as he saw him that he was not mistaken—he was the man to guide him, to lead him to reach the three stages of consciousness spoken of in the Scriptures –*sat-cit-ānanda*.[6] The Swami had something majestic about him, something as wide as the sky. In the very moment of giving himself up to the Master, however, the boy knew in the depths of his being that he already possessed the freedom he wanted to find. It had been revealed to him one night when he was barely nine years old. That night the sky with all its stars had entered into him, throwing him to the ground in a swoon. He had never spoken of it because there were no right words to describe it, but the secret bloomed in him like a lotus when he heard Kikirchand sing; it filled his heart and tears ran down his cheeks.

He gave himself passionately to this Guru who was absolutely necessary to him, holding nothing back, repeating to himself: 'I love him, I am going to serve him, to follow him, for he is my Thakur.' The Swami was thirty-eight years old. Elegantly dressed, his hair falling in curls to his shoulders, a ring on his right hand, he gave the impression of belonging to the world rather than to a monastic order. He had learned from several teachers the practical disciplines that gave directives for life. Open, natural, with great yogic powers, this man embodied a mystery.

For three years, the Swami's visits were repeated at regular intervals. In between, the father of the family used to go to visit him, each time coming back transformed, full of stories of spiritual disciplines and ecstatic states which he told to his wife. His young son listened with a growing hunger for a life like that for himself.

The Swami was planning to settle in Assam, where the government was giving away land to anyone prepared to drain it. This was virgin territory, swampy and malarial. A first group of disciples was ready to accompany the Swami and dedicate themselves to the service of their fellow man while living in accordance with the law of the *sāstras*. To struggle against untamed nature, virgin forests, and wild beasts seemed to go hand in hand with the conquest of the inner nature.

A decisive moment arrived. One night the father woke up his son in order to have a talk with him. 'Listen. In a year you will be sixteen; you will be a man. You will become the head of the family, for I have decided to go with your mother to live at the feet of the Guru in Assam. Your grandmother will take care of the younger children. Money has been set aside for your studies. You will become a doctor like me.'

The boy, who had never spoken openly with his father, felt the earth giving way under his feet. Out of respect he was bound to obey and he said not a word. How could he have cried out, 'I, too. I want to go to him—he is my Thakur! All I long for is the life described in the Upanishads, to serve the Guru and to reach the goal!'

He remained silent and for seven months struggled with himself. At last, one night, he pulled the bolts, went out, closed the door behind him, padlocked it, and went away without taking leave of anyone. He visualized his Thakur in a halo of freedom, but when he arrived there, nothing he had expected was given him—no teaching, no discipline. Life in the ashram-to-be was a medley of the sounds of hammers, saws, and picks. It was centred entirely on unconditional love for the Guru and self-effacement. The one call was to action: 'Work for the Guru!' which meant digging wells and ditches, cutting down trees, building houses. In his devotion, the young man accepted all the circumstances as they were. He worked without thinking, to the limit of his strength. Sweat and tears together streamed down his face. He did not notice them.

After a few months, news came that he had been awarded a State Scholarship on the results of the University examination he had sat for before he left. The Guru made the decision: 'Well! If that is so, then you go and study! I shall need a well-educated man like you later on.'

And so the young man went away for six whole years, first to Dacca, then to the University of Calcutta. He worked hard, dreaming of his Guru. When he came back to the ashram for vacations, the Master made him welcome, kept him constantly at his side, and told him in detail about everything that was going on. The disciples considered him the great favorite—the poet who sang his devotion and was able to open all hearts. He was liked because what he said drove out fatigue and transported the mind above the realm of the senses. He served the Guru in all things, fanning him during the oppressive nights, attending upon him in little details. Love of the Guru filled his life.

After passing his examinations brilliantly, the student was getting ready to return to the ashram for good. On his last day in Calcutta something occurred that left its mark on his life and changed its course. On the way to the station where he was to take the train for Assam, he looked around him as for the first time and, relaxed, smiled at the people, amused by everything he was seeing, absorbing the life around him.

A fog came down. He shook himself as though he were coming out of a long sleep, his limbs numb. Where was he? He shut his eyes. In a vision, he saw the gentle banks of the Brahmaputra, the vast sky, himself standing between earth and heaven in his own freedom. He heard the murmur of the water running over the pebbles. Who was he? A wandering Bâül? He was seized by an irresistible impulse to go towards the South, all the way to Cape Comorin, to see the goddess Kanya Kumari[7] with his own eyes, in her eternal waiting, the infinity of the seas, the infinity of freedom.

He decided at once that he would take a ticket to Kanya Kumari and that he would not return to the ashram. He arrived at the station and took his place in the line of travellers waiting to buy tickets. For a long while there in the crowd he knew the joy of being in harmony with himself. But when he came to the ticket office window he found it impossible to utter a single word. He felt pushed from behind, jostled. Then he distinctly heard a voice saying: 'One third-class ticket to Jorhat in Assam.' He shut his eyes and knew that he had just been swallowed by his Guru.

When he arrived at the ashram, a complete change in his way of life was awaiting him. Books were put aside. He took his place as a novice beside the other monks, the diggers, the plowmen, the woodcutters. The life was hard. The Guru imposed silence during the work. The clearing of the undergrowth was dangerous, drinking water was lacking. As soon as land was cleared, seed was sown. No communication with the outside world was allowed, no correspondence. The Guru gradually exerted his hold over their being through an obedience automatically accepted. During the night, long hours of meditation broke down resistance. The heat was heavy, humid, the air filled with the barking of jackals.

In this effort, the novice lived torn between his dream of freedom and the body that had been brought back to where he no longer wished to be. His devotion was drying. He was absent from himself, lost. A nun who lived in the ashram upset him greatly. It was the first time he had spoken to a woman and this one was old enough to be his mother. One day she showed him the image of the Iṣṭadevatā she was worshipping covered with flowers, and she said to him, 'Just as I have put that beloved image in front of me to focus my concentration, I can also break it. At that moment, the Divine, if it pleases Him, can choose to enter into the heart and live there. You should know this and never forget it.'

The Guru was anxious about the mental state of his favorite novice, who was escaping from him. He consulted several of the older ones about it. How could he bring back this rebel, whom he needed for his work, and attach him to the Guru for good? How could he prevent him from thinking? He decided to make him take the vows of continence on all levels (*brahmacarya*). Between the Guru and the novice the silence was broken, but the young man who had been brought back against his will resisted; the cocoon of paralyzing tenderness was torn. He asked, 'What do you want from me? Where are you leading me?'

In this confrontation, both spoke openly—the Guru of attachment, the disciple of freedom. Finally the novice gave in before the power of the Master. The required vows were pronounced, but they included a condition: 'I accept to work for you in full obedience, but let me not have cause to regret it later on. My path is the one which leads to the ultimate freedom.'

Several years passed.

The handful of disciples who had followed the Swami to Assam had now increased to about fifty, making it necessary to create an autonomous institution. The property included the buildings where the monks and the novices lodged together with a few old couples and children of the lay disciples who were being brought up in the ashram. The ashram had its own school, a dispensary, a printing shop, weaving rooms, grain lofts, gardens, orchards, and rice fields. As time went on, the Swami who had been its creator had become, inevitably, an administrator, working day and night for the community. His urgent preoccupation – other groups having grown up in the nearby provinces – was to name his successor and have him recognized. The only one who was capable of taking over from him was his favorite novice, but would the latter, with his independent character and the aim he was pursuing, be likely to accept the *sannyāsa*[8] without which he could not be the head of a monastic institution?

The novice was working twenty hours a day, consumed by the tasks he was obliged to fulfill and by his thirst for the infinite. From time to time, an affectionate impulse made him break the silence and plead with his Master: 'Stop, I implore you! Do not go on enlarging your work. You are getting caught in the net. Give it all up. You are being eaten up by your obligations. Return to inner life. Leave everything and do not look back! Go and sit under a tree in the forest and meditate. I will take care of you. I will go begging for you…' But the Guru, entirely identified with his work and its problems, could no longer detach himself. Then the disciple became more distressed: 'I beg you to stop! The spirit of the ashram is dying. Each effort is useful in its way, but only up to a certain point. If the effort is maintained by will alone, it is no longer in tune with the natural rhythm of creation, and disintegration sets in.'

The Master was quite aware of this, but to struggle against the established current had become impossible. The first impulse of the disciples, who had come to live in total renunciation, had little by little changed into unreasonable demands. In the course of the years, anniversary feasts had multiplied and all the poor came running to the ashram to be fed and clothed. Although the crowd flattered him, the Guru had no more illusions, even concerning the children, all sons of his nearest disciples, who had been entrusted to him by their parents so that they might grow up in the atmosphere of the ashram. He said, 'It is possible that some of these children may open themselves to the light, but also that some of them may become thieves. In that case, they will be perfect thieves, because they are being fed and raised in the force, the energy and the sight of the Guru.'

When the question of accepting sannyāsa was put to the novice, he asked for three days to think about it. For him sannyāsa was not only a formality that was needed in order to be put solemnly at the head of the ashram—for the salvation of the institution; it demanded a lifelong commitment of himself. In the course of the years that had gone by, he had blindly followed the rules established by the Guru: obedience, breaking from the family, poverty, continence, a constant discipline of the mind in order to attain an impersonal state—a kind of 'little death' in which, if the stray impulses of the mind haven't given a wrong direction to the effort, true being could be born. But the aim was still the final freedom.

At the end of the first day of reflection, his heart torn between loyalty to the Guru who showed him such attachment and his own intense desire for freedom, the novice put a question to himself: 'Does the required sannyāsa bind me inwardly?' The second day, he said to himself, 'If I accept, I shall work in full obedience, but who will be responsible?' When he woke up on the third morning, he knew the answer: 'Nobody and nothing can be binding on me. I am a Bâül. I am free.' And so he said to the Guru, 'Do whatever is useful for you. Inwardly, nothing can bind me.'

The ceremony of his sannyāsa was very simple. According to the ancient Vedic tradition, the novice, calling the sun to witness, says three times, 'I renounce, I renounce, I renounce.' The Guru directed him to celebrate his own funeral service in order to burn his past. After that, the Master handed him the rough-hewn staff, the emblem of the monk, and prostrated himself before him. According to the law of the sāstras, they were now equals.

Symbolically, the new monk, Swami Nirvanananda,[9] possessed nothing but a gourd (*kamandalou*) made from a dried fruit and his staff. But the Guru took the stick from him saying, 'If I do not take it from you, you will go off and will not do my work!' The new monk did not flinch. Although he was voluntarily bound to do his Guru's work, his mind remained free. Deliberately, at that very moment he made a vow that was to create an obstacle to the life of automatism that faced him: 'The day the big tree at the ashram door disappears, in one way or another, that evening, I shall leave…'

More years passed, very hard ones.

The Guru had retired to Puri, and from there he travelled from city to city, always talking about the ashram, encouraging people who wished to go there and live. On this level, the ashram was a success; money flowed in. The old disciples busied themselves with settling in the newcomers.

Swami Nirvanananda lived under greater and greater pressure with a load of obligations on his shoulders and, like Sinbad the Sailor with the Old Man of the Sea, he had to carry his Guru at the same time. One day he counted the number of years he had been working for the Guru, serving his human ambition, and felt free to leave. The ashram was prospering in its new direction. He was no longer necessary. He took his kamandalou and left. The same evening a violent storm tore down the tree at the door of the ashram.

But he felt miserable as he departed, for all opposition to the Guru had fallen away. Now he could but love him in his weaknesses with all the tenderness of bygone times. He felt baffled, full of a grief which he knew would last for a certain time according to an exact law.

He vanished. He gave up his name.

The experience of death in oneself, which he had lived through little by little in the course of the years, accompanied him. He made his way to the Himalayas. At the end of his strength, he dragged himself to an ashram where wandering monks were received.

He remained there, on his rope bed, feverish, with no one to care for him. There is no mutual help among sannyāsin. If one of them dies, his body is burned or cast into the Ganges. How could there be room for pity in the vows of renunciation of oneself, since sooner or later all men have to throw off this used garment which the body represents? The miracle is to descend lucidly to the very last vibration of conscious life. That is the moment when a new birth can take place. One day in his weakness this man without identity saw a brilliant light before him and knew that he was not going to die. The ordeal was overcome.

He recovered, but he was no longer the same man. A long period of wandering began for him. He never speaks of those years. If questioned, a smile flits over his lips and he answers with a poetic phrase that leaves an aura of mystery. Friends told me of having met him in various places, although it was never possible to establish any chronological sequence in his travels or in the events of his life.

His former tenderness for Swami Nigamananda remained the same. Although he had rebelled, he continued to serve his Guru by respecting his monastic vows and by devoting himself to the study of the Vedas which was to fill his life. They saw each other again only once, in Assam, and spoke openly about the divergent ways of the search for the self which had occasioned their parting. The disciple revealed himself in such a way that the Guru, blessing him, gave him full freedom to follow his solitary way. He had become an *atyashrami*, one of those who are beyond all rules and all disciplines of an established order and who are recognized by the tradition.

With his long beard framing his thin face and in his white robe, he was sometimes taken for a Muslim *pīr*, sometimes for a Hindu sādhu. For his part, he smiled at his freedom in a society full of taboos. He allowed a direct contact with people to take place, but at the same time he was like an empty shell filled with the sound of the ocean. I have heard him say, 'What a strange experience. I cannot bind myself to anyone. They are in me, but I am not in them.' This objectivity, so devastating in appearance, helped the growth of our work on ourselves with a merciless lucidity supported only by his look, amused and full of confidence.

One of his childhood friends once came across him in a northern city where, just for a bare living, he was preparing students for different university examinations. He had taken the name Anirvân. The professor in him was just another role voluntarily assumed. So, many hours a day, like a factory worker, he set himself to the work of translating the texts he considered necessary for the people who gathered around him once or twice a week. Soon other friends began meeting together in neighboring towns, each group organizing themselves so that his ticket from place to place could be paid and his visit assured.

The whole of life was his Guru and at the same time his field of action. He wrote to me once:

> *What people expect from me may not come about. All I can do is to be true to myself and sincere with others. I do my best not to hurt people, yet every one of our movements creates a reaction, however slight it*

> *may be. We cannot avoid it. All we can do is to accept this with good grace and without complicating things.*

For him, any place was a good one in which to live an inner life and carry out one's task; even a room on a noisy street of a big city with electric lights burning day and night, the sounds of the market place, children shouting. The conditions under which he lived were extremely modest, difficult and complex, but he made light of them. He said:

> *If you walk for a long time carrying a burden on your shoulders, you get more and more tired, whereas the same burden will weigh nothing at all if you float it down a river. Is life not a river? My work also floats downstream. All my life, I have tried not to burden myself with cumbersome things. But how hard it is to live simply, not to amass things and thoughts. Of their own accord they pile up around you and in the end become a weight. At that point, one has to know how to slip between them like an eel and escape. One must never allow oneself to be caught.*

For years he has lived, and stayed for a while, only in those places where his freedom was completely respected. No one ever knows when he will go away, for he follows his own law, which is secret.

Endnotes

1. *A classical grammar book of the fifth century B.C.*
2. *One of the six classical schools (darśanas) of Hindu philosophy, founded by Badarayana or Vyasa and the one that is best known in the West.*
3. *A Hindu Bâûl assuming a Muslim name 'Kikirchand Fakir' whose songs were very popular then.*
4. *Lord, the Divine incarnate. A name given by every disciple to his Guru.*
5. *Swami Nigamananda (Joy of Vedic realization), died 1935. His place of burial is in Halisahar, Bengal.*
6. *Pure Existence, Pure Spirit, Pure Bliss.*
7. *Kanya Kumari, the fiancée whom Shiva forgot and who waits eternally for her beloved.*
8. *Definite entrance into monastic life, with all the vows this entails.*
9. *'Joy-of-Realization-of-the-Void.'*

Chapter 5

Everyday Life

One question bothered me: 'How are we going to live together, we who are of such different backgrounds, with such different customs?' My Hindu friends put it in their way: 'How are we going to bear our *karma* together?'[1] Then Sŕi Anirvân told us a story.

> *In life, one has to know that one is at the same time the cat who eats the mouse and the mouse who is eaten by the cat, for life, as it comes to us and the life which is in us, takes these two forms simultaneously. But can I understand who I am if I do not know my place in the universe? When this is seen, then I discover that the one who is first eaten is the first to be liberated, while the other has a heavier karma to bear. If I accept my responsibilities in the situation in which I find myself, then the struggle or absence of struggle, in one way or the other, becomes the secret dignity of my inner being.*
>
> *The fervent disciple of a sādhu went one day to beg in a village and there a peasant took a dislike to him and beat him with a stick. The disciple behaved according to his own understanding and did not hit back. On his way home, deeply immersed in himself, he forgot all about the peasant and the beating. But his Master saw the marks on his face and asked, 'What happened to you?' 'What?' asked the disciple. He could remember nothing. When the Master*

insisted, he searched in his memory and remembered what had taken place. 'And you didn't hit him back?' asked the Master. 'Why did you not share your aggressor's karma? Now go back and see what is going on because of you.' The disciple returned to the village, but from afar he saw flames. The house of the peasant who had beaten him was on fire.

Our life was made up of periods of work interrupted by periods of rest or of communal life. Each of us had his special task about which we did not speak among ourselves, for tacitly everything was related to that voluntary commitment. This gave flexibility to our relationship with one another. At the same time, my own solitude weighed on me, for in that 'present' in which there was as yet no relief, I had no criterion to go by. Sŕi Anirvân spoke to me about it as a potter might have spoken about a vase he was modelling. 'Why not break it and begin over again? In that case, one has again to knead the clay, soften it with water, and begin from scratch.' I accepted inner work interpreted in that way. What kind of clay was I? Constant, minute observation of myself was beginning, though I did not know where I was going —but I had complete trust in the potter.

The evening meal—always the same—milk, boiled potatoes, butter, salt, and sugar—brought us all together. The food was just food and not meant as a diversion for the eyes or greedy taste. After a day of individual work and concentration, we enjoyed an open conversation, speaking about our experiences, about our difficulties with ourselves. Sŕi Anirvân listened to us with patience. 'In a ground that has not been plowed for a long time, one cannot sow wheat right away,' he would say. 'We are at the stage of preparing the ground. Various crops must be sown and plowed back into the soil to make it fertile.'

In the evening, when Sŕi Anirvân came back from his walk, and if there were no visitor announced for a private interview, the hour belonged to me. Outside, nightfall—the moment when the crows made great circles in the sky. We used to speak about the little facts of our lives and of my life, for all these details began to have a meaning related to a reality that still escaped me.

For several weeks a young Hindu woman came to give the lessons in Hindi. She had a degree. A servant came with her and waited for her, stretched out like a lizard in the sun. My tutor took me through a real course on the *Ramayana*, at the same time explaining her profound contempt for foreigners. To her I was not a foreigner. I listened, apparently without reacting, putting my hand over my mouth, as Hindu women do to hide any expression. One day she announced that she was leaving me, for a reason which was only a pretext: a relation's marriage in some far-off province.

Another incident: The village woman who came to cut the grass on the terraces used to steal lemons from the neighboring gardens in order to make me an offering. One blow with her sickle and the fruit fell into the skirt held up to receive it! She explained, 'You are my mother, God makes the fruit grow, and I pick it, for you.'

The peasant who regularly brought me his rice from the village, used to sing at the top of his voice: '*Jai, Jai, Sitā-Rām, Jai, Jai* ... like an automaton, happy in his poverty, absorbed in his song. My 'weekly' beggar woman, who came on Mondays for a day's food, used to stroke my shoulder as if I were her sister. Both of them spoke to me about the 'golden breast of our Divine Mother.'[2] 'Ah, yes,' Sŕi Anirvân explained, 'these simple people get food from the essence of the spirit which for them quite naturally takes on density in matter. This idea is far more ancient than any philosophical idea of power assuming a form. In the Vedas, the earth is not yet heavy matter. It is spirit and from its essence the Divine Mother is born. Simple people have not forgotten this, for their chemistry is nearer to the truth than ours, therefore they are better nourished than we.'

One evening, while we were talking, a voice was heard far away singing, '*Namah Shivaya* ... (O Shiva, I prostrate myself before thee)' on two low notes, a *re* and a *mi* a quarter tone lower. The rhythm was that of a quick march. The invocation came nearer and nearer, louder and louder as it approached the house, then faded away in the forest. An echo carried it back for a long time. Sŕi Anirvân said, 'A great sacrifice has been offered up.'

The chant of the priests who accompany the dead to the cremation ground is quick and hard. One hears it from a distance in the mountains, for the way down to the river Koshi is long. A little group of men go by at a run, with the body on an uncovered litter on their shoulders. Their chant runs with them through the dust, in time with their steps, in time with their breathing. The voices are guttural:

Ram Nam satya he
Satya bolo gatta he.
(The Name of Rama is truth,
Revealed truth is liberation.)

Once a week in the afternoon, Sŕi Anirvân received three of the town notables, very old men. Their heads were shaven except for one lock on the top and a fringe of white beard. They carried knobbed walking sticks. They came to read aloud an Upanishad. Sŕi Anirvân gave a commentary on each verse, which became for them the support of their thought in the following days. The text was chanted in Sanskrit, the commentary given in Hindi. The three men would sit facing Sŕi Anirvân. I had the right to sit on a cushion a little to the rear. If I did not understand what was said, I could see in their eyes what they were receiving; felt in myself the immobility of their bodies, their inner silence which allowed the Being to open. All my attention was focused on approaching this quietness in my disobedient body and vagabond thoughts. When the lesson had come to an end and our guests had risen, I saluted them by 'taking the dust from under their feet.' They would then make a sign of parting and blessing, a little hesitant since I was a stranger. Sŕi Anirvân, unperturbed, looked on with love in his eyes.

One day only two of them came. After the lesson, Sŕi Anirvân told me:

Our missing friend died two days ago. One morning he saw the hand of death (Yama) *coming towards him. He understood the sacred sign and took leave of each of the members of his family; then he went up alone onto the hill, forbidding anyone to follow him. He sat under a tree and tied himself to the trunk with his shawl. He cut off his topknot of hair and placed it in front of him, with all he had on him—his watch, his wallet—all the while reciting the prayers which made him a monk. Then, gazing straight before him, he recited the prayers of consecration. When his eldest son found him, he had been dead for several hours. Each of us may well wish for a death like that in full self-consciousness.*

Among us, the pupils, the atmosphere was not always so relaxed as it could have been. One of the Bengali women having been allowed to cook a special dish, there followed a series of special dishes in competition, a reaction to the moderation that was demanded of us. Sŕi Anirvân liked extreme simplicity. Food should be considered merely as material used for nourishing the spirit. The first mouthful of rice was raised to the forehead in salutation; some verses from the Bhagavad Gita were recited mentally with the next four mouthfuls.

Sometimes criticisms were exchanged among us, and there were moments of impatience disguised by extreme politeness. I often felt myself walled in, in a heavy body with no life in it other than an intense pain. And the others—what was going on in them? Their presence reassured and irritated me at the same time. I knew that if I had said, 'I shall never reach anything,' Sŕi Anirvân would have reminded me of a certain Puranic story:

Some devotees in a mango orchard were talking among themselves. Each one knew the kind of mango which grew in his province. Soon they began to count the different varieties of trees in the orchard and in the end began to quarrel about the way they should be grown. Suddenly the owner of the orchard arrived and, much surprised, said to them, 'Why do you not eat this beautiful ripe fruit hanging on the branches instead of counting the leaves on the trees?'

Endnotes

1. *Karma is the occult force of* prakriti *(Great Nature) which brings people together for some secret purpose.*
2. Hiranyavaksha aditi.

Chapter 6

STUDY

I often heard our visitors ask Sŕi Anirvân, 'Why do you not publish your teaching?' and his answer was:

> *At the time of the Vedas, the Master spent many years giving instruction to the 'chosen man' to whom he would transmit the spiritual knowledge he possessed. Nowadays, because of printing and communications facilities, spiritual science has become an affair of the market place. If one considers the march of time, it is just as important to talk to trees as to talk to men, for the tree and man are both part of Great Nature. The sage has to work in harmony with the slow evolutionary transformation, without concern for the enormous waste it entails. When Sŕi Aurobindo speaks of the transformation of species, he is looking into the future. In fact, the passage from one species to another takes millions of years; during that time the sage is responsible for the survival of the vital spirit.*

Sŕi Anirvân sometimes gave us to understand that he was 'doing his time in the Himalayas' to be in communion with the earth which prays. The earth prays; it leads people to wish to know the mystery of the Void. Just as one always returns to the fundamental teaching of Patanjali,[1] so one day he would return to Assam and Bengal. He said, 'My ambition is not very great. It is to live a life rich in impressions, luminous to the end; to leave behind a few books embodying my life-long search for truth, and a few souls who have caught fire. My aim? Simply to inspire people, and give them the most complete freedom to live their own life. No glamor, no fame, no institution—nothing. To live simply and die luminously.'

For many years he had been working under a yoke without losing his freedom. 'Work does not find me,' he said, 'because I never search for it. If it is thrust upon me, I devote all my energy to it and then when it is taken away, I never look back. Once it is done, I forget it, for the only thing I care for is the idea that "I am"—that idea is at once an individual, a cosmic and transcendental law in itself.'

When Muslims looked at him, they asked, 'Is he one of us?' Some Hindus, not yet freed from form, would question him. Then Sŕi Anirvân very humbly explained: 'I must tell you that I never wore the ochre robe of my own free will. It was put on me by my Guru, who attached great importance to everything that had to do with the idea of institution. He himself always dressed elegantly, like a man of the world. It is true that this robe never had much meaning for me and that is why I discarded it one day as easily as I had put it on.'

I did not yet know all the methods that Sŕi Anirvân used in order to test us. One day a group of ochre-robed monks, the most distinguished of a well-known monastery, came to visit us. They were curious to see a Cultural Center in process of formation where, under different forms, the inner experience was recognized as identical in substance. One of the monks asked me casually, 'But, if I am not mistaken, this must be where Sŕi Anirvân lives?'

This was in the morning. Nobody ever disturbed Sŕi Anirvân at that hour. Nevertheless, I went and knocked on his door. Surprised, he asked me, 'Do you personally wish that I should come?—Yes? Then in a few minutes.'

When I went back to the monks on the veranda, they had embarked on a very learned philosophical discussion while eating the fruit that had been served to them. In a little while Sŕi Anirvân appeared and, like an anonymous mendicant, sat on a stool to one side, his scarf wrapped around his face. He looked so pitiful that the discourse continued and nobody paid any attention to him. After ten minutes Sŕi Anirvân asked me in a low voice, 'Do you agree that I can go away?' He got up and left discreetly. The monks had not stopped talking. That evening, at the study hour, I was still blushing.

On the occasion of the visit of some friends of Sŕi Anirvân from Allahabad, we had the 'class' at an unusual hour. A white sheet spread out on the floor of the library marked the space where we sat together. Twelve years later, I still have a mental picture of our group: three women in white saris with red borders, five or six men of different ages, among whom were two lawyers and a doctor in a long buttoned frock coat with a white cap on his head. Nobody took notes.

Sŕi Anirvân had put the following question: 'What is the function of the interiorization of consciousness?'

On this occasion he said:

> *The too-facile affirmation that man is spirit but born of the flesh needs some sort of introduction. Every religion makes a distinction from the start between the natural man and the spiritual man, which is the reason for the great importance given to a sacrament marking the passage from the one state to the other. This sacrament has a social significance; in Aryan society, it formally admits the child to partaking in the spiritual heritage of the community, or else it can also remain secret; but it is always a bond, like the reins that in a visible way link the horse with the coachman of the symbolic team described in the* Katha Upanishad.[2] *Our attention needs to be directed to the factors that make it possible to approach the individual sacrament* (diksha), *for it is in fact the actual commitment to a particular spiritual discipline. Such a commitment is voluntary; it is the 'setting forth' on the spiritual adventure with no possibility of return.*
>
> *But this all-important moment which separates the natural man from the spiritual man also separates vital values from spiri-*

tual values in an artificial manner, whereas conscious evolution is nothing but a process of inner continuity, strangely similar to the growth of a seed. For the young plant to open out, an atmosphere composed of two categories of values is absolutely necessary. While favorable surroundings can modify the vital values so that the latter may better reflect the mind, a training is necessary before the mind is able to control and utilize properly the vital values. A broadening of thought can be observed chronologically. In the Vedas, *the word* 'karma' *designated only spiritual work, while the* Bhagavad Gita *spiritualizes all forms of activity, including the unconscious and psychological movements of life. It then becomes a question not only of a rise in level, but also of a deepening and widening of consciousness, which is the aim of spirituality. There is no divorce between the aim of spirituality and the aim of life, which is growth. Spiritual search is a conscious effort to grow by harmonious assimilation and at the same time an intensification of consciousness.*

But how many steps to climb! As soon as we have set out on the way, we try to spiritualize every instant of our life in a conscious or unconscious manner. Should the unconscious effort be supported by favorable social conditions or by a rudimentary inner need, it is already a preparation for a conscious effort, for the entire process depends on the dynamism of consciousness in search of clarity. Indeed, a sort of clarity comes as soon as the sensory values of animal life begin to be transformed into values of the understanding. The power to handle ideas is a conquest of consciousness. But though sensations may be clear and precise, the way they are understood by one person and another are very different. Sensations, even badly interpreted, are the only instrument a man possesses at the beginning of his search to put an order into his experiences, to shape his way of life, and to discover the laws of Great Nature.

On this level, the repetition of experiences related to the senses gives him a power of control. It is a help for creating his own inner world, although the values of this still only derive from outer influences. In the long run, this position is discovered to be false, for par-

ticular facts, even held to be true, still belong to the world of the senses. And the crucial point in the problem, paradoxically, is to grasp the universal on the ideal plane in order to project it onto the particular. Such is the pivot on which the spiritual effort turns: to transform the given values to the point where consciousness becomes dynamically free in its enjoyment of the 'I'. It is here that the interiorization of consciousness comes into play. This is the inescapable first step to be made. One of the ṛṣis *of the* Upanishads *clearly formulated its law: 'Pure Existence* (sat) *pierces an opening to project itself into the phenomenal world.'*[3] *Human consciousness obeys the same law, but the result is a degradation and a blunting of the conscious energy. To maintain the fire of life within it, the process has to be reversed.*

And Sŕi Anirvân said further:

If formulated in an abstract way, the call to observe oneself seems fantastic and even alarming at the beginning, yet to look into the depths of oneself is a necessary stage in the evolution of consciousness. Since it is an aim to be pursued in everyday life, the way of going about it must be clear and all the possibilities foreseen. What is more, it must be known that a certain quality of imagination will necessarily be utilized by the thought. In other words, it is necessary to 'imagine'[4] *what pure thought will be and to know at the same time that pure thought will only arise when the habitual automatism of thought is suspended. The same applies to our life, when in the midst of our occupations, a temporary and voluntary suspension of all activity is necessary to clarify our consciousness. Even if that moment is very short, consciousness will discern, in a flash of perception, what comes from the outer world and what from the inner world. But to exert any control whatsoever, one must first of all be able to control one's own thoughts. Therefore a control dictated from outside—let us call it a voluntary discipline—must play its role until the inner being is revealed.*

Another evening, Sŕi Anirvân sketched for us a picture of the development of independent thought in India in order to lead up to the question of the Bâüls and the Sufis.

Modern Indian follows intellectually a philosophical religion which is composed for the most part of Samkhya[5] *with a little Vedanta. Every cultured person knows it. In this connection, the word 'Hinduism'—rather vague and broad—can include and satisfy every curiosity. But what is tragic is that cultured society, from the time of the Upanishads, has completely turned away from the religion of the people. Popular beliefs, in their Tantric forms, with a background of Vedism, are intentionally ignored and the Hindu monks who teach Vedanta in Europe and in America, by tacit agreement amongst themselves, keep silent on the subject.*

In their family life, the people follow the autochthonous religion which the Aryans found in India when they arrived, an essentially practical religion far from any written teaching. This religion, still very alive, is founded on the close relationship existing between woman who embodies the power of śhakti[6] *and the earth. Though this cult of the woman was not formulated in a particular philosophy, it breathed life into all the philosophies, which without it would have lacked all radiance. It gives name and form (*nāmarūpa*) to the power of the primordial energy, so that the believers of all faiths can apprehend it. The greatly worshipped 'Divine Mother' was born and made incarnate to pour forth forever her grace and blessings on those who call upon her. The Divine Mother made her way into the temples, took her seat on private altars, was enclosed in amulets. She accepted a thousand names and forms, for an abstract symbol is not sufficient, anywhere, to nourish the heart. For those who worshipped her, she became the outlet for their strength, their passion, their despair, and their tenderness.*

On their arrival in India, the Vedic Aryans, who formed the aristocracy of priests and warriors, worshipped the spiritual principle of 'sunlit life' in a ritual that was far beyond the understanding of the aborigines. So that they might also worship the sun, but on their level, the simple people merely gave human features to the sun—who became Vishnu-the-Radiant. This was a spontaneous concretization. It followed, historically, that one of the Vedic princes, Krishna, who would never accept the throne even though it was his by right, espoused the cause of the people and denounced the rituals and sacrifices from which he was excluded.[7] *Certainly he wished to be free, but without ever himself becoming the sannyāsin whose spirit and form he praised in the Bhagavad Gita.*[8] *Because of this, Krishna personified forever the 'way to liberation' for all the oppressed and became for them the All-Powerful-Divine-Lord. For a long time before the story of Krishna was written down, it was passed on by oral tradition. He is represented as having been taken by force from his royal surroundings and brought up by villagers. He is above all else the Child-God playing with the* gopis[9] *and, in the Bhagavad Gita, the Lord who teaches. His greatness lies in having transformed daily existence, with all its sufferings, into sacrifices for love. Thanks to him, the poorest man, though hungry, plays his flute and sings his love without complaint.*

Another evening, we took up again the question: 'What are the forms of pre-Vedic religions that give life to India?' Sŕi Anirvân said:

They are very much intermingled. The generally accepted idea is that everything Vedic belongs exclusively to the Aryan culture does not mean that everything Aryan is Vedic, for as soon as the Aryans arrived in India, some of them refused to submit to the authority of the Vedas and were persecuted. These heretical Aryans, driven out as though they had been undesirable nomads, went away and settled on the eastern boundaries with their free thought, their democratic way of life, without gods, without kings, without castes. If we look back to these beginnings, it is because they show how independent thought has been literally suppressed in India since Vedic times. Secretly, however, it became the great 'subterranean current' of force that inspires us, causing flames of living spirituality to spring up here and there;[10] *these flames are extinguished at a given moment only to blaze up again, later and elsewhere, with equal strength.*

Here we come to the history of the well-known rebels, independent souls, which is at the same time the history of the great Gurus. They are known in history under the name Vratyas[11] *and are only spoken of with contempt! With the passing of time, silence fell on the subject of this minority who had dared to defy the fierce Vedic orthodoxy. If the* Vratyas *are mentioned in some of the writings, it is always in harsh terms: 'They are the ones who, without having been initiated into the Vedic cult, speak as though they had been … they are the ones who claim to play the Guru without being Gurus …'*

Although the Vratyas *did not observe the Vedic forms of worship, they believed in a great Being who can be described only negatively; here we recognize Shiva:*

… in the beginning there was the One.
From Him everything emanated.
He who knows this Vratya
is called vidvan vratya …

Very soon this great Being, free from all slavery, became the prototype of the living, liberated man, of the Shaivite monk completely indifferent to Vedic orthodoxy. This wandering monk, roaming about naked, his body smeared with ashes, possessing nothing but his gourd, so impressed the people that he soon occupied the foreground, leaving the priests far behind.

Another wanderer, equally free from all social rules, appeared at about the same time—the Bâül, a counterpart of the 'Man in the heart,' of an inner state which can be attained only by personal discipline.[12] *Since the Bâüls did not recognize caste distinction, since they had no temple, worshipped no God and made no pilgrimages to sacred places, they were considered to be rebels. As soon as India was invaded by Islam,*[13] *Sufis of all lines of descent joined with them.*

> *They became like one family, singing the same songs, playing the same instrument. Together they followed the same precepts: to submit to and obey the 'Man seated in the temple of the heart,' to respect the secrets of others, to use money simply and without attachment, to expend themselves for the good of others, to show themselves strong with the strong and humble before the weak.*

The Sufi who was among our guests said, 'What I am I do not know. If you have a Guru, you have no more head, but only *fanā*, that sensation of infinite expansion which is the Void. Your intuition is fed by the immensity of the Guru's intuition. I absorb what he gives me, "I am," until I am filled to overflowing. It is not I who have touched the Guru's coat, it is he who holds me by the hand.'

The Bâül travels in the Void
in which all voices resound
O Bhagavan …

Endnotes

1. *The author of the Yoga-Sutras, who probably lived in the second century B.C.*
2. *1.3.3–4.*
3. Chandogya Up. *6.8.4.*
4. *Based on a knowledge of what is real.*
5. *See p. 76.*
6. *The primordial energy, the conscious force of the Divinity, the Divine in action, the feminine aspect of the One.*
7. *Kings belong to the second caste, the Kshatriyas.*
8. *6, 1. The Bhagavad Gita is only one of the scriptures containing a wealth of practical spiritual instructions.*
9. *The shepherdesses.*
10. *Śrī Ramana Maharshi is a striking example.*
11. *They are often described as 'the savage hordes.'*
12. *The Shaiva represents the Purusha aspect and the Bâül the prakriti aspect of the same spiritual discipline.*
13. *In the eleventh century.*

Chapter 7

Problems

The Brahmins who gravitated around us lived for the most part in Almora and were lawyers. They took time to visit each other, smoked water pipes together, and conversed on matters to do with God, the temple, and the priesthood, as well as on those concerning their large families, the town, and the land. Each of them had two or three disciples (*chelas*) attached to their person to carry out all their wishes—to carry a message, to write letters, or quite simply to keep them company. These were young men of the same caste learning to play their role in society, or some distant relative of the family, or students in charge of the children's education.

Our friends were all orthodox. My relationship with them was excellent because as one who was serving Sŕi Anirvân, I had a recognized status. While I observed all their rules of conduct, I also imposed my own rules when they came to visit Haimavati. 'Be careful,' Sŕi Anirvân warned me. 'They will forgive your failure to keep the rules of others, but they will not be tolerant if you fail to obey your own!' My rules had to do with the practical facts of life at Haimavati. The stone flags in the rooms were washed every morning. No garbage such as fruit peelings was to be thrown in the garden. I asked the women not to dry their washing on the bushes, the stairs, or the roof. These demands, minimal from my point of view, went against habits and raised a conflict in myself. The rule I imposed on myself was never to ask a question and never to ask a favour.

There were difficult moments when I felt far removed from my own culture and yet unable to understand the customs of the people around me. With Sŕi Anirvân I never reacted in this way for he had the art of making me live from my own substance and not from his; he gave me the strength not to be weak with myself. With my Hindu friends, I looked for the point of contact where direct communication could take place. We spoke about the same efforts, but we did not have the same reactions. Certainly I succeeded in mastering my own, and in this way I learned a great many things about myself. I did what was expected of me, I said the words that were supposed to be said, but when I went back to my room, I asked myself, 'What am I doing here?' And my answer to myself was, 'You are watching yourself live!' It was impossible to cheat, for there was no one to approve or disapprove of anything I did, there was only 'me' becoming my own obstacle. And the game was worth playing.

The isolation in which we lived finally created a curious phenomenon. It was as though a cloak of mist distorted the outlines of things and transformed the abstract values of what we were looking for. Whereas Sŕi Anirvân had always spoken about the harmonizing of the ego within the radiant being, we began to get lost in talk about 'the destruction of the ego.' The psychological poverty of my Hindu friends was concealed within an exaggerated sense of their own importance. In fact they were imprisoned by caste, family customs, and life routine. The direct consequence of this state of things was a continuous dream described in a cosmic vocabulary and used as an escape from life. Such was one of the many problems brought to Haimavati and laid before 'the one who knew' so that he might direct the mind towards another dimension. The great difficulty was passivity. Many begged for the Master's blessing and wished to live in his orbit, for it is easier to exist in his shadow, to watch him live, to rejoice in his asceticism, than to struggle oneself. A process of dissolution (pralaya) gave a glimpse that one is far closer to God in death than in life. Subconsciously, each one wished to die or retire from the world, to 'get out of it,' no longer to bear the weight of it. To leave everyday life for the sake of finding something else—a stability around an impersonal axis—meant an almost superhuman effort in this land which had become a museum of rites. But if this effort were directed towards action and towards the liberation of the self, a solution could be found without having to destroy the ego.

Sŕi Anirvân said:

> *If you truly wish to see your conditions as they are, you must realize that from childhood on, even with a highly developed intelligence, you have no chance of making a choice in the circumstances of your life. You grow up in a hierarchic order, your career is predetermined, you are given the wife with whom you will make your earthly journey. These conditions of respect and obedience are ideal for being completely free in spirit. Great Nature allows nothing to escape from her. Repetition exists on all levels: movement, attitudes, speech follow a known gradation which ensures the continuation of the species in the same pattern. The centripetal law is allowed full play.*
>
> *But where is this freedom to which you aspire? It has to be paid for dearly. The ashram life which appeals to you is only family life transposed into a broader frame. The Guru is the father, the* Guru-patni *is the mother, with all her prerogatives. The change in the pattern would only be in the orientation of your vocabulary bondage towards a movement rising in a spiral, around an axis which goes from the nadir to the zenith.*

The Europeans among us found the solitude hard to bear. Any physical effort required at that high altitude[1] and in the tropics, combined with the anguish aroused by the strangeness of the landscape, created tension. Unlike the Hindus, the freedom of the Europeans to accept or to destroy all elements of their private life, including even their stay at Haimavati, aroused a whole range of emotions. At a certain time, the body, having accepted new habits which were often uncomfortable, reacted violently. Our guests would escape into the forest for long hours at a time on non-existent pretexts: some dry wood to pick up, a new path to be discovered, a lost sandal … they would come back with explanations that nobody was asking for. The Hindus, more accustomed to communal life and to the tensions of the inner life, merely said, 'I am at my saturation point,' and with a slowing-down equal to the eagerness of the first days, they would allow themselves long periods of retirement. Sŕi Anirvân let it all go on. Everybody was suffering in one way or another, like an iron bar when it is thrown into the fire and then beaten on the anvil to give it the required shape.

As for me, my task was to be 'alone' in the midst of civilities, offerings, demands, and ironies. Did our guests have any idea that my heart very often bled to see their inner hunger? In the evening, in front of Sŕi Anirvân, it was my turn to beg and plead until he made the little movement of his head that meant it was time to get up and go away. We were all playing a game under pressure.

Traditional techniques affirm that although one cannot change one's character, one can nevertheless become free from it by making it sufficiently supple. What remains at that point is not a residue, but the very foundation of being, stripped bare. If this basis were to disappear, it would be death. 'One must have experienced the process,' Sŕi Anirvân used to say, 'before undertaking a more advanced discipline. To fashion a gold ring, the jeweler uses pure gold and an alloy. He is a smelter when he works in the descending movement, an artist-engraver in the ascending movement. He is liberated only when he sells his jewel. It would be madness to believe in a possible liberation without having voluntarily descended many, many times to the foundation of being, to know the mysterious seed in us where the life of Great Nature is hidden.'

One of our guests, a man of sixty-five who was a lawyer, spoke to me of the daily discipline he tried to follow. For several years he tried consciously to limit all his desires to three major principles:

- *to try to live in the present moment which fills all space and time;*
- *not to give more importance to transitory happenings than to a monsoon rain which falls violently and may stop at any moment;*
- *not to waste time on things that are outside immediate concern.*

The fact that he consciously refused to let himself be drawn into what did not concern him meant not interfering in the fate of other people. In life, this man was like all others; but face to face with himself he evaluated his resistance to the current of life. When he came to the ashram, his questions to Sŕi Anirvân, even more than the answers, showed him the direction to follow. 'How,' he said, 'can one ask a question which is true from the beginning to the end?'

We received news that S., a friend of Sŕi Anirvân, died in Delhi. He left a wife, five children, and parents who were dependent on him. Nobody ever knew who he was. In the family group he lived according to the consciousness of the group and made it a discipline of introspection from which he derived all that he gave to those around him. Sŕi Anirvân said often, 'He knew how inwardly to create the solitude that is propitious for divine delights. He has gone away with his secret.'

The Hindu women who came to Haimavati felt quite at home after a few days, even though they had to give up the habit of drying their washing all over the place! They spoke a mixture of Hindi and Pahari, the dialect of the mountains, which I found difficult to follow. I had to discover by myself the depth of their spiritual quest, all that they knew and how they were the cloak of nothingness which the men threw over their shoulders. My life as a Western woman, my work, my travels did not interest them. I could easily have appeared for them as a professional storyteller!

Their world seemed to me at first to be very small, but soon I became interested in their devotions and discovered how the Brahman, nameless and formless in manifestation, interpenetrates life in an active way, makes everything the senses allow us to perceive divine: the wind, a perfume, a song, a tree, a fruit, an animal, and particularly the husband and the child. Anything could become the logical support leading to the undifferentiated Divine. While the men had spoken to me of the Vedanta philosophy, unconnected with everyday life, the women, through the Tantras, perceived every single thing as animate. In the mountains, the gods have no sculptured image. The stone cup placed on top of the little square temples represents the being who offers himself to heaven to receive grace, rain, abundance. In the shade, big pebbles marked with a red dot hold the power that unites heaven and earth. Each woman had in her Shrine a little of the sacred earth of Badrinath and Kedarnath, the two temples from which one makes the ascent to heaven.

The first time I was invited to step over the wall of orthodoxy of a Brahmin family in Almora was on the third birthday of a little boy. For the occasion the women of the two families, the Pants and the Joshis, were wearing a special shawl on which was painted the emblem of their clan (*gotra*). The glittering of the many feast-day saris looked as if the house were flowing with gold. Traditional hospitality required my hosts to receive me as though the Divine had knocked at their door and at the same time the caste laws forbade that I should eat with them! To save the situation a compromise was found. While the grandmothers, the aunts, and the widows were watching the child being blessed by the priests, the younger women watched me eat alone like a princess surrounded by her court. Then they led me by force into the presence of the goddess of the house, who was also draped in the shawl of the clan. A joyful impulsive curiosity kept us all close together until it was time for me to leave just before sunset. I could not be late. Sri Anirvân's disciple had to be home before nightfall.

Whenever I went out from Haimavati, I never failed to meet sādhus on the road. Their life intrigued me. They went by, carried forward by their vision, begging their pittance though often ill-received in the poor valleys. Some of them had a definite itinerary; others, like dead leaves, were blown by the wind from place to place. All obeyed alike the same rule: not to stay more than three nights under the same roof. Some of them had the bearing of princes in disguise, others were ragged or had their body smeared with ashes. Whoever they were, with their beautiful names—'Abandonment-in-God,' 'Joy-in-Austerity,' 'Pure-Vision-of-the-Infinite'—they had the tradition with them, for the renunciation, of which they were the living symbol, was envied by many. They were part of the totality of the anonymous efforts by which the mass is leavened. In a word, their search and mine were somewhat the same.

Higher knowledge is certainly not to be picked up on the trails in the Himalayas, nor yet is it hidden in the caves; but it exists for the few, for those at the stage of direct perception. One evening, we translated from Kabir a few lines from a text written half in Urdu, half in Hindi:

The Puranas and the Koran are only words
but behind the veil of the words, I see . . .

The water in the ghats[2] *is cold, the Gods are mute,*
but I, Kabir, am hot-blooded and I have a tongue . . .

Endnotes

1. *About 7,200 feet.*
2. *The stony bank of a river where ablutions are performed.*

Chapter 8

Lessons from Life

Our young servant was called Prem (which means 'divine love'). It was the first time he had served in a house where there was a foreigner. Though quite unaware of it, Prem was destined to be my teacher in many realms. Sŕi Anirvân never gave orders—a sign, a look was enough. He was always served first. I gave orders, but they would not be carried out unless they were given indirectly since Prem belonged to a high caste. It was up to me to know what he would never do, and make arrangements accordingly.

Prem, the passive witness of all that went on, managed very cleverly to be always respectful and contemptuous at the same time. Barefoot on the stone slabs, he came and went inaudibly with an absent-minded aire. In the evenings he lit the oil lamps and went to sit on a wall in the garden. Soon the sound of his flute would be heard. He could neither read nor write, but he was good at sums! His mistakes in arithmetic were just little tricks tried out to see whether I was a real mistress or not. His sleepy mind irritated me. Sŕi Anirvân said one day, 'Well, then, teach him to think! In a few years Prem will perhaps own a tea shop and be a member of the village council!'

Prem tolerated the wildcat I had brought from Lohaghat. She followed me about everywhere, but allowed no one to touch her. Sŕi Anirvân often said, 'Pussy is your disciple. You are responsible for her. She is a perfect cat, who shows it by doing her own cat business very well.' In the evening she used to come into the room where we were talking and take up her position in front of a hole between the stone slabs and the outer wall. She would stay on guard there for hours without moving. She knew perfectly well that sooner or later a rat would come through the hole because there were no other holes and plenty of foolhardy young rats! When one did come, she was ready. No struggle, no playing about. One snap and her teeth were in the back of his neck. She then threw him into the air to break his spine, exactly as a panther deals with his prey. 'Are you as vigilant and watchful as Pussy?' asked Sŕi Anirvân.

This cat provoked an incident with Prem that had a great effect on my behavior. I had bought a drinking glass in town for a flower vase. One day Prem poured boiling water into it and it cracked. Prem said, 'It is Pussy's fault.' I answered back, 'Liar!' and there was anger in my voice. I looked up and saw Sŕi Anirvân on the doorstep. I felt I had been caught doing wrong without knowing why. Nothing was said in front of Prem, but in the evening the Master said, 'It was you who were wrong in answering like that. When you have found out and understood why, we will speak about it.'

Six years later the question came up again when I was visiting Sŕi Anirvân in Shillong and we were talking about impressions received from our surroundings.

> *Do you remember Prem? You two were obeying different laws. The influences around him were too different for him to understand them. He was never sure of approval and so he was slow in everything he did to have time to affirm himself, to have confidence in his reactions. In his own eyes he could not make a blunder—what would he have explained to his family? In front of something incomprehensible, isn't the simplest thing to accuse the other? Don't we do it all the time because we don't trust our reactions? Prem asked himself no questions, his life was a series of impulses, while your Pussy was perfectly in harmony with the laws of her nature. Our reactions are fed by the laws we recognize and they in turn lead us back to the great cosmic law.*

Several of us went one evening to hear a sacred chant (*kirtan*) led by Narayan Maharaj.[1] Seated in the lotus posture, Narayan was as beautiful as a young god. He was about forty. His face, without a wrinkle, was framed in black curls. His shawl, draped over one shoulder, left his breast bare. A necklace of crystal beads and *rudrakshas*[2] signified life-death, Tantrism, and Shaivism. He accompanied the chant with *taraks*, a kind of castanet. The rhythm died under his hands, only to come to life again without a pause. Little by little the sacred ecstasy began; the movement of his right arm wrapped the fullness of his voice around him, his shoulders swayed from right to left. Narayan was like a tree bending to the storm. He sang a sacred word, a *mantra*, which was repeated by his audience in the same tenuous, vibrant rhythm. Feeling was at its peak.

This went on for a long time. And then, quite suddenly, Narayan was silent. In the abrupt stillness, he stayed with his arms uplifted, his body rigid, living an emotion he communicated to us. His face reflected an intense joy … then, slowly, he came back to himself, murmuring as if to the gods, his body relaxed. His taraks had slipped to one side. Earlier, the skin of one of the drums had burst and at that moment his face had reflected intense pain. Something had broken. Then he had gone on with his song.

I did not recognize myself in those moments of shared exaltation. Later, I asked, 'Who is Narayan?'

Srî Anirvân said:

> *He is a great artist. His song fills him. It is astonishing to follow his movement around the axis of the body. He is as supple as the seaweed in the sea; he gives the impression of being transparent, full of light. Has he been feeding on milk and honey? He sucks in the atmosphere around him and swallows three-quarters of it to feed the sap of his ascending force. The remaining quarter is for whoever happens to be ready to take it. A pure being like Narayan—the least sexual desire would kill him—feeds the soul of those around him for a long time. He brings a warm sensation which leaves a recognizable taste. But as soon as the mind begins to play with it, all that is fundamen-*

tally primitive in such adoration is spoiled. Reason condemns it and drives it out; then adoration comes in by the back door and becomes worship of movie stars, of a life of luxury, of sex.

Tagore used to invite Bâüls and Sufis to chant kirtans at his house. Many of his poems were born in such an atmosphere. Sŕi Ramakrishna experienced ecstasies of the same kind and his great disciple, Swami Vivekananda, was one of the greatest sankirtanists *of his time, though in the West he never spoke of it for fear of criticism. In orthodox Islam, too, there are those who break down the barriers, like Raihana Tyabji, the pīr of Kanpur, and others. For them,* bhāva *and fanā are words which reveal exactly the same creative joy.*

Years later, Sŕi Anirvân used the same words—bhāva, fanā—when he said, 'Ramana Maharshi was like the trunk of a tree, the pīr of Kanpur like its foliage, Narayan like its flowers. The one drew sap from the earth, the second was a breathing in of life-giving air, the third was the perfume of flowers. But they were all fed from one and the same root. What can a Master truly do for his disciples? He can do no more than create the phenomenon which breaks down resistances and invade by surprise the soul of the one who opens to him—this is the only possible way.'

That same evening Sŕi Anirvân told me the story of a Hindu woman who was to arrive the next day. Her name was Pushpa. Her story began on the day the River Damodar rose furiously out of its bed, carrying everything with it. There were many deaths. Hundreds of villages were destroyed before the waters became calm and the flooded land reflected the clouds passing overhead.

Sŕi Anirvân continued:

My Guru opened a camp to take in the victims of the flood and sent out teams to help them up and down the river. One of our men saved Pushpa's mother. She was half unconscious, clinging to a tree with one hand while with the other arm she was clasping her baby tightly to her. Her husband had disappeared before her eyes. They brought her to the ashram where she became a humble servant. And so that was how Pushpa happened to grow up there and unfold into a fine young girl. Everyone loved her. When she was ten years old, the Master decided she should be married. We had had with us for a year a young novice from the same district and the same caste as Pushpa. This was the man the Guru chose. It was a curious fate for that young man—he had come to the ashram to become a monk and now the Master was giving him a wife!

My Guru gave Pushpa a dowry as though he had been her father and sent two monks to represent the 'bride's family' during the marriage ceremony. Beautifully adorned, Pushpa looked like a goddess. When the feast was over, she came back to live with her adopted father, according to custom in child marriages.

From then on I was put in charge of Pushpa's education. Until she was fifteen, her husband only came back to the ashram on feast days. He had found a good job in his village, took her home with him, and their married life began. Two years later Pushpa, to her delight, had a son, but the baby died in infancy. Faced with death, the young mother remained a spectator of her own grief; people heard her saying, withdrawn into herself, 'This is how it happened—the child smiled … and then it was all over.' 'All over' to her meant that she knew her married life was finished, for she could not have another child.

Pushpa adored her husband with all the ardor of an eighteen-year-old. A year later, when she felt sure of her reactions, she said to her husband, 'Shankar, you must take another wife, for I do not dare raise my eyes to look at your mother so long as she has no grandson in her arms.' Before speaking to Shankar, she had made inquiries about a young girl and told him about her. Shankar said nothing, so Pushpa went ahead and arranged the marriage. Then she went away and made a long pilgrimage in the mountains. When she came back she said to the second wife, 'May there never be any bad feeling between us. Shankar is yours. You are there to serve him in everything. I chose you to give him fine children.'

Pushpa had made her position clear. She was skillful in everything she undertook. Sometimes she would take some money from the bag in which Shankar kept his savings and would go away for a while. Where did she go? Nobody knew except Shankar. Sŕi Anirvân continued:

> *She used to come and visit me and she still does. Each time she brings questions which have ripened slowly and are filled out by her experience. She listens to what I say with the intelligence of the heart that perceives what is hidden by the obscurity of the ego. You will see her tomorrow night. She has discarded so many things that she tastes life at its source. What she understands, she makes use of. And from here she will take away only what is true for her. Because of this, people are happy to be near her. Without knowing it, she transmits a living reality, but if ever she comes to realize it, the miracle will come to an end, for Great Nature will no longer work for her in the same way.*

The next day Pushpa arrived with the innumerable baskets, bags, and bundles which my Hindu guests always brought with them. She was small and slender, and wore a Kashmir shawl over her shoulders. Her hair was covered by a fold of her sari knotted round the neck in the manner of Bengali women on their way to the temple. She prostrated herself before Sŕi Anirvân. As she was getting to her feet, she caught sight of me. She gripped me by the shoulders and leaned her head on my breast. Her lips were murmuring tender words I could not understand. With one hand she wiped away the tears that sprang from my eyes. I was very much older than she. All the time she was with us, she behaved to me like a loving daughter, always keeping for me the place next to Sŕi Anirvân. Her awareness enriched our hours of silence. She always seemed to me contented—sorting rice or pounding spices or whatever she did. How simple life was with her! Sŕi Anirvân gave her very little time, but she did not ask for more. When she had left again with as much enthusiasm as on her arrival, Sŕi Anirvân said:

Pushpa plays with time. Life has taught her that every sensation lights the flame of a little lamp in us. What matters is not to have at the same moment opposite sensations that would start a big fire. With only one sensation at a time—but that sensation has color, smell, sound—it is even tangible. This sensation has an identity! Something in us knows perfectly well where it comes from and what it is worth.

Pushpa had to spend three days and three nights on the train to get home. She traveled third class, in heat and discomfort, with an inward smile on her lips.

Endnotes

1. *Sŕi Narayan Swami of Soosa, died around 1958.*
2. *Seed of a fruit.*

Chapter 9

The End of Haimavati

It was four years since Sŕi Anirvân had sent out the call to his pupils: 'Come, everything is ready for you!' One evening he said to me, 'It is all over. The experiment at Haimavati has come to an end.' I did not answer. I knew it, but I would not have been able to say when it had come about.

It is amazing to see how rapidly dissolution takes place when nobody holds on to the fluid matters that enter into play. I did not attempt to stop this movement of dissolution and at the same time I was careful not to let fear enter into myself. Fear could easily have poisoned my reactions or created sufficient lies to reassure the inner being. I wanted to keep my eyes wide open and follow what was about to happen. I only said, 'I know it. The pupils we were expecting did not come.'

'The Great Nature (prakriti) of India is not ripe,' said Sŕi Anirvân:

> *Everything is too fragmentary. There is no unity yet in time. But the dream has been born and is powerful, even though lacking a body.*
>
> *What are we in the play of the great forces in action? An instrument, a means, a tool—nothing more. Let us watch this movement of dissolution taking place as it wishes; it will disappear of itself at a phenomenal speed. We are witnesses to the deviation that comes about directly after any effort. Do nothing to hinder this natural*

> *cadence. In any case you could do nothing without interference by the ego. And the ego in this case would be pure pride.*

This conscious dissolution under the law was no accident; it found its own way like a phrase in music seeking another tonality. If the pupils who were supposed to have formed the nucleus of a stable team in our work had established themselves at Haimavati, this would have meant for me a task I had agreed to undertake for the next ten years. Influenced by their orthodox background, by the pressures of family requirements, they had not come. Nevertheless, they existed, and Sŕi Anirvân was certainly going to use their energy in some other way. So far as we were concerned, the money sent from Hyderabad, Calcutta, and elsewhere had already been sent back and nothing remained but to close the house. Later, I received a letter from Sŕi Anirvân, which summed up the situation as follows:

> *What we created remains intact; Haimavati exists. It is an idea, a real idea. We had a twofold aim, that of creating a very broadly conceived Cultural Centre and of preparing a retreat for those who were attracted towards spiritual research. What was lacking in our plan will come of itself, little by little, without a plan. All is* māyā,[1] *which is the mystery of life.*

The house was taken to pieces as quickly as it had been put together. Sŕi Anirvân wished me to return to Europe, to take the 'living idea' with me and allow it to grow freely as he himself was going to do in Assam. He foresaw that it would take me at least three years to find the right irrigated land in Europe in which to plow my furrows. To give me confidence for this new spiritual adventure, he threw a bridge out between us, as light as a spider's thread. 'I shall stay here for another three years,' he wrote, 'but nothing will survive of what we created together except our common effort. To feel oneself "aspirated" by the ascending law is nourishment for the whole of one's life on earth. You are going away, rich from having put your effort into an ascending law. If you are not destined to taste the fruits of this effort, it means your task is to cultivate the ground, to till it.'

A few days before we left, he brought me a book which had recently appeared and which had been sent to him from Allahabad. He had read it through in one sitting.[2] 'Read this carefully,' he said. 'It contains ideas that are very dear to us and that have been your food in these past years. Look for the people who are working in this direction; they are living for a conscious reality. You will find among them men and women who are capable of carrying an idea. This will be your first duty on arriving ... and you keep me informed of what steps you take until you are carried by your own current.'

The time of departure came near. I knew that the time lived close to a Master is a period of initiation into all the requirements of life as a whole and that the true discipline would begin for me only when I went back into the world.

At that moment, the freedom you have acquired will give you a new sense of values in your new surroundings. Live your life leaning up against the vault of the sky and with your feet well planted on the earth. Move constantly between the one and the other, remaining aware of the movements of Great Nature. It is this constant movement that is to create the matrix of the Void in which you will find yourself face to face with yourself. It is now up to you to formulate your own discipline. Above all, wipe out the past. You will be called upon to participate in different kinds of work. Enter into them and give your thoughts, your blood, your warmth, but remain free. Do not allow yourself to be eaten up by the autointoxication of your law of gravity; live with your law without going round and round in circles. Never accept any money that would bind you. Money is useful, but if you are not able to use it and remain free, then don't touch it! You know a great deal about the laws. Take what is good in them and ally it to what is good. Never go beyond what you have understood, nor what you are able to live. Principles alone are right. Do not confuse them with the interpretations that men produce. Sow seeds, water them if you are able. This is the most we can do.

I was quiet within myself when I left. At one moment when I needed reassurance, I asked, 'Have I made progress in these four years that have gone by?'

'You have gone far. Before this, you were putting ideas together, crumbs of information related to knowledge. Now that is over. You are taking the time to live a totally different life.' And he put a mango into my hand as he had on the day I arrived.

Sŕi Anirvân left first. I took him into town as far as the bus that goes down to the plain. As we had done every day, we each folded our hands and took leave. Neither one of us spoke. We exchanged a look, very strong. When the bus had gone, it struck me that I had never touched his hand.

A week later I received the following letter:

> *Today is your last day at Haimavati. It is also the anniversary of the day when I became a Bâül, forty-one years ago. Go forward! free and without fear, go ahead like Devahuti,[3] the mother of Kapila. May life and death be one and the same thing for you.*

Endnotes

1. *The power of illusion; the veil covering reality and the divine force producing the illusion.*
2. *This was* The Psychology of Man's Possible Evolution, *by P. D. Ouspensky (London: Hodder and Stoughton, 1951).*
3. *See pp. 77.*

Part Two

TALKS ON SAMKHYA

Śŕi Anirvân

Chapter 10

A State of Sahaja

The *Katha Upanishad* says: 'The aim is to attain pure Existence (sat).' He who has realized this has a clear understanding of what reality is. Pure Existence is the Truth beyond life and death.[1] That you exist is a fact! And your existence is nothing but a manifestation of that which is universal and transcendental. So your existence becomes oneness (*kaivalya*) in which there exist the two principles of Samkhya: Purusha, which is the spirit, and Prakriti, which is 'that which is manifested.'[2] Spirituality cannot be acquired; it can only be derived from these two principles.

Open yourself up to the sun of pure Existence (sat) as the bud of a flower opens to the light. Then the Truth will flow into you. Impatience spoils everything! There is a Bâül song which says:

The stars, the suns, and the moons are never impatient.
Silently, they follow the stream of pure Existence, as the true Guru does.

Now, this pure Existence, lived with a wide-open heart amid all the circumstances of life, is in itself the state of *sahaja*—a state in which the mind is freed from all duality. The motionless mind knows 'That' which has neither beginning nor end, which is free in its very essence.

Sahaja is a yoga for the same reason as all other yogas. It is a path that leads to the discovery of 'That with which one is born,' the pure being living in the temple of the heart.

Sahaja can be defined as follows: 'That which is born in you, that which is born with you,' a state of pure essence. The body, the spirit, the impulse of life and intelligence are all there. Nothing must be rejected or mutilated, so that 'one and the same thing' can be consciously established.

That is why Samkhya, which is the path by which the state of sahaja is attained, speaks a great deal of the waking state that is the normal level of all activity. It also speaks of the state of consciousness interiorized in dreams, which later becomes the state of deep sleep. The fourth state, that of inner awakening, is the mark of deep sleep. Shankaracharya[3] instructs us about these four different states in his philosophy.

In sahaja, there is a fifth state, that of a totally awakened consciousness; it contains in itself the four states of wakefulness, dreaming, deep sleep, and the state in which deep sleep exists along with the other states. There is no longer any differentiation between the various states, all of them being unified at a single point.

From that moment on, everything becomes your food. Everything is one and the same thing in you. Then you are faced with a new task in the realm of sensation and relaxation. It becomes a question of forgetting oneself, of voluntarily obliterating oneself, which is a letting go in a region that is very subtle and hard to discover.[4] Voluntary forgetting is a task that is just as difficult as accustoming one's mental faculty to remembering the details of self-observation. It is only approached much later, when memory has become submissive and fulfils its true role.

This is slow work and a true discipline in itself. The effort to forget ceases when the contraction that determines the field of work disappears. Without contraction there can be no directed effort. When this effort is recognized, the contraction disappears and is at once replaced by a very special kind of attention coming from very far away. This attention is indifferent to what is going on and yet it watches closely. It gives no orders and does not know impatience. It simply watches how Great Nature (prakriti) operates, for even in the subtle domain of voluntary forgetfulness prakriti has still to be reckoned with.

To wish to forget is, in fact, impossible. Forgetting proceeds from a principle without any form. When your being is invaded by a movement coming from the heart and the mind, you are just like an empty vibrating bell filled by the echo of a sound coming from elsewhere.

Accept within yourself the idea that you have only twenty-four hours to live. Let those hours be full of clarity to help you to accomplish your task. Do not allow them to be tarnished. They have been entrusted to you. Those twenty-four hours are your eternity. In the face of this three-dimensional day, it is impossible to imagine the future. Do not attempt to stretch the time, nor to divide it nor to lengthen or shorten it. Everything is so full and at the same time so empty!

The discipline of sahaja begins with the acceptance of the whole of life just as it is. The heart opens up to receive it and to live it. As for intelligence and logic, they will seek in Samkhya the necessary strength for finding the key to the enigma of existence. Sahaja then appears like a path illumined by the experience of inner being.

In practice, Samkhya is a technique to realize the expansion of sahaja. Neither the one nor the other takes into account gods, demons, paradises, hells, or formalism of any kind, in the course of inner effort. The point where Samkhya and sahaja converge is in the whole of life, which becomes in itself the object of meditation. Therefore serenity within oneself and a right relationship with life and one's fellow beings becomes a way of being.

He who practices a spiritual discipline (*sādhanā*) will use Samkhya to learn how to look at the movements of Great Nature in all its manifestations without interfering with its movements, to recognize its imprint on everything and to observe the ability of prakriti to pass imperceptibly from one plane of consciousness to another. Not to react to any of its movements would, in fact, mean, to live in the very heart of life without being affected by it. But at the beginning, this state cannot be taken for granted, for it is not merely by observing the movements of prakriti that one becomes its master.

The disciple will turn his gaze upon himself and discover, although he had never before seen it, the countless inner disturbances created by everything in him that says: 'I like and I do not like; I want and I do not want; it's right and it's wrong,' and so forth, which prevent him from noticing that in himself there is a stormy prakriti identical to the one that exists around him.

How can he dissociate himself from that prakriti which until he dies will always be for him his life, his mind and his body with all their functions? At this point traditional Rajayoga comes to help. This yoga, through its graduated disciplines, brings the body to a state of conscious joy, one's life to a state of equanimity comparable to complete rest and one's mind to ecstasy (*samādhi*).[5] In this state of equanimity, all the automatic movements of prakriti and its unconscious play can be perceived. Always, in following this inner discipline, the ideal of Samkhya is to learn how to stand back, and the ideal of yoga is *vairāgya*, which means to learn how to observe oneself dispassionately and without judgment.

Long and meticulous work is indispensable in order to discover that emotion of any kind creates a passionate movement which takes man out of himself. In this case yoga teaches how to check any impetuous movement by emptying the mind of all images. The superabundant energy is thus brought back to the self. But the purpose of Samkhya is that this energy, having returned to the self, should also be directed consciously towards the outer life, that it should become openly active without disturbing the inner or outer prakriti. In this way life-energy is purified. It becomes creative. Of course, this state can only last for a few minutes, and the ordinary man immediately reappears with his train of habitual reactions within the play of manifestation.

This moment of illumination (*sattva*)—and this word is right even if the moment be brief—is a look into oneself and at the same time a look outside oneself *śivadṛṣṭi*. Symbolically, it can be compared to the piercing look of Purusha into himself and upon the active Prakriti around him. To accept Prakriti in its totality is pure sahaja. In a subtle manner, beyond 'I like and I don't like,' it brings a possibility of modification in the densities of the intrinsic qualities (*guṇas*)[6] of the lower prakriti and shows the path by which a higher Prakriti can be reached.

Learn to return voluntarily to what is fundamentally primitive in you, carefully hidden and disguised in the realm of instinct, intuition, and sex. This conscious return will produce unsuspected reactions and induce outbursts of all your dormant impatience. If you were a tree, they would all of them be branches issuing from the same trunk. One cannot cut off one branch without damaging the whole; cutting several of them would cause the death of the tree. All the branches together form the canopy of foliage.

In the wind, the foliage is in harmony with the whole forest. It is in the foliage that the birds nest and sing. May this picture help you in your spiritual discipline, even if it is very hard. If something obscure lingers in you, it means that there must still be an attachment somewhere, just as in the tree there are knots which hinder the rising of the sap.

You can absorb ideas and make them your own. You can freely create ways to express them. That is what the force in you can do. Perhaps I can help you to discover your own power but only by suggestion. If you open yourselves up and discover who you are, I shall be pleased.

A great *tapasyā* awaits you. This word means personal austerity and voluntary discipline.

The expression 'voluntary discipline' connects two ideas: that of heat and that of light. These are clearly the creative energy and the wisdom so often described in the Upanishads as being together the first manifestation of the creative urge. One of the Upanishads even goes so far as to say that it is a radiation devoid of any specific characteristic; that is, without form (*alingam*).

True tapasyā means to be one with the creative power of Prakriti. It brings us close to Great Nature as she really is. One voluntarily drops all accumulations, all that has been acquired, and returns to what is simple and innate. Austerities, both mental and physical, to which many a seeker subjects himself, are only the fumbling means adopted by ignorant souls wishing to attain that entirely natural end.

Allow your power to radiate, and may this radiation be your discipline. Hear the resonance of this call in you and, without tension of any sort, have the courage to plunge into the depths of your soul. Do not listen to the sophisticated sayings of the wiseacres who teach with pomp and ostentation.

Understood in this manner, tapasyā is the progressive development of limitless intuition. There are two kinds of tapasyā. One in which I always say 'yes'—Tantras, and one in which I always say 'no'—Vedanta. The true seeker who says 'yes' is a born poet, for he finds himself obliged to translate everything into exalted thoughts and language. His poetry plays the role of a science of transmutation.

In sahaja there is a close correspondence between the Bâül and the Sufi, provided that the 'underground current' of spiritual life brings the mind of each one to grasp the secret and to live it in his own light.

As soon as one attempts to describe Hinduism in terms of circles and cycles, and Sufism in terms of four degrees, one is lost. Immediately one enters the world of division and quarrels.

How is it that the Sufis have discovered the content of the Upanishads, that freedom of which they sing, when, in fact, the Upanishads are unknown to most of them? Each one, at his appointed time, must break the shell in which he is enclosed, so as to penetrate into knowledge; just as a fully formed chick must break out of the eggshell if it wishes to live its life.

In the final stage, there is no longer any discipline but only an uninterrupted consciousness of being. If the entire being is immersed in sahaja (the Sufi call it fanā), I 'know' how, in myself, without efforts the current of a right relationship is established, which dissolves everything false or halting in my relationship with myself and with my fellow men.

The Bâüls and the Sufis tread the same path in life and drink from the same eternal source; they are above every kind of sectarianism. They do not practice any formal initiation; they speak, however, of two kinds of initiation.

One is compared to the sun touching the bud of a flower, inviting it to open. A power is transfused from the Master to his disciple simply by radiation, without ritual or words. That is all. The bud of the flower retains all its individuality.

The other initiation, at a still higher level, is compared to the sun which absorbs the dew into itself. At a glance the Master recognizes the real disciple, whether he be a Bâül or a Sufi. His look captures the reflection of the disciple's being as in a mirror; then the eyes of the Master and the eyes of the disciple close. But the current between them will continue to flow eternally. This is called the process of saturation.

But the time comes when the Master becomes an obstacle to the flowering of the disciple. The cult of the person falls away, and also the cult of devotion to ideas. The question arises, 'Why do I obey?' And the answer is, 'The Guru of the Guru of my Guru is walking ahead on the same path as I. Can I reach the source by myself alone, making do without any intermediaries?'

That is the beginning of a long and undeclared war with many painful stages against the Guru. The true Guru will be aware of this struggle. He watches closely the disordered movements of the disciple. His kindness is such that he speaks with his disciple about the one who walks ahead, about the Laws of working on oneself; yet he does nothing to attenuate the struggle which has begun.

At the end of this stage there is sahaja when the disciple finally opens the eyes of his heart and understands that he has gone astray. On this subject Keshab Das[7] has said, 'I discover that I am what I was, but between the two there are only complications. Now, I see. ...' The aim is the Truth, through which the unity of all things can be perceived. This truth is sahaja.

The Master of a Bâül or of a Sufi teaches nothing directly; he merely stimulates his disciple by suggestions. Once initiated, the disciple feels that a force drives him forward, but he will always have to struggle alone in the world around him, in the very heart of all life's complications.

My one ambition has been to learn how to speak without words. That is, to be the smoke of a fire that others do not see, or the sound of music that others do not hear. It has taken me fifty years. Two ideas have always been in my mind. The first of these was to be the traveler who follows a trail with a precise goal: to touch God and to serve Him. The second was the idea of expansion: to know how to flow out like a gas without any destination, for the ṛṣis have said, 'Those who have attained pure Existence (sat) become the One.'

So many people come to see me who only want words! If I do not speak, they are upset. So I speak in a poetic way and that keeps them occupied for a while.

But where are those to whom I can entrust a task in life, one single task that would be the expression of their spiritual fervor? If you are not a plowman, what do you know about plowing? If you are not a man of action, what do you know about a task to be fulfilled? In the seed-bed of thought, action, prayer and meditation coexist in the sensation of being, and action is not what men have made of it—something subjective and hypocritical, far removed from the centre of being.

You do not know that all creation is born of an action? To live is also an action. To live could be the fact of acknowledging the 'Man in the temple of the heart' and serving him perfectly.

Endnotes

1. Rigveda *X, 127.2*
2. *Prakriti has a capital P when indicating a higher Prakriti and has a small p when indicating a lower prakriti.*
3. *The greatest master of Advaita philosophy (788-822).*
4. *This means a forgetting of the ordinary 'I', that is, the superficial structure of the individual.*
5. *The state of ecstasy comprising different degrees.*
6. *See page 80.*
7. *16th century.*

Chapter 11

SAMKHYA

Samkhya is, above all, the practical philosophy transmitted by Kapila, who lived in the far distant past.[1]

Samkhya gives a clear idea of the 'Purusha-spirit' and of 'Prakriti-manifestation' represented by 'Great Nature.' The latter is manifested essentially in a mechanical manner, like all the cosmic Laws which govern us.

I know how difficult it is to explain deep spiritual values. That is why I think the best link between the things of the beyond with the things of this world is that of practical psychology. Psychology speaks a universally known language.

Samkhya is the only religious philosophy that speaks a psychological language, hence a scientific language. Everything can be explained from the point of view of Samkhya. It is the basis of the Buddhist *pitakas*,[2] as well as of the Sufi precepts. It is no more concerned with rites or with dogmas than are the Upanishads.

Nothing exists, in any realm, that by deduction does not proceed from a higher Law. There comes a time when one must submit to such a deductive process. This process is pure Samkhya; it is the inexorable descent into Prakriti, under pressure from above of the great Will. From that moment onwards everything functions in a mechanical way: the higher intelligence (*buddhi*), the soul, the ego, all the centers of the human being, each one with its natural intelligence. The mechanicity functions from the moment when connections start between the different levels of the being: its inner organs of perception (*indriyas*) or senses, its constituent elements (*bhūtas*) and densities.

When 'he who knows' affects the descent voluntarily, and reaches the lowest point, that is to say, the nadir, his being becomes radiant. At that moment he enters consciously into the discipline of a clearly conscious upward movement.

Man is by nature inductive; he gropes his way forward and goes blindly along. Woman, on the other hand, is by nature actively passive, for her function is to create the child. From her are born husband and father. All manifestations, mind, soul, life, matter, have come from her. In that respect she is the 'Divine Mother,' the foundation from which the slow ascent towards the source begins.

It is said in the *Bhagavatam*[3] that, at the time when Samkhya arrived on the earth, a woman was the first to benefit by it. This woman was called Devahuti.[4] She represents the higher Prakriti. Devahuti realized this knowledge to its ultimate limit. Having rejected everything that was not the pure and luminous 'I,' she is said to have wandered in nature, completely naked, radiating light. At the moment of death, she transformed herself voluntarily into an inexhaustible river in order to water the whole earth and allow hundreds of thousands of beings to quench their thirst for knowledge.

The spiritual science of Samkhya can make a saint out of a man who no longer has any faith in God or in himself.

In the beginning, Samkhya appears to be appallingly dry and lacking in love, for imagination and any kind of emotion are strictly set aside. But when the inner being has recovered his lost equilibrium and discovered the equilibrium which he had thus far never felt, he is nourished by a pure love which no longer has any root in human love.

The adept of Samkhya finds his point of support in his own inner attitude, in a conscious effort to understand 'what there is.' To reach this attitude, he makes use of everything that he has discovered, everything that he has experienced up to the time when he begins his search. His material consists of events in his life which enlarge his plane of consciousness, harmonize the microcosm that he is, and reveal the relation existing between the known universe and the unknown universe around him. Even if he has neither a prayer nor a petition, he has, on the other hand, an attitude of openness. He questions and he observes. He searches within himself for a familiar sensation so as to face the perfect and absolute cosmic Law which unfolds. He knows that it is through overcoming obstacles that the inner being will make a fresh effort to attain a wider level of consciousness. To hold to this openness entails attentive vigilance and an immense work of amassing details upon details, until the first of them are clearly perceived. To lead such a life is to live a prayer.

The following example, taken from a Tantric text, formulates it like this:

> *Let your body become hard like dry wood. Then your inner felicity* (rasa) *will be like sugar syrup. Let the fire of your spiritual discipline (sādhanā) purify this syrup until it becomes candied sugar; this candied sugar will at first be brown, but finally it will become as transparent as rock crystal. May your inner felicity resemble rock crystal; then your love will be as pure as Krishna's.*

In order to taste this experience, there are two methods on opposite levels. In the one case, stimulants and drugs are utilized by the physical body. In the other case, the spiritual body consciously becomes more and more refined and, in full awareness, reaches a strictly graduated interiorization. This conscious lucidity will then be continuous like the tracks of a caterpillar on the earth.

Then a stage of knowledge will be reached, that is, a knowledge that is searching for itself and gradually discovers itself. At its highest point, after a very delicate attunement, this knowledge becomes true compassion or pure objective love.

In Vedanta and for the Vedantist, if felicity is not reached in the complete passivity of all the centres of the being, the upward path is nothing but renunciation and frustration. Vedanta denies all reality, while the Samkhya discipline affirms that everything is reality (sat). In prakriti, which by nature is mechanical, three densities have to be acknowledged and gone beyond—matter, energy, and spirit—to reach finally the cosmic force that contains them all. Higher reality, or pure Existence (sat) beyond manifestation, is expressed by the unity of these three densities. Behind it stands Purusha.

The essential condition of this discipline is the possibility of absorption which continually increases until it becomes total. To start with, everything appears heavy and opaque, like a clod of earth that little by little, as understanding broadens, appears like pure rock crystal.

The soul's felicity (*vilāsa-vivarta*) is the state in which the unreal becomes real and vice versa.

In attempting this a Christian risks himself with difficulty, for he has to take into account a 'sinful body' which weighs very heavily. The Christian places his point of support ahead of him in God, who gives him strength and consolation. He prays, invokes, and gives thanks. He is a worshipper (*bhakta*) before his Lord (iṣṭadevatā). The great majority of Hindus are also worshippers.

In Samkhya, several themes for meditation are taught which date from the time of the Vedas.

For example, the idea of the opposite pairs of zenith–nadir (what is above and what is below), or Purusha–Prakriti, is graphically pictured by two points linked by an ideal line going vertically from the zenith to the nadir. But in living experience one perceives in meditation that it is quite different. Actually, these two poles of zenith and nadir are not opposites, but are joined in a continuous movement that starts from the zenith, describes a vast semicircle to the right and reaches the nadir at the bottom of the curve. After having penetrated the nadir, this same movement re-ascends to the left towards the zenith, forming the same semicircle as on the right. It gives a picture of a large round vessel with the nadir at the bottom.

The energy that descends from the zenith is fully conscious of its movement. In full force it condenses, breaks down any resistance on the way, and penetrates the inner being which, having seen it coming, has hidden itself, coiled three and a half times, in the nadir. This coil is what the energy has to break up.

A Guru of Samkhya explains this state as follows: energy penetrates the dark night until the energy itself becomes inert and without reaction. At that very moment it becomes entirely one with the heavy matter.

In the nadir of prakriti, the threefold coil represents the three distinct and complementary qualities (guṇas) of prakriti itself. In the descending movement, white (spirit), red (energy), and black (matter) follow one another in the order of the colors at sunset. In the re-ascending movement toward the zenith, the colors follow one another as at dawn: black (matter), red (energy), and white (spirit).

The last half-coil remaining besides the three coils of the guṇas was, during the entire process of the descent, the hiding place of the active consciousness of Purusha. It represents the last redoubt of the individuality-spirit through which the re-ascent can take place.

In this picture, the conqueror, conscious of the road he must follow, resolutely penetrates into the darkness of matter and its heavy densities to reach the very heart of prakriti. To complete his course, he has to break down the last half-coil of prakriti which is holding him back. Only then will he emerge from the struggle a hero.

Throughout the conscious and voluntary descent into the heaviness of the human body down to the nadir, a clear vision makes it possible to perceive what will be the ascending path starting from the nadir, for the stages and steps of the descent are analogous to those of the re-ascent.

There is also a theme of deep meditation which consists in seeing the three guṇas as if they were concentric surfaces, one within the other. Thus, we have the picture of four concentric barriers which delimit them, one within the other; the one delimiting matter is outside, those delimiting energy are inside, as well as the one in the center which delimits the spirit. The space in the centre represents a zone of perfect calm, the Void.

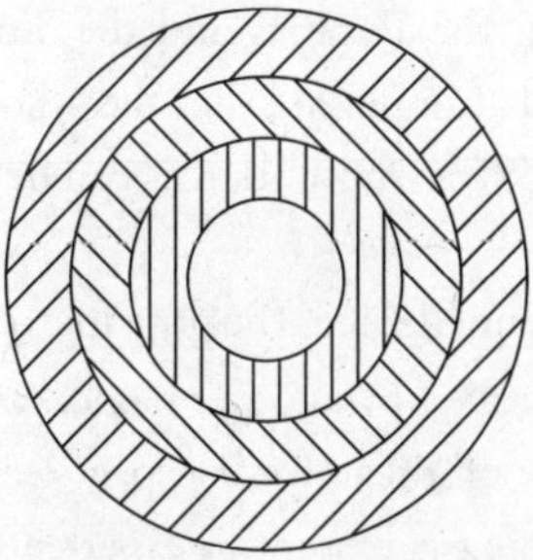

As soon as the perfect calmness of the inner space is perceived, the image of concentric surfaces is obliterated and the fact of existing is now experienced but very subtly, as if a state of active consciousness could be compared to a thin streak of light which at the same time is filling the sky. The result is an all-encompassing sensation of fluidity along the spinal column. The sensation is that of a very fine vibrating matter ascending from below. This sensation is like the radiance of light which fills space.

The three guṇas constitute the equilibrium of Purusha. Whatever takes place, the constant balance between the qualities and the substances that compose the guṇas remains. They move always in the same order, that is, from matter (*tamas*) to energy (*rajas*), then to spirit (sattva), or, in the reverse order, from spirit (sattva) to energy (rajas) down to matter (tamas). At the moment of sunrise and sunset, one can feel in oneself the very delicate transition from one density to the other, from one quality to the other and see the change from one color to another. That is why, traditionally, these are the moments in which the guṇas form the background and the theme of all meditation.

There are two Samkhyas: the first is philosophical, the second, mystical. Philosophical Samkhya, formulated by Ishvara Krishna,[5] is recognized in India as being the system of basic thought that indicates to the *yogi*, as well as to the anchorite, the ascending path of spiritual search. It is a profoundly negative philosophy which had an influence on the whole of life in India in the Middle Ages. This is all that is known of Samkhya in the West.

But this Samkhya is also a mystical path, enshrined in the Vedas and the Upanishads, which, in the course of centuries, has found its free and clear expression in the Puranas and the Tantras, especially in the later sacred scriptures. It can be said that the whole Tantric way of life is none other than a Samkhya whose sources can be discovered in the most ancient Vedic verses.

In this, the world is not denied. The principle of supreme bliss (*ananda*) is recognized, but it is called by another name, *samprasāda*, which, in the Upanishads, is the state of 'dreamless' sleep, a sleep in which the spirit is awakened within. Nothing is present to experience anything at all. There exists only a calm joy which can carry over into the waking state. There is no question of fleeing from pain, but rather of experiencing it as the embrace in which Kali enfolds Shiva prostrate beneath her. This is technically described in the Tantras by the word *viparitarati* (or the inverted coitus), in which the Purusha is passively accepting even death and destruction from the active Prakriti. Evil and pain, from which the world-negating Vedanta assiduously turns away, are transformed here into bliss.

But the mystics have added something further to their experience. They have felt that, for a realized soul, suffering itself is no more than a ripple in the current of bliss. It was in reference to this that Sŕi Ramakrishna[6] was able to say:

> *Everything is sat-cit-ānanda. Even my suffering is only a part of the experience of existing and it has very little place in the total experience of 'being', in the consciousness of bliss.*

From this profound experience, Samkhya, integrated into life as it is in the Bhagavad Gita, looks upon Prakriti as being threefold: the lower prakriti (*aparā*), the higher Prakriti (*parā*), and the highest Prakriti that is our very own (*paramā* or *svīyā*).

The philosophical Samkhya takes into consideration only the lower prakriti, which is merely a complex of the qualities of sattva, rajas, and tamas, permanently intermingled, although one of them must necessarily predominate. But a pure quality (*śuddha sattva*) can also exist, which is neither touched nor soiled by rajas and tamas. This, then, would be the highest Prakriti that is many times mentioned in Puranic and Tantric literature. This idea of pure sattva reigns over all the practical philosophies of the Hindu mystics.

This pure quality is nothing other than eternal bliss (non-existent in rajas) and eternal illumination (non-existent in tamas) co-existing in the spiritual being. This is the entire concept of sat-cit-ānanda common to the mystical philosophies of Samkhya and Vedanta.

Vijnana Bhikshu, a great Master of the school of Samkhya in the fifteenth century, has given us the following metaphor in connection with Purusha and Prakriti:

> *Prakriti is Purusha's wife; she is shrewd and peevish. She gives Purusha no respite, until he becomes so harassed that he finally says, 'I am going away, do what you like!' Then Prakriti runs after her husband in tears, implores him, and clings to him. …*

These are the two ways of dealing with prakriti, before and after having realized what she is. The cosmic Law closest to us tells us, 'As soon as you become detached from prakriti, everything follows you.'

Swami Rama Tirtha[7] has given us another picture:

> *If you turn your back to the sun, your shadow is in front of you. You can try to catch it, but you will never succeed. But the minute you turn to face the sun, your shadow is behind you. If you move, it follows you. You can make it go where you wish. The sun is truth, the shadow is Prakriti.*

It is easy for us to talk about the changes in our consciousness, the broadening of our understanding, but not so easy to speak of the readjustments of our relationship with the world, for the matter of the body is heavy. And the many envelopes of the body (*koṣas*) are not mere illusions, as the envelopes of the mind often are.

Purusha can do nothing for us, since we are the slaves of prakriti. Purusha is outside of time and beyond our understanding, whereas prakriti exists in time. It is at once the aggregate of the qualities (guṇas) that we can evaluate and the aggregate of the movements and impressions (*saṁskāras*) of all those qualities that make up our life. Purusha is a flash of perception, while prakriti operates in an integral mechanism.

Between the two there is the sacrifice of Purusha, which in time takes on a form. For example, the efforts of the Buddha can be perceived by us. If we talk about the efforts of the Buddha on our scale, we have a certain perception of something. But of what?

An exact relationship exists between prakriti, which moves spontaneously, mechanically, always in circles, and Purusha, outside of time, which merely looks on at what is happening. In spiritual life, this relationship appears at the exact point where voluntary detachment breaks the bonds which have been established by prakriti. In the life of the Buddha, the period of detachment is represented by the first half of his asceticism. Later on, while looking from afar at what is happening, he becomes increasingly interested in the game in which he no longer participates and observes the smallest errors of each participant. Then, without hindering their manner of playing, he urges them by his spiritual strength alone to stand aside like himself, so that they, too, can watch the game. In this way, at the proper time, he gives them the chance to see the prakriti from which they are withdrawing, as he himself sees it. The subtle energy that is here described has become the aura of the Buddha; it is simply the lower prakriti transformed and illuminated.

In active spiritual life, one proceeds only by negation. This constant negation, for Christians, has become resignation. We must not forget that whereas in Hinduism there is no beginning and no end, in Christianity there is no end but a beginning. The way of love (*bhakti*) has its place in the attitude of negation as well as in the attitude of resignation.

The path to the attainment of the state of 'divine soul' is extremely long with precipices on both sides. This state of 'divine soul' is limited to a very few and, even so, is always subject to the Laws of the all-powerful and mechanical prakriti. Jesus Christ himself was crucified; nothing was able to prevent the action set in motion by prakriti, which on our human level works exactly like the cosmic Laws and with equal intransigence.

Prakriti contains everything that exists. It is the divine womb of all manifestation. In prakriti one can observe three different degrees:

1. *Everything of which we are made: soul, intelligence, ego, life, mind, and the animal matter of our body.*
2. *The very principle of our possible evolution on all planes of our psychic and physical being.*
3. *The divine energy (śhakti) in its most subtle elements.*

In one sense, all is materiality. In the Vedas, the word *tanu* means the body as well as everything to do with incarnation, and the word *ātman* means the spirit and everything connected with its energy or life. These words are interchangeable and are constantly being used for one another, since they both express the same materiality. There is no difference between spirit and matter; it is only a question of different densities.

When a piece of coal is white hot, it is impossible to say whether it is burning matter or a cluster of flames symbolizing the spirit. Here we have a phenomenon of transubstantiation that is visible in the heart of the spiritual experience.

The essential characteristic of India is that nothing is ever rejected. What was a simple Vedic sacrifice has been transformed in the course of centuries into a ritual of such complexity that it suggests a banyan tree sheltering at one and the same time a temple, a mosque, a saint, a bandit, devotees, animals, manure, and so on. It is a real jungle in which one can easily lose one's way. In it one finds 'this and that and also That.'

Hence the hoarding of objects in the Hindu temples. The minute one accepts the idea of form (*rūpa*), one can throw away nothing. Who is to decide what is true or false? Everything is of equal importance and equally worthy of attention. Each form has a name (*nāma*) and significance. This is so on every level.

The 'too much' has a logic of its own, and logic is very far from the Divine. In the ceremonies, the forms have become all important and have driven out the spirit. Man plays with materiality with consummate art, without being aware of the mechanicity of prakriti, and without discovering that he is its slave.

One cannot change the course of prakriti, which goes its way according to a determined plan in the order of universal things and according to immutable Laws that it does not know. It knows only its own law. It does its work excellently and faultlessly. The energies divide and subdivide up to the point of feeding the cells of our body. They penetrate the heart and penetrate every drop of blood. At this point the body is an expression of 'That.'

Men are tossed about and carried along by a wave of which they cannot get free, but they can swim in the direction of the cavern of the heart. The seat of immobile consciousness is there. The movement of the wave has then ceased for these men, because they have put their attention to another order of reality. In the cavern of the heart they touch the immutable. One has to follow this proeess with an inward look and feel the pulsation of life. There is a known relation between the pulsation of life and the movement of the outer wave just as there is a relation between the pulsation of life and the immobile consciousness. This movement is continuous. A sudden stop would mean death.

So long as we are immersed in prakriti, in ourselves and in life, we are governed by it, by its movements, its sudden jumps and its cosmic rhythms. Without withdrawing into ourselves, we can have no control over our prakriti.

It is impossible from outside to know whether the driver of a vehicle has control over himself or not. If he has, he can stop when he so decides. He knows that the wheels of the vehicle turn because of him. He is in control of his personal prakriti, which in its turn plays its role in a vaster Prakriti. The latter is itself the field of action of the great cosmic Laws.

There are two ways in which Great Nature constantly reacts toward Purusha: it remains in the center of the movement, not to be drawn to one side or the other; or it follows the movement all the way. In any case, one must turn to the Void, which is the beginning as well as the end of all things.

Conscious energy (śhakti) implies continuous growth which, even if it is not apparent and seems to start from darkness (tamas), is nonetheless real. It passes through the red-hot glow of active impulse (rajas) before reaching the whiteness of the rarified state (sattva). This whiteness in life is the state of awakened consciousness.

Thus, we have to raise ourselves up step by step from the plane of gross matter to the plane of awakened consciousness, and thus come back to heavy matter, retaining in ourselves as long as possible a continuous and right sensation. We are constantly harassed from outside by multiple shocks which bring forth in us either the desire to see God and experience a moment of illumination, or the anguish of death prowling in the shadows and bringing a state of deep depression. The dawn symbolizes the intermediate power of śhakti. It is the light that begins to shine in the heart of the dark night.

Perched on the shaft, the driver of the bullock cart sees the two big wooden wheels turning at the same time. One of them is life, the other death. Both wheels are equally necessary for the balance of the cart. [8]

Discover in yourself the faith that shakes the world. Never say 'Perhaps,' but say 'Yes' right away. This helps you to discover reactions in consciousness, to observe them and to make a choice. You must not accept the slavery of automatism in your reactions. Cut it off. It is possible. Refuse categorically to be the slave of your reactions. Have a deep desire to master them.

Accept primordial Nature as it exists in time, but withdraw from it and observe it from the plane of Purusha. The plane of Purusha is the plane of the spirit. This step is pure Samkhya. Believe that your evolution is possible even if your development is extremely slow.

Expect nothing whatsoever from anybody. Men are nothing but blind instruments, tools without freedom, driven by an invisible power that they do not even wish to know, for their eyes are not open. It is important to know whether our philosophy of life is effective. Only when circumstances overwhelm us do we see the movements of prakriti that surround us and notice that we ourselves are an integrated part of prakriti.

Then what we have perceived of pure Existence (sat) nourishes our inner being, no matter what for us has taken outwardly the form of victory or defeat. It is useless to regret the past. In our life experience, we have acted according to our understanding and our possibility at a particular moment. This is an inescapable Law which holds us in its orbit as long as we are the slaves of prakriti.

As soon as one withdraws consciously from prakriti, if only for an instant, its movement ceases. One emerges from it having touched the point of creation. This point gives an extremely pure sensation. It is often reached through 'spiritual death,' which is beyond all energy, beyond cogitations of the ego. But the disciple should not desire at all costs to escape from the grip of prakriti, for it is the field in which his own movements can be discovered, closely studied, evaluated, and used.

Every time the boatman uses the oars—they are indispensable only when going against the current—he causes a rupture in the normal flow of the river. It is the same in the flow of life. To go consciously against the current creates an opposing movement which will be manifested in one way or another.

Every movement that starts abruptly is always wrong. It comes from an unconscious reaction in our own life, or from anguish in front of the unknown, that is, the fear of death. One must always allow the 'Life principle' to run its course between an action and the decision that precedes it, and thereby allow the normal rhythm of the movements of prakriti to take place. Prakriti will assert its rights and create enough obstacles to strengthen or to cancel the decision before there has been any action.

It is said that thoughts that are a part of prakriti are of a very subtle matter. Because of that, one can learn to control them and no longer to feel one with them. When you are able to direct your thoughts in a more objective manner, it proves that you are already dissociated from them.

Every time you discover that you are dissociated from prakriti, even for an instant, it means that some of the elements of prakriti in you have been liberated. But the secret remains, that if we emerge from an impure prakriti, it is only to enable us to go towards a purer prakriti. This is the way of a sahaja discipline lived in the midst of life. The follower of such a discipline works to coordinate his efforts towards that end.

There are two ways to escape from the chain of prakriti, since everything on every plane exists in such a way that experiences are endlessly repeated. Both of them are very exacting.

One of the ways is upward and consists in the initiation into sannyāsa of the monks who roam about India wearing the ochre or the white robe, or of the layman who resolutely enters, at a particular time in his life, upon the hermit's 'cave life' in order to live a spiritual experience.

The other way tends downward. For man and woman alike, it is like the degradation of prostitution: the abandoning of castes and of the social framework. By this movement they deliberately cease to submit to the true Law and put themselves under a lower set of laws.

It is not giving that counts, for giving remains a proof that one has something to give. What counts is to experience the most complete dissatisfaction with oneself and to see it with open eyes until one gets down to bedrock. This is the movement that causes prakriti, uncovered and unmasked, to react.

At this moment something as yet unperceived can begin to break through. It is the energy (śhakti) that becomes the matrix or the Void. There only can something take shape and be born when the time comes. Bedrock represents the eternal Prakriti busy with ceaseless creation, for such is her function, indifferent to everything taking place around her. This is one of her movements. She has another movement, opposite to it, which must also be discovered. According to one of her Laws, she gradually pushes her children into Purusha's field of vision. Meeting the piercing look of Purusha, whose function it is to 'see', is an instant of total understanding, a giving up of oneself. How can one describe that look? What one knows of it cannot be communicated. And besides, it would be useless to try.

All one can do is to wait with much love and be ready to meet it. Is it possible to guess when Prakriti will make this gesture for you? Is it possible to know why she does so?

It is essential to build one's life around two principles: that of letting go and that of contraction. The moment of complete, conscious 'letting go' is when Purusha is in dissociation from Prakriti. Such a moment lasts only as long as several very calm respirations; this creates the naked universe, stripped of the 'I'. Correctly speaking, this is not meditation, but rather an attitude of interiorized life. Sŕi Aurobindo lived it for forty years isolated in his ashram[9]; Sŕi Ramana Maharshi lived it during his whole life in his rarely broken silence.

Expansion is the creative movement corresponding to introspection. The one inevitably leads to the other, that is, expansion of itself leads to letting go when one finds the inner point of balance.

A fundamental idea is that of conscious identification with the forces of Nature. Its significance is vast. It means full expansion in complete relaxation. But one cannot actualize anything without first having let go of everything!

What can I do? Faced with this question, the best thing to do is to do nothing on one's own initiative. The idea of expansion has to be properly understood. There can be no expansion except through love. In love we emerge from our little ego. But this love has to be impersonal. I can speak about it by using the Vedic image of the sun, which radiates energy and thereby illuminates and creates. This is the essence of its expansion. It is not attached to anything, yet it attracts everything to it in its kingdom of light. Expansion does not mean doing something; it means *being* and *becoming*. The capacity to do flows spontaneously from the capacity to be.

Purusha 'is,' whereas Prakriti 'is' and also 'does,' but always from the center outwards, exactly in the way the very delicate green shoots sprout from the germinated seed. This seed in itself is Purusha folded back on itself, motionless and at the same time the creator of the movement of life. You must know this, and then feel in yourself that you are both Purusha and Prakriti. This is the Samkhya version of expansion.

I often wonder who orchestrates the dangerous games of nations, who it is that in a given year devours the sap of life and in another year gives it fresh vigor. All this is the work of prakriti. How clever she is at creating mountains out of a grain of sand! From afar Purusha watches her at work. He smiles! To tell the truth, prakriti also laughs while pretending to be absorbed in the work on which her heart is set!

The important thing in all of this is to keep calm and to smile while taking everything as it comes up just as seriously as a child would. Then forget it in the next minute! There will always be heavy obligations for you to carry, but you can lay them down, one after the other, as you move forward on the road of life.

These obligations are like black clouds accumulating in the sky. When they become heavy enough, they burst of themselves and disperse. In time, obligations disappear by themselves.

The secret is to accept everything, but be very careful not to be attached to anything whatsoever!

Endnotes

1. Rigveda *X, 27-6.*
2. *Teaching of the Buddha in Pali. Collected by his disciples a hundred years after his death.*
3. Śrimadbhagavatam *or* Bhagavatapurana *is traditionally attributed to Vyasa, the author of the Mahabharata.*
4. *See p. 196.*
5. *The author of a treatise called* Samkhya Karika, *in the third century A.D.*
6. *Śri Ramakrishna died of cancer of the throat in 1886, at the age of fifty-four at Dakshineswar near Calcutta.*
7. *Rama Tirtha, who died in 1906, went to the United States after Swami Vivekananda's time. While there, he spoke magnificently about Vedanta; he created no organization, saying, 'The whole of India is my ashram.'*
8. *Taittiriya Brahmana.*
9. *Śri Aurobindo appeared only four times a year before his disciples, on the days known as* darsan.

Chapter 12

LAWS—POWERS

In India people strive for these powers:

- *to reach God;*
- *to make God appear objective;*
- *to have a clear sensation of the 'I';*
- *to eradicate every difference between 'you' and 'me';*
- *to materialize the divine Laws and worship them as they are represented in the form of gods.*

If man of 50,000 years ago were to return, he would see that man has not changed, either spiritually or in his deep reactions. The whole of civilization is only the outward appearance (māyā) of what is manifested (sat). So why then should the Hindu believer not look for a means to escape from this slavery?

This cosmos to which we belong does not hold us in slavery. It is what it is. For us it represents the continuity of a power, of a descending Law with, here and there, one ascending soul, one in a million says the Bhagavad Gita.

Such a soul radiates its own light; it touches other hearts because it has 'passed through the death of the ego and the birth of the being.' It is nourished by the Void. In the Void, absurdities evaporate spontaneously.

He who has lost faith and builds it up again slowly and cautiously by means of the science of Samkhya, the logic and mathematics relating to cosmic Laws, knows by experience why the world holds together; but the instant he tries to formulate the mathematical equation, he will fail and fall.

Great Nature in her eternal recurrence represents a form of prakriti that the human heart can comprehend. She expresses the force that has two opposite movements, the one ascending, the other descending. Their role is to bring mankind and organic life on earth into the play of cosmic Laws. She shows the mechanical aspect of the Laws, in which man, according to his stage of evolution and inner attitude, sees miracles, ironies, or absurdities, or no matter what else, in order to escape the grip of eternal recurrence. At the same time, he refuses to see the harmonious operation of these cosmic Laws.

This concordance is beyond human logic, such logic being only a form of the unconscious and mechanical functioning of the ego.

The world is a bazaar where everybody is shouting at the top of his voice to attract attention and make his little bargain. Remember that success or failure means nothing in the play of the Laws. All depends only on how the game is played. Thoughts are a thousand times more powerful than words. Be quiet in yourself, be calm and silent in the agitation around you. Let the powers act without allowing the human law, subjective and narrow, to interfere. The great powers act by impregnating the nerve fibers of the earth.

The whole of life is the immensity of the darkness of night (*varuna*) and the immensity of the light of day (*mitra*). The multiplicity of the circumstances and conditioning, to which we are subject in time, must not distort our inner vision in relation to darkness and light.

Then, in the intermediate light between day and night, we will clearly distinguish the broken lines which are the Laws as they come down to us, insofar as we are able to understand them. The work, for every one of us, is to learn to recognize them steadfastly and patiently, one after another.

Power, even in its most subtle and essential vibrations, includes two directions: one is positive and the other negative. Words such as truth, life, essence, should only be used with caution, for they contain in themselves an implicit source of opposition.

All the Vedic sages (ṛṣis) repeatedly taught that spiritual life proceeds by jumps, by upward thrusts, whose trajectory, being subject to the Law of gravity, falls down again from the apogee of its course to the lowest point. This fall is what starts eternal recurrence. We live and are fed by the visions of 'those who see', and there will always be new ṛṣis and new disciples.

In these times, the ṛṣis' vision serves only to create disciples. Disciples are necessary so that what is brought by the ṛṣi can make its way into life. But the more the disciples are attached to themselves, the more mediocre they become, interested only in defending their rights of seniority, their ashram, their Master's thought, without engaging themselves in the process of creation.

In summary, the ṛṣi's vision does not seem to belong to those who gather around him, but is a testimony to 'That which is' for a much wider circle and for the sake of a continuity that will establish itself. This vision is a state of impersonal consciousness; it is what keeps the world in an exact relationship to the Laws. To impose a name on it is to limit the vision and lock it in a closed circle.

There are three important points to recognize in the ascending spiral representing the evolution of man: the point of sunrise, the point of the zenith, and of the 'High North' (*uttaram*), which is the summit reached by the trajectory of this ascending spiral. The High North is the point where a new light scale begins to develop.

This direction toward the High North is also directly related to the solstices. The sun travels toward the north from December 21 until June 21 and the days lengthen. From the time when the sun moves toward the south, the days get shorter. That is why Yama, the king of death, is represented as living in the south and Shiva, the god of life and death, beyond the north. Moreover, the east is the origin of light, the west is the house of the Void. These indications are scrupulously observed in the building of a temple or of a house. The position north-east always indicates the very action of the Law in our life.

For an action to be in accordance with the Laws and be a part of them, two forces must support it. One of them is the Void, which generated the action, the other the energy and freedom of its movement.

Such a mode of action is established in a right relationship between Guru and disciple. The Guru says to his disciple, 'Go and fulfill this task and know that even here I shall be the Void of your movement. Feel this deeply in yourself.' These two forces can also co-exist in the same person, which is the state mentioned in the Bhagavad Gita: the action is born from the vibration of the Void.

The best illustration of this is the story of a nun chosen by the king of a state to become his queen. The sannyāsinī finally accepted on condition that she be given an isolated room in the royal palace to which she alone would have the key. She used to go there every day. The king, jealous of the radiance of the queen, decided one day to follow her there to steal her secret. The room he saw her enter was bare and whitewashed. A sackcloth robe was hanging on a nail. The queen took off her rich attire and her jewels and put on this beggar's dress. Then she meditated for a long time, seated on the ground. At last, she turned around and said to the king, 'Here I am "myself," the woman who loved God alone before she became a queen, and who still loves only God, in His divine play.'

That queen has no name. She is part of Indian folklore.

An impulse pushes us to follow the way of the spirit, Purusha. We must not stop to ask: 'What is this impulse?' It is there so that we may follow the ideal and constantly make it grow. No backward steps! This impulse has to be cultivated because it belongs to the ascending Law.

Opposing this, prakriti holds us fast in the wheels of her perfect machinery. One can be satisfied there and sleep in peace. Prakriti asks no more of us. She has a very strong power of gravitation, and drags back to herself beings who were ready to escape. She brings them back very skillfully for she needs our lives for her own purposes; she needs humus composed of the constantly renewed heavy and fine matter which our lives bring to her.

As regards any personal discipline, you must follow the right course.

What you get through intuition can never fail you. The whole attitude can be summed up in a short sentence: 'I know that, I feel that, I am that.' Let the powers work deep within you. The pain that results is that of a new birth. If inclination for inner work lessens, do not worry. Creation starts in darkness. Out of nothing comes the force of śhakti. Let yourself be carried by the stream; do not struggle. Not that you will reach the shore; your destination is to become the ocean itself.

We know that there are seven planes: three above and three below and a seventh which serves as a bridge. The three lower planes generate the physical, emotional, and mental; the three higher ones generate pure existence (sat), pure radiant energy (cit), and bliss (ānanda), which is the joy of creation; the seventh plane (rasa) is that on which things are carried out, that of the mother standing between the father and the child, permeating both.

In the Tantras the lunar days are divided into three groups of five. This fivefold pattern symbolized the power of the Virgin-mother. In each group, the days stand for joy (*nandā*), harmony and welfare (*bhadrā*), victory and power (*jayā*), consecration and sacrifice (*riktā*), plenitude (*pūrnā*). Śhakti is pictured as a little girl growing into womanhood. The first stage is her childhood; the second, her adolescence; the third, her youth; the fourth, her maturity; and the fifth, her completeness. Beyond is the Void. The same applies to the three lower planes: physical, emotional, mental. Analytically speaking, beyond śhakti is the eternal spirit known as *nitya-ṣoḍaśī*, and still further beyond is complete emptiness, *nirvāna-kala*.

The full moon symbolizes the blossoming and fruition of the hidden moon's creative activity working in darkness. This is why peasants who are in contact with the earth sow seeds for flowers during the bright phase of the moon and for edible plants in its dark phase. The dark ray of creation is spoken of in the *Katha Upanishad*.[1]

Following is the scheme of the seven planes:

Father	Mother (the bridge)	Child
1, 2, 3	7	4, 5, 6

There is always a gap, a no-man's-land, between two planes. Otherwise there could be no creation. The Buddhists were right in saying that 'everything' comes from 'nothing.'

The intrinsic qualities (*guṇas*) of prakriti are what bring gradual degrees of modification in the transition from matter to spirit and vice versa. These modifications are everywhere and on all planes. Energy (*rajas*) is the element of fermentation. The *Bhagavatam*[2] gives an excellent comparison between the entire process and a piece of wood catching fire. At first there is no fire—a state of inertia (*tamas*); then comes smoke—a state of energy (*rajas*); and then heat and light—the rarified state (*sattva*). So whenever we try to break up inertia on the human plane, we must be ready for confusion, misunderstanding and rashness; these things are bound to happen. The whole world is rajas, storm and stress, otherwise matter could not become 'luminous spirit,' or 'harmonious multiplicity' like the petals of the lotus, which is the symbol of the One.

Dissolution is often necessary before real creation starts. You cannot always be looking for something. You must stop somewhere and let things grow within you. There is a rhythm of creation and a rhythm of dissolution, symbolized by the dance of Shiva. At first this dance is violent, full of convulsive movements with steps marking life and death at the same time. The ṛṣis have called this part of the dance *tāṇḍava*. Its duration is related to cycles. Gradually the dance changes into the gentle dance of balanced force, where the rhythm becomes so supple that life and death are near each other and can be felt in the same movement. The ṛṣis have called this rhythmic vibration *lāsya*.

Herein lies the true creative possibility of śhakti, of which the violent tāṇḍava of Shiva is the cosmic background. The balance and deep significance of life lie in dissolution. This is what makes life a constant renewal. Accept things just as they come and one day the light step of lāsya will be yours.

There are two movements in creation. The movement of interiorization always precedes that of exteriorization. It is represented in the following imagery: according to the Puranas, creation was to come from the four united principles, the four sons of Brahma.[3] But when Brahma had created them, instead of going down to earth and manifesting themselves outwardly, they went back into their father's bosom and became the force of withdrawal, from which there then issued the 'Seven Sages' or 'Seven Laws' that participated in the creation and continue to maintain it. These two movements, interiorization and exteriorization, are to be found everywhere, in creation as in de-creation, or pralaya, that is to say, the creation that undoes itself spontaneously, beginning from the end. Creation is in itself birth and death, whereas de-creation is in itself death and birth.

It is difficult to conceive of the transition from rarefaction to density even though it is the very process of all creation. We realize, or rather we imagine, what the Void may be, but to follow the process of the ether becoming the earth, which would be the genuine realization of creation, is far from our understanding.

You rise to the heights and are often aware of the process, but then you suddenly bump your head on the earth. Of course, you bring the flavor of the ether down with you but still you cannot re-create it. The attempt has been given up as almost impossible by the author of the *Brahmasūtra* who remarked: 'You can become one with Brahma in knowledge and bliss, but you cannot become one with him in his creative power.' The explanation is something like this: you can die consciously, but you cannot be born consciously. If you could do so, your birth would be a divine birth, an incarnation.

Through the ages man has pursued his quest beyond death through idolatry. Even nowadays man's search starts with idolatry and it is very important to see that it ends with it, too. If matter becomes spirit, spirit likewise must return to matter. That is why the greatest spiritual Masters of India never denounced or gave up idolatry. Not even Shankaracharya.

Through his Guru's teaching, the Hindu disciple discovers, in the spiritual discipline he follows, how to put into daily practice the Laws of Shiva Mahadeva, the supreme Lord, just as they are described in all the sacred texts. These Laws are illustrated by three aspects of life—creation, preservation and destruction—and by two movements, the one from above moving downward, the other from below going upward.

A disciple will hold to this imagery so long as he expects to receive everything from his Guru. He may continue to do so during several successive lives, unless the idea of evolution is born in him. There comes a time when the disciple recognizes the obstacles that he must face and go beyond. He discovers that this has to do with the Law of three in his own nature and in his development.

Three Laws govern life: the Law of growth, the Law of expansion, and the Law of intensity. All three are illustrated by the 'tree of life', showing how this tree grows, how it spreads out its foliage, and how it sinks its roots deep into the soil.

One must be firmly rooted. Such is the first Law. Then grow and assert yourself. At that moment open yourself, stretch out your arms to feel your radiation around you, and then bring the universe back to you with your head held high, for it touches the sun. Be deep, wide, tall, truly like a tree of life.

Śhakti, insofar as it is the power of matter utilized by Purusha in its manifestation, still depends on Purusha. It is by nature opposed to Purusha, so that between the two a life-giving current may be established. As soon as śhakti appears, it already contains in itself the three initial Laws which give it its material density.

If Purusha chooses to play an active role, its śhakti will always be passive. On the other hand, if Purusha chooses to be passive, its śhakti will always be active. While the passive element stands back, the active element takes different forms. Each form or each movement gives rise to new Laws which, if the movement ceases, will be reenfolded within one another and will return to the initial force that gave them birth.

Thus in Shaivism, Shiva, representing the spirit, is always passive, and his śhaktis, representing various aspects of manifestation in the world, have different functions under different names: Uma, Gauri, Annapurna, Parvati, Kali, Durga, and so forth. In Vaishnavism, on the other hand, Vishnu is the active element. He is the creator who has manifested himself in different forms in different incarnations,[4] displaying a gradual voluntary evolution. The constant activity of Vishnu is to maintain the world, whereas his śhakti is secret, inner and completely passive. She is called Sŕi, meaning beauty and harmony. She is the symbol of the lotus in full bloom. Sŕi is the secret in the heart of a woman.

The sound (*bīja*) in the sacred word (mantra) is the vibration which causes matter to pass to spirit, or conversely, spirit to pass to matter. Hence its great importance in spiritual techniques. Every being has his own vibration which, in either a clear or confused way, is equivalent to a formula of coagulation or of a possible dissolution. On the horizontal plane, in ordinary life, this mantric vibration is expressed by a configuration (*yantra*) which is the basic individual diagram used by the force emanating from oneself at no matter what degree of materialization.

This force flows out in complete disorder. It is instinctive. It obeys all the outer attractions and associates itself with all the automatic movements of prakriti, whatever they may be. Those who are conscious of the power of this spontaneous force direct their effort towards preventing its uncontrolled emanation and towards canalizing it without producing any mutilation.

Then one must learn to know it, to guide it, to love it as it is, so as to tame it and give it a way of expression. The sacred sound (bīja) is that very force which, when necessary, is used against itself. This has nothing to do with the invocations or sacred words (mantras) which are repeated to create a state of openness or surrender; but only with the seed-syllable itself.

There are four Tantric Laws that concern Unity:

1. *Cosmic unity* (brammāṇda), *which is, in the expansion of the self up to touching the sky, a passionate love for the sensory universe in all its forms, until it brings within ourselves the vibration of the Vedic formula: 'The earth is my mother, I am the child of the earth.'*
2. *The psychic unity* (prakṛtyanda) *existing between the real inner*

being and the ego with all its impulses. This unity is the thread of life connecting all experiences lived through up until our discovery of knowledge.

3. *Causal unity* (māyānda), *which is the progressive discovery of the forces and Laws within the heart of Prakriti.*

4. *Spiritual unity* (śaktyānda), *which is the harmonious association of our soul, our essence, the 'I,' and the force of life, the most subtle Prakriti.*

There is a basic rule for approaching any one of these Tantric Laws, which is to understand that the body is the instrument of life. It follows that any stiffening or hardening, that is, any tension in thought or in body, prevents a conscious extension towards the infinite.

Now, as regards the spiritual quest: if you consciously hold within yourself three-quarters of your power and use only one-quarter to respond to any communication coming from others, you can stop the automatic, rapid, and thoughtless movement outward, which leaves you with a feeling of emptiness, of having been absorbed by life. This stopping of the movement outwards is not self-defense, but rather an effort to have the response come from within, from the deepest part of one's being. This process reverses the natural movement of prakriti and brings back energy to its seed form. Let this become your way of communicating with others.

Something in yourself is awakened, and by this interiorization you begin a movement in the direction opposite from what is taking place outwardly. Thereby two movements are produced in you. One of them goes outward and the other goes inward. The latter is the movement of the higher Prakriti uniting with the immobile Purusha. This is the moment in which prakriti surrenders, in which there is no struggle.

The Law of life is the same. As the physical cells build the body, the germ cells are concentrated within and retain their energy for a later creation. We imagine that we create by projecting outwards, whereas real creation takes place through suction and absorption. When this power of absorption becomes natural, you discover that creation, radiation, communication and all similar processes come to you spontaneously.

In Samkhya, this spontaneous creation is called *dharma-megha*, or the cloud of energy that pours forth multiple powers, for behind this creation there is the Void.

All spiritual search is directed towards a shining point, which can be approached only from the periphery of a big circle and in many different ways. Samkhya is the logical science that makes it possible to see the movements of prakriti and to dissociate oneself from it on the plane of life itself. This is the opposite of the attitude of so many seekers who, in order to escape from the clutches of prakriti and turn away from it, run away from the world to follow a primitive discipline that mutilates their life to such an extent that it no longer has any connection with reality.

Feeling oneself dissociated from prakriti does not mean that one has become her master. To master prakriti requires inner work and attentive observation of śhakti's energy. This energy is a fully awakened power which is not yet tamed. Only when prakriti is conquered and mastered does Life within life, in the midst of all prakriti's erratic movements, become the state described as Shiva-śhakti in the heart of the cosmic Laws.

The whole theory of the Void is that of the luminous ether (*ākāśa*). Sound (*śabda*) and speech (*vāk*) come from ākāśa, and therefore also the idea of a creator God who in order to manifest Himself, uses five elements and five sensations.

The five elements belong to God, to the descending Law; the five sensations belong to man, to the ascending Law. To approach a direct experience, we have only the authority of the Sacred Scriptures and the experiences of the saints and yogis who have gone before us. The work of transformation in the course of evolution can only be done by oneself on oneself. A Master, of course, can activate it, and fellow disciples can help in sustaining the effort, but the seeker will be entirely alone throughout his attempt and many times he will confuse the means with the end to be attained.

Some notions are occasionally given but always in a veiled form which can be interpreted in different ways, such as:

One must be subtle enough to feel the presence of the mother, for life begins with an odour…
One must be subtle enough to discover where the father is, for life ends with a sound…

In studying the Tantras, one discovers progressively, thanks to sound and by means of sound, how the idea, by taking on density, gradually becomes the object that is perceived. The two linked words 'Shiva-śhakti' create the vibration by which the spirit takes on the density of matter. Every time this double word is pronounced one must refer also to what it contains in the ascending Law, for it is the passage from one level to the next. In every sensation pertaining to the ascending Law, each movement begins with heat, continues with the materiality of food and light, and reaches luminous ether, that is, the Void.

The three Laws of śhakti always remain veiled. They are the Laws of pure Existence (sat), of pure Spirit (cit) and pure Bliss (ānanda). Another Law, however, the Law of phenomena, is projected on to the screen of consciousness.

The first of the three Laws is that of pure Existence, sat; although having the appearance of complete immobility it is in itself a vibration or a movement. This inner vibration is the source of all existing movement. The first movement is a straight line between two points and it is this straight line that represents the immobility of Shiva. Prakriti appears and takes possession of the pattern of straight lines, weaving onto it her pattern in the shape of a spider's web, with broken lines forming angles, surrounded by concentric circles.

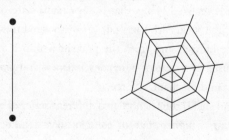

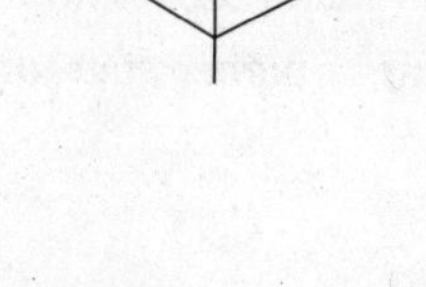

Finally, by the force of śhakti these curves detach themselves from the horizontal plane to form a spiral ascending around its own axis.

The second Law is that of pure Bliss. Ānanda is the result of the movement having taken place in consciousness, a calm movement like an undulation of the water. This undulation contains life, which is in itself the very essence of śhakti. This pattern of flexible undulation is nevertheless made up of short broken lines.

The third Law is that of pure Spirit. Cit has a very definite function between the vibration originating in the immobile source and the wave that is the essence of śhakti. It is the awakened consciousness and its role is to unite sat with ānanda.

In one way or another, it can be said of sat that if I look within myself, I see that śhakti draws me inwardly. I become conscious of the immobility of the world and of the straight line between two points representing Purusha. Of ānanda it can be said that if I am conscious of what is around me, I project myself outward and enter into the very play of śhakti. At that moment I feel all the waves passing over the water as being the pulsations of life itself. On the other hand, cit, the pure consciousness of the spirit, observes what is happening between sat and ānanda.

The expression Shiva-śhakti reveals the ultimate reality beyond the concept Purusha-Prakriti of classical Samkhya. Shiva-śhakti is the state of the fully realized being, that is, an inward state of enlightened consciousness. The seeker who has not yet dissociated himself from the prakriti outside himself and from the prakriti within himself, sees the immobile Purusha as a state of pure consciousness and prakriti as being an unconscious and mechanical force.

Prakriti and śhakti thus denote two different states of consciousness, the second being a higher state of consciousness tending towards the limitless. Prakriti is a kinetic energy, whereas śhakti is a latent potential energy returning to itself and containing in itself all the possibilities of development of prakriti's movements.

The inner fluctuations and commotions in the course of spiritual discipline (sādhanā) can be expressed schematically, according to the modifications in the passive and active qualities involved.

The lower aspect or exteriorization	prakriti—Purusha
	+ −
The higher aspect or interiorization	Shiva—śhakti
	+ −

From the point of view of Samkhya, Prakriti can be an active energy only if it has a passive substratum opposing its movement. This fact is represented mythologically by Kali (time) dancing on the naked body of Shiva (infinity). From the psychological viewpoint, consciousness is the surface of a mirror across which reflections of movement pass rapidly. Consciousness remains immobile.

In the mystical experience it is known that Prakriti in movement and immobile Purusha are but one. Here the *Vaishnavite Tantras* bring a clarifying element to Samkhya by saying that the visible movement in Prakriti is Purusha's movement permeating it. The two are no longer dissociated. Spiritualized Prakriti is nothing more than the form of Purusha. Mystically, this gives us the following scheme:

Prakriti—Purusha:	the two movements of existence having become one
Krishna—Radha:	the mystical couple par excellence

Krishna, as Purusha, is fully conscious in the midst of his activity. Radha, in her transcendental love for Krishna, is in ecstasy (samādhi) even in her role of prakriti. Psychologically, according to Vaishnavite Tantrism, Radha, through her passivity, becomes the substratum of the activity of Krishna-Purusha. The roles are thus reversed, producing the following diagram:

Shiva— passive consciousness	Kâlî + active *prakriti*
Krishna + active *Purusha*	Râdha— effacement in love
Shiva—Râdha are *nirguna*	the transcendental aspect of existence and power
Kâlî—Krishna are *saguna*	the phenomenal aspect of existence and power.

That is why, in India, so many children are named Kali-Krishna.

The Tantric scriptures reveal the necessary deviations making it possible for creation to escape from the ceaseless mechanical repetitions of prakriti.

If there were no deviations, one could easily imagine creation taking place without discontinuity between the immobile Purusha and Prakriti manifested in its numerous aspects. But the primordial energy of śhakti constantly produces deviations, both in the subtle densities of the spirit and in the coarse densities of matter. Once set in motion, this process cannot stop. Therein lies the whole chance of creation towards a possible evolution, and man's opportunity to move upwards, provided that the deviation by broken lines turns upwards in a spiral (*kuṇḍalinī*). The amplitude of their curve can be very wide without change of direction.

The curve of deviation can also be repeatedly retraced on the horizontal plane, attracted by its point of departure. In that case, because of the endless repetitions that will take place, the primordial energy will be frittered away and finally lost.

The figure '3' represents the 'Law of three,' which contains in itself the whole of life. In the beginning, there was the One, Purusha. From its inner vibration, the One projected its opposite, as light casts a shadow, which is its substratum. In this movement, spirit-matter, bound by the energy which belongs equally to the one and the other, can become perceptible. This can be demonstrated in the following manner:

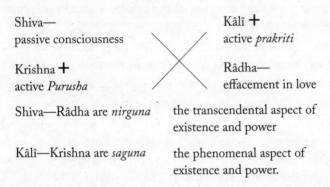

One is the 'I'-subject manifested by light—sattva
Two is the 'I'-object manifested by shadow—tamas

Between the two aspects of I-subject and I-object the perpetual movement of life develops, that is, all forms of manifestation on the lower plane of life. This perpetual movement of energy is rajas.

Thus life, through the energy of rajas, is a development of movements acting between the two poles of sattva-tamas. From the plane of rajas, which is ours, a certain state of consciousness can exist in which it is possible to perceive what is above (sattva) and what is below (tamas).

What is above can be known by sudden intuition or glimpsed through imagination, but it is impossible to reach it without a shock provoked by the vision itself. A thorough discipline of the mind is the indispensable preparation for this.

What is below is the weight of ignorance, the inertia of the primitive prakriti. It is also the field of individual work. Before discovering the stages leading towards sattva, one must become familiar with the opposition of heavy matter.

The energy of rajas proceeds from śhakti, which holds sway in the space between sattva and tamas. The energy of rajas is the desire that creates life. Without this desire, that space would be the Void without movement or action. Actually, life exists only through a deviation of energy, through a propulsion which sooner or later returns to its starting-point.

This movement of exteriorization and of interiorization seems to vary in its possibility of extension according to one's understanding of it. In fact, one is in front of a point ● (*bindu*) which contains everything in itself. When energy creates a movement, this point becomes a straight line. To return to its starting-point, a deviation is a necessity. The straight line will break and, through broken lines forming angles, will return to its starting-point.

Three angles are necessary for a movement to enclose a space and thereby create a surface, a form. This form is a triangle. Every action can be described as a triangle. If the angles are equal, the action is perfect and balanced. The three lines are the qualities of prakriti (guṇas) and the space is that of śhakti spread out and in balance. Śhakti can also gather itself together at the central point (bindu), which signifies—in a perfect action or in a perfect meditative state—the union of śhakti and Purusha, a state of perfect awakened consciousness.

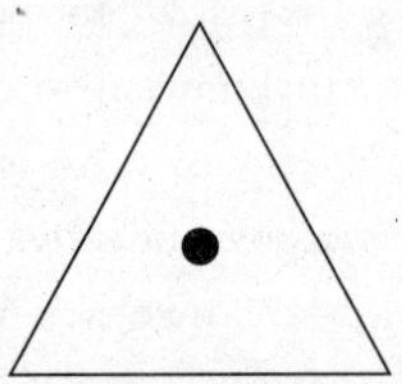

But life is full of distorted and falsified actions, that is, of triangles with unequal angles in which the central point has been displaced in relation to the center of the perfect triangle. The deviations are caused by unconscious subjectivity, by the desires and greediness of the individual prakriti. Innumberable triangles can be formed on the base (tamas) of the triangle, which are projected up to the line of consciousness. This line is not continuous; it is made up of an infinity of points that represent short moments of consciousness.

The following diagrams serve as illustrations:

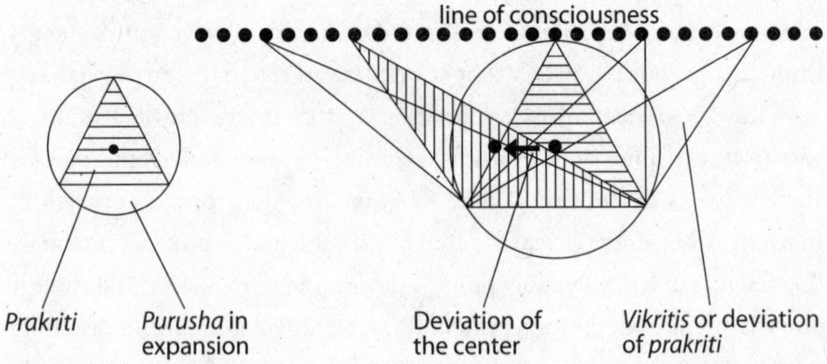

While following a spiritual discipline a man tries, at a certain time, by interiorization during active meditation, to feel in himself the mobile qualities and tendencies of the inner being. It means coming into contact with the world in which his own Law of three functions. On our level of understanding we can perceive the triangle of our life formed by the three guṇas and the numerous irregular triangles formed by our actions.

The subdivision and expansion of the three guṇas (tamas-rajas-sattva) in relation to the three fundamental intrinsic qualities of the primordial prakriti make up different worlds in accordance with the relative distance of these worlds from one another. The greater the subdivision of the guṇas, the greater is the subdivision of the Law of three. A seeker can never have access to any world higher than his own unless he has completely absorbed in himself the guṇas of his own world to the point of being one with them. This means that his inner equilibrium is then brought into accord with his prakriti.

In the following diagrams, the figures indicate the number of guṇas in each world. From one world to the next, the number is multiplied by two, whether the worlds are taken as in the cosmic order or as worlds interiorized in man. The number represents the subdivision of the Law of three which becomes heavier the further it moves from the primordial prakriti. Three guṇas are added in each world to the sum of guṇas from the preceding world.

The triangle shows how three broken lines enclose a surface. This surface has two dimensions, but there is a third dimension to be attained, in conformity with a Vedic Law indicating three successive stages. They follow one another in the manner indicated below:

1. The stage when the potter's wheel sets up a circular movement.
2. The stage when the clay placed on the wheel becomes malleable; the circular movement can then give a form to the clay, but it still remains on the same level.
3. The stage when a spindle is fixed on the wheel. The clay at once comes up in a spiral. The hub will even reach a point slightly higher than the spindle-axis.

3 *gunas* of primordial *prakriti*.

3 + 3 = 6 + 3 = 9

9 + 3 = 12 + 9 = 21

21 + 3 = 24 + 21 = 45

45 + 3 = 48 + 45 = 93

93 + 3 = 96 + 93 = 189

189 + 3 = 192. …

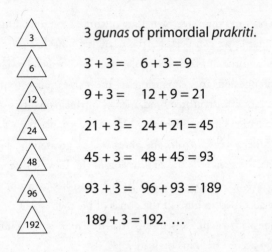

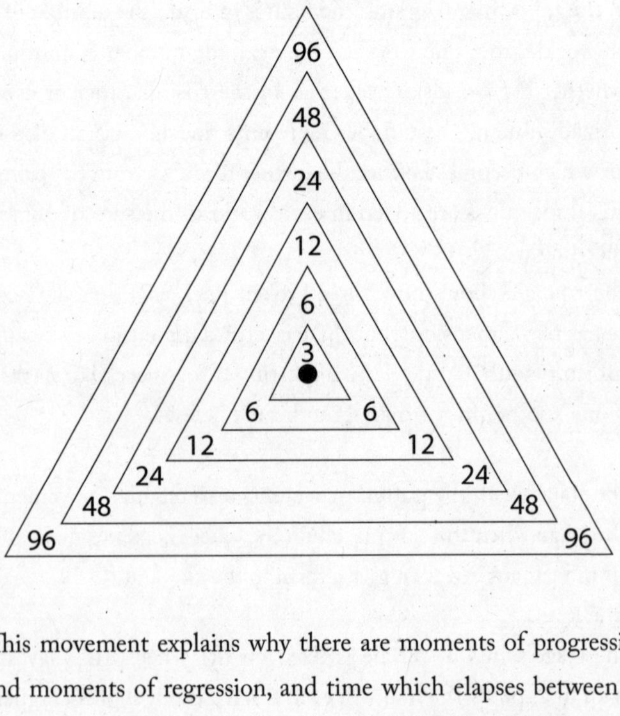

This movement explains why there are moments of progression in life and moments of regression, and time which elapses between these different movements. In spiritual experience, every man ought to aspire to raise himself around an axis, and every woman to become a perfect triangle in order to create perfect forms.

In the following diagram the seeker stands between two triangles. He who devotes his life to spiritual search, thanks to his inner discipline, absorbs the śhakti of the triangle of the infinite ideal which is above him. Below him the downward pointing triangle contains all possible forms of manifestation.

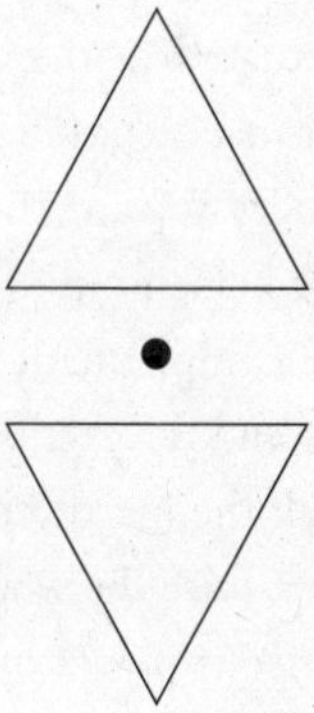

Perfect yoga in the heart of life is represented by the two integrated triangles with a single center. A Master is one who voluntarily enters into the manifested prakriti. His disciples and pupils are so many reflections of himself which he recognizes without being attached to them. He stands in the center of the two triangles.

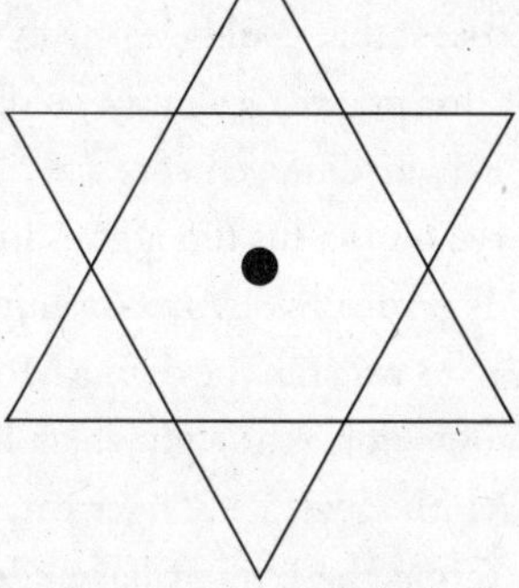

As regards the symbol of the triangle, one should know that Tantric esotericism represents śhakti as the water chestnut (*Śŕingâtaka*), a peculiar pyramid-shaped fruit growing in swamps. There again you have the idea of density.

The radiation of energy has two movements, one of them centripetal and the other centrifugal. The interaction of these two movements produces the luminous sphere of all existence, technically known as bindu, the point which is situated in the center of the pyramid. Creation may appear and start from any point, going either from the center outward, or from the periphery toward the center. Śhakti never stops creating, whether she spreads herself out or concentrates herself within. In fact, these movements are complementary to one another, just as are the phenomena of denseness and rarefaction.

What we need is to break the inertia that hinders or slows the passage from one state to another. I use the word tapasyā in speaking of this movement, and the instantaneous power of transformation in this passage, whether it be centripetal or centrifugal.

The Vedas tell us that we have a 'Father in Heaven' and a 'Mother on Earth.' They are linked together by the atmosphere full of clouds, full of quarrels between the gods and quarrels between the demons, full of book knowledge and all the philosophies of life. The sāstras and the puranas bind us with chains called spirituality, orthodoxy, politics, castes and economic conditions.

What does man possess that could eventually free him? As often as not he is unaware of it, for prakriti jealously holds him under her sway. And yet most of his instinctive movements are right. His original, very primitive nature can serve him in his thought as in his feelings. And this is his chance, for he will gradually discover in himself a higher spiritual force which will lead him to worship the divine Mother in one or another of her aspects, and an animal force through which he will identify himself with one of the divine Mother's vehicles: tiger, cat, swan, peacock, etc.

The cosmic Laws act on the level of our understanding, but we are able to perceive only a very few of them. As a result, we can adapt the conditions of our life only to those Laws we have recognized. The cosmic Laws operate in time. And the notion of time, beyond our limitations, is unknown to us. What consciousness of time do people in India have? This concept is difficult to understand until you integrate it within yourself.

The Tantras indicate a method to realize the zero value of time. Technically, this value is called bindu. It is said that the pronunciation of a sacred formula (mantra) takes three *moras* and a half. The half is the point (bindu) which contains the all and is attained by drawing in the consciousness through seven stages, each stage in a geometric progression with different intervals: ½ + (1/4 … 1/8 … 1/16 … 1/32 … 1/64 … 1/128 … 1/256) … of a mora.

In reality, this is the alternating movement of consciousness in an inner concentration lasting as long as the recitation of the *japa* (sacred formulas) until one comes in contact with the Void. This bindu, more subtle than the atom, and Brahman, 'the Vaster than the vast,' are the same. Both are the Void. Time moves between the two. Between the two, there are the coils of manifestation like the coils of the serpent which represents the innate force (śhakti). This innate force, also called kuṇḍalinī, is the operative force between the two modes of the Void.

Endnotes

1. *2.2.15.*
2. *1.2.24.*
3. *The God of the Hindu trinity in his creative aspect.*
4. *There are ten incarnations of Vishnu (*Bhagavatapurana, *Bk. 1, Chap. 3).*

Chapter 13

MASTERS AND DISCIPLES

The disciples, in no matter what ashram, are not attracted primarily by pure metaphysical research, but by the person and the radiance of the Guru, who becomes for them the beacon-light on the path, the ideal made real. Thus the rule of 'loyalty to the Guru' immediately comes into play. The Guru's authority (*Gurudom*) is boundless.

Traditionally, without even being expressed, the Guru's promise to his disciples is as follows: 'I am here to lead you toward liberation. Do my work obediently and you will be saved. You will know the highest ecstasy and will be freed from the round of births and deaths (*saṁsāra*). If I go to heaven, you will come to heaven with me; if I go to hell, you will come to hell with me ...'

The Guru's responsibility is immense; he takes upon himself the karma of all those he accepts. For their part, the disciples are happy to throw their burden on his shoulders. Is the Master great enough to wish that one of his disciples will one day be more renowned than himself? If he does not wish it, a descending Law immediately operates. Owing to the Guru's hold over his disciple, there is often something morbid in their relationship, like that of father to son when the son is doomed to remain a son without ever becoming a father.

In the preliminary part of the Samkhya discipline, the disciple's relationship to the Guru is compared to a seed that has been buried in the earth. The seed is left to develop by itself in the heart of what feeds it. It absorbs the Guru. It will become a plant, bearing foliage, flowers, fruit and seeds. In so doing, it transcends the ground in which it grew and becomes directly responsible for its relation with Great Nature and for the life it contains in itself.

An attitude particularly conducive to rapid progress is that of total obedience to the Guru in all things: thoughts, attitudes and actions. The aim is to become the well-tilled ground the Master needs. From tradition, everyone knows that with rare exceptions this field, plowed with such care, will only be used in a future life when the right impulse will take possession of it. This slow and deep preparation is most important.

Great is the illusion of the man who believes that he can reach the goal after a few months of efforts! His ambition will be stopped at precisely the point where he becomes conscious of his personal destination (*svadharma*), of his own law as it seeks its own way in the midst of cosmic Laws. This is equivalent to discovering the Divine that lives in the heart, to serve it, to worship it but nothing more. A wild rosebush can be forced to produce big flowers of its kind, but a wild rosebush will never be able to produce anything but wild roses; any grafting promised by a Guru would mean that he is an imposter. And pseudo-Gurus are legion! This moment of self-knowledge is crucial. It means the death of the illusory ideal and often brings violent reactions. But if the ideal becomes interiorized, that moment of consciousness will be a feeling of unity on the level of the understanding attained. Here we are in the very heart of the living power.

At the beginning, a Guru and his disciple are like a mother and child, joined together by the umbilical cord. There is no tension whatsoever in this attachment. If there were any, it would mean that the 'psychic being,' which is to grow and develop between them until it becomes the 'heat' of their blood, would never take shape for lack of necessary substances.

This psychic being must be nourished with care. It is both cause and effect, meaning that it exists out of time. That is the reason why there is no longer any 'why' or 'how' in a well established relationship between Guru and disciple. Master and disciple can each say to the other: 'I am you. . . .' The same vibration animates them. One day, the 'child' between them will disappear, when certain vibrations mathematically reach a known point of reabsorption. Then, life in its reality becomes the Guru.

There are four kinds of devotees:

1. *He who becomes a devotee because he is in danger.*
2. *He who wants to obtain grace, help, health, security from the Master, or simply to live close to him, for his own sake.*
3. *He who has a thirst for knowledge. In such a case, the Master's physical person and way of life are of little importance to him.*
4. *He who* knows *without being aware of it, who by nature is good soil. Such a devotee welcomes obstacles on his path because they increase his determination. He has his own roots. For him, what matters is to live an experience, no matter how difficult.*

Does a Master care for this last kind of devotee? The situation is illustrated by the story of Lord Narayan, who one day was resting after having stationed two faithful guardians at his door, Jayā (victory) and Vijayā (total victory), to drive off intruders. Two ṛṣis arrive from afar and ask to see Narayan. A violent quarrel breaks out at the door of the god, so much so that the ṛṣis curse the two guardians. Awakened by the noise, Lord Narayan appears, bowing to the ṛṣis; at the same time he is also greatly upset, for nothing can erase the curse the ṛṣis have called down. It must take effect. So Narayan says to his two guardians, 'Since you have been cursed, you must enter the round of births and deaths, but I can allow you to choose your fate. Do you wish to be born among my devotees or among my enemies?'

'What will be the difference?' ask Jayā and Vijayā.

'If you are among my devotees, it will take you seven lives to reach me; if you are among my enemies, it will only take you three!'

And so it happened that Jayā and Vijayā willingly became great enemies of Narayan, constantly aware of their hate and therefore constantly remembering the god in spite of the severe obstacles they had to overcome to draw near him.

The relationship between Master and disciple is established by an infallible Law, with a view to the esoteric transmission of the cosmic Laws and their functioning. Once this relationship is clearly established, one can neither break out of it nor make decisions for oneself, nor wish to sidestep the Law once it has been recognized and one's part in it discovered. That would only be mental self-deception.

In this connection what is most difficult to attain is the surrender of the mind, because for some time, until a real new birth takes place on a different plane, this surrender seems to be a state of alarming torpor. To accept this state of passivity is always painful.

During all this period the subjective attachment of the disciple to the Guru exists in contrast to the objective love of the Guru for his disciple. What the Master can transmit is neither an idea nor a form, but a means. The *Kaushitaki Upanishad*[1] describes the traditional way in which the dying 'father' passes on his power to his 'son'.

It can be interpreted as the passing on of power from the Guru to his disciple: 'Let me place within you my word, my breath, and my vision; what I perceive, what I taste, likewise my actions, pains and pleasures; the concepts to which I have been attached, and my search itself. In you I place my spirit and my consciousness. I give you the breath of my life (*prāṇa*). May power, sanctity and honors go with you. ...' The son or disciple answers, 'May your words be fulfilled. ... Go in peace!'

In the life of the Buddha, this moment is the one when he set the wheel of the Law in motion within those around him, saying, 'Go, and speak of the Law for the benefit of many. When the soil is well tilled sow one seed of knowledge in it, nothing else, and go on further.'

Every Guru has only a very few key ideas at the root of his teaching. These ideas are the very ones that brought him to his realization. No others. He will constantly bring his teaching back to the fruits of his personal effort, which keep his spiritual experience alive.

Some Masters try to express these ideas by a single key word, others dilute them with explicit formulations in order to pass them on to a larger number of disciples. So there are two methods, that of interiorization and that of exteriorization, which the orthodox Hindu recognizes at once. Both of them are traditional. Both of them demand total sacrifice and cost dearly.

No Master transmits the totality of what he has received. As soon as he feels in accordance with the Laws known to him, he utilizes them like chemical formulae, transmitting only fragments to those around him. On the other hand, no fragment of knowledge is ever transmitted before the disciple has perceived it or had a foretaste of it. In summary, the Master is nothing other than an indispensable intermediary between the Laws and those who are ready to discover them. Nor does he ever teach more than a tenth of what he knows. Likewise, air is only a tenth part of ether, and water only a tenth part of air, and so forth. It cannot be otherwise. The Master cannot allow his strength to be further utilized. This explains why there is such a rapid degradation between the level of the Guru and that of the third generation of his disciples. A well-known cosmic Law comes into play here.

What is important to the Master, after having consciously reached the zenith of his upward curve, is to see the downward curve with equal consciousness and to choose the point from which he will teach. This point will keep constantly moving in response to his own living search.

Every saint or Guru speaks according to a particular 'principle,' adopted and faithfully served, in which lives a hidden Truth. The Guru is perfectly aware of this. This fragment of Truth belonging to ultimate reality is the only thing of real value, whereas the principle in itself, on the human level, merely helps to create the strict form of a discipline.

Certain sacred formulas (mantras) have been revealed and many commentaries written. Their form is known, even to the number of vibrations in each letter. But only the Guru knows their bījas, which are his potent semen or seed. He never reveals them. Were he to do so, he himself would become like an empty vessel. Whether the death of the Guru occurs after he has passed on his seed or after he has let it be reabsorbed in himself is of no importance, for the disciple who is a Master by nature will have found by himself the exact resonance of the bījas in his Guru's mantra.

In the Tantras, the mantra has four forms:

1. *It is given in a detailed form as in a hymn* (stotra).
2. *It is condensed into one formula* (mālā).
3. *This formula is condensed into a single word (nāma).*
4. *This word becomes only a pure sound (bīja).*

The mind must be led from the hymn to the bīja, which is the seed, the pure vibration that gives birth to the psychic body of the disciple.

There are great Masters and small Masters. Both of them do exactly the same work, for great Masters are for great disciples and small Masters for small disciples. The relationship between Master and disciple is the same in both cases.

The disciples, because of their avidity and competitive spirit, are always anxious to discover the sources from which their Master has drawn his knowledge. Some of them ask questions, discuss and argue; others even demand proof. And what do they find? Nothing worthwhile, for the Master transmits what has become his own substance. It is through this substance that the disciple will taste what he is able to assimilate of any given Law.

No matter what stage he has reached, a disciple must learn not to talk about what he has received. All experiences, spectacular and fleeting, are no more than the vision of the level he is trying to reach. To believe in them and talk about them is a pure illusion of the ego. Because of this, a period of silence after each experience is a wise measure of protection.

Sometimes, faced with a difficulty of understanding, the disciple blames this on his Guru and goes away; he is driven downward without being aware of it, caught by the Law of gravity. And so he becomes a parasite in the spiritual search, fed by his ego.

Every great Guru, when the time comes, drives away, from himself and from those close to him, the disciple to whom over a long period he has given a great deal. He releases him from all bonds, blesses him and entrusts him with a special task to fulfill, for 'there cannot be two tigers in the same forest.'

The disciple who is called upon to leave is fundamentally different from the disciples who live under the direct inspiration of the Master. He takes away with him a seed to be sown where he goes. He leaves without anyone knowing it, after he has secretly received from the Master the 'gift of power' which will be his support in life.

This is the origin of the tradition of wandering. The one who goes away changes his name. His trace is lost. No one asks about him. On the lower vital plane, the wildcat, when the right time comes, drives her kittens away from her. At the risk of their lives, they must find their own living space and hunting ground.

The disciple who leaves possesses nothing except the fact of his belonging to the Laws, for he has been fed by the Guru's essence. Either he will grow and develop with fresh vigor, because of the very separation he has lived through and the difficulties that await him, or he will perish without anyone hearing about it. In the latter case, he becomes humus useful to prakriti, a humus with a definite function to fulfill, however humble.

On the other hand, most of a Master's disciples remain close to him all their lives. They are a necessity for the Guru, just as the presence of the Guru is a necessity for them. These disciples have a precise role to fill. They are the fine matter which the Master uses to manifest his work in Prakriti. Without them the Master would be merely a radiance, but through their presence these disciples establish the circle in which the Master's vibrations create the ferment of possible evolution.

Until the disciple assumes his responsibilities, it is the Master's stomach that works and digests for him. But the disciple continues to question his Master: 'Who are you?' Krishnamurti answers by saying: 'I have never read any sacred books. ...' The disciples of Ma Anandamayee[2] cut things short with the words: 'She has never received anything from anyone, since she already knew everything when she was born!' even though they themselves have put forth the same question a hundred times! The same question has also been asked about Gurdjieff[3] who has been a pioneer in the West, far ahead of his time—hence the virulent attacks directed against him—because he instilled the broad ideal of possible evolution into the current of thought. One could answer with another question, 'Who can tell what the Pathans, that proud people of the Northern Frontier, are made of?' They were originally Aryans who became Muslim after having been Buddhist; but above all, they are to this day the sturdy children of their own land. In a like manner, just as the river Triveni unites three sources, so the knowledge of Gurdjieff has at least three different sources in the East—Vedism, Buddhism and Islam.

Gurdjieff was, of course, a real *cārvāka*, that is to say, a rebel against learnedly expounded orthodoxies that constrict the mind. He behaved like the mystics and powerful Gurus who, at a given moment, have called the crowds to them. Likewise, Sŕi Ramakrishna in his exaltation used to climb to the roof of the temple at Dakshineshvar near Calcutta and, weeping, would cry out, 'Come to me from everywhere, disciples! So that I may teach you ... I am ready!' Others, like Sŕi Ramana Maharshi,[4] through their silence and concentration have compelled those who approached them to ask themselves the question, 'Who am I?'

Among 'the independents' wandering about, there were those called cārvākas because they rebelled against all learned, expounded orthodoxies. Some have found fame without looking for it. Some have allowed followers to gather around them. Others have repeatedly fled from the slavery created by the excessive solicitude of their disciples. Still others have accepted this bondage with a definite aim known to them alone. Many of them have lived incognito in the midst of the world, hidden in the crowd and have died without leaving any apparent trace. Since the cārvākas have never been written about, it is only indirectly, through the reactions they aroused, that their name has circulated by word of mouth. The orthodox followers of every tradition have pursued and persecuted them, considering their freedom and influence too great.

Should one attempt to say what cārvākas are? It is written that Brihaspati, a Vedic sage,[5] was their ancestor. Fragments of their teachings are scattered throughout the *Katha Upanishad*, the *Mahabharata*, and also the Buddhist texts, since in the time of the Buddha, their voice was listened to very attentively. But their enemies gave such distorted descriptions of their positivist, anti-ritualist philosophy centered on the search for the 'I' that later they hid themselves with their well-guarded secret. They knew the paths leading to knowledge.

There is an enormous disparity between quality and quantity; quality hides within, whereas quantity spreads outward.

He who possesses the gift of captivating the imagination of the many and of transforming it into creative imagination is a born Guru. When a lamp is used, its light loses none of its brilliance, but when one takes a pound of sugar out of a bag of provisions it leaves an empty space in the mass of material. When receiving the *darśan*[6] of a Master, one touches the spirit itself, but as soon as one makes arrangements to stay close to him the 'downward curve' begins and the Law of gravity immobilizes the spirit.

One cannot escape from this Law, nor from its process of materialization. Owing to its constantly moving densities, matter will always be either somewhat more or somewhat less receptive to spirit.

The Guru sees what is happening with an intelligence that is not the intelligence of his disciples. He dwells at the center of an esoteric circle which, of course, carries its own limitations; but this circle is far above the circle in which the disciples move. In comparison with them, he is living in knowledge.

However, the Guru is well aware that this knowledge is relative, and that he himself is a seeker in relation to knowledge existing in the circle above him. A Guru who thinks he has reached the end of his search would be an imposter; a disciple who imagines him thus to satisfy himself would be a fanatic, cutting himself off from the Laws, from the ascending and descending movements that support life.

Why would you want the moment of knowledge to last? Even Brahma cannot keep what he creates for himself! Everything springs from him and immediately flows out. Millions of gods or of Laws at once take possession of it. We are a humble part of those who are trying to swim upstream. And what do we find? Close by we hear the repeated calls of Krishnamurti, who is becoming impatient, because, despite the shocks he produces, Great Nature does not transform itself. He halts people caught in the circumstances of life and cries, 'Stop! Understand who you are! Understand what you are doing!'

Elsewhere, in the sphere she governs, the Mother of Śrī Aurobindo's ashram declares, 'O Nature, material Mother, you said that you would collaborate in the transformation of man; and there is no limit to the splendor of such collaboration.' The unfolding of time enters into play here, in the very play of prakriti.

Ma Anandamayee was the first in history, faithful, more-over, to the Buddhist tradition still widespread in Bengal, to roam about Northern India, stopping to sleep and eat only in temple resthouses, completely cut off from the rhythm of life. For years she lived almost continually in ecstasy without any relationship with her surroundings. She returned gradually to the human state, at first unconsciously through a known process. Now she has voluntarily returned within the rhythm of Prakriti to transmit her experience to those around her and teach a way of possible expansion.

And what has Gurdjieff, with his broad shoulders, created for those in the West? Surely a field of prakriti corresponding to their own possibilities. This prakriti is arranged with care to offer many toys, instruments to use, and all kinds of 'intelligent absurdities,' which one wishes to keep in one's hands, hide in a strong box, or piously preserve in memory because of the love to possess things. This same prakriti will also reveal the many steps to climb to approach the goal without depriving anyone of all the possible ways to break their neck.

What tools will the Master use? The ones that suit him best. What difference is there between a bare room like the one in which we are speaking together now and a room filled with a hodgepodge like a bazaar? The Master utilizes the means that are needed to bring his disciple to him. Some day perhaps, if such is his wish and need, he will take the very bones of his disciple, crush them, make a pie out of them and offer them to the gods. He can make use of the trust the disciple has placed in him, his submission, and even the essence of his being (bhūta), to the uttermost limits.

So what remains of the disciple, once his bones have been crushed?

Nothing. For him it is death. There are deliberate deaths in which the blood flows, as in many temple sacrifices where the bodies of the decapitated goats keep on jumping and twitching until all life departs. What is it that is freed by death? There is also the secret of dogs, those beasts branded by the curse of impurity, who hide under a bush to die with a dignity the sannyāsins envy and hope to have at the moment of their own death. One of the hardest commandments in the initiation into sannyāsa is: 'When the day comes, know how to die like the dog, with dignity, unnoticed.'

Does the disciple know that by his death he is serving the 'essence of the Guru?' Can ashes know what use they have? If he so desires, the Guru can swallow up his disciple. He can use the liberated energy, just as we do in eating the food we need. The interdependence of functions exists; it is right and normal. The Bhagavad Gita states clearly how few out of a million pass through the narrow gate. But the aspiration is there. How can we know what is above us, since we only control the relationship of the planes of consciousness that we have acquired? That is why death in the 'Guru's essence' is the highest goal we can desire. We cannot lift our prakriti any higher. The best we can do is to unify, in all our reactions, the raw material of our nature with the movements of the spirit and to place these reactions in the heart—the heart that becomes the 'seat of the Guru' (*gadi*). This movement in itself is the voluntary death of the ego. It is only in this voluntary death that the Guru sees what is permanent in us: the fact of existing (sat). He can only give it form and animate it. In this he is like the Creator in Genesis, removing one of Adam's ribs to free the divine śhakti who is ready to give birth. Without this shock coming from above, no transformation is possible.

Another transformation is to give birth in ourselves to śhakti's child. This child will manifest a different prakriti than ours, different in quality. The child will call right away for a plaything. He must hold something in his hands to have the pleasure of throwing it on the ground, of picking it up, of giving it away, and taking it back, without any logic in his movements, just for the sake of moving around and discovering what life it. So always surround yourself with plenty of toys, for yourselves and for others. . . .

Endnotes

1. *2.15.*
2. *Śri Anandamayee Ma (1896-1983), a great Bengali Saint.*
3. *Georges Ivanovitch Gurdjieff (1877-1949).*
4. *Śri Ramana Maharshi (1879-1950) who spent most of his life in silence near the sacred mountain of Arunachala.*
5. *Teacher of the Vedic gods.*
6. *To be in the Master's presence, to be seen by him; the establishment of a current between Master and disciple.*

Chapter 14

Method and Teaching

How can one conceive of pure Existence (sat) in the heart of life? A characteristic feature of thought is to transmute the concrete into the abstract; and in the end, thought becomes interested only in the abstract. It is a kind of escape. The relation with life is then simply cut off. But when man, impelled by his desire to know himself, resolutely looks into himself, he resists the temptation to be carried away by the abstract.

In this regard, the energy that has been withdrawn from the outer realm will quite naturally become more intense as it reaches the inner realm. If this intensity is merely the repercussion of a shock coming from life in the world, it may devastate the field of consciousness. Having been damaged, consciousness no longer has any aim. But if this intensity is knowingly guided, it can lead to the perception of pure Existence (sat), in which the polarity between subject and object is resolved in a feeling of identity.

This experience, in which the dualities arising from the polarity of consciousness cease through natural absorption, lies beyond all other experiences in the midst of life. It is a creative matrix which gives birth to new forms. This is an important experience even in its very early stages. During a certain period the need for quietude can be dominant, but to attribute to it a negative value would be to fail to recognize the rhythm of Nature. It would be more exact to see it as a prelude to the need to create. In fact, when a pupil plunges into himself, his force appears to be lost. This force will reappear, but where and when? It is precisely during this period that the true Guru gives active protection and support to his disciple.

We look on confidently at all the movements of interiorized consciousness. It seems sometimes to be passive, inert, like dead matter, but actually it is a living force with a quite definite quality of feeling. In this respect, a perception has to be evaluated according to the quality of energy it frees in the realm of feeling and in the realm of will. In the realm of will, it becomes dispassionate and disinterested action, and in that of feeling it becomes the sublimation of some fundamental emotions of the heart.

In practice, quietude can easily appear like a high place from which to face life's problems. In that case, the technique to be followed consists in counterbalancing all positive energy with negative energy, knowing that both come from the Void. Without deviation, consciousness then takes a direction that it will maintain. All along the way its own vigilance is able to transform the emotional movements it encounters, even to the point that one can speak of the absorption of shocks through an absence of inner resistance. This is not inactivity, for will is present, operating in the realm of time with a clear vision of what reality is. This vision (*kavikratu*) has already been described by the Vedic sages.

The 'space-time' concept of the Upanishads has become the measure of existence in which everything 'moves without movement,' for all movement, in the end, is merely the displacement of what is contained in a seed, a seed that is self-sufficient, withdrawing into itself if it chooses. Thus, a seed of thought can, at any instant of its development, intensify its energies in perceiving its existence. It has no necessity to evolve, and yet it does evolve! Therein lies the mystery beyond intellect, the static state of the dynamism of pure Existence (sat) in life.

In the sāstras there is an oft-repeated precept that one should never speak in vain of one's spiritual experiences. If you do so, it shows that you have nothing yet in your own being that is valid and able to preserve the current of power that has come down to you. He who readily talks about himself is like a little child who runs to his mother to tell her about everything he came across while he was playing.

Before you speak about an experience, you must learn to observe it in silence for a long time. First, it has to find its place in you, to be clarified and to bear fruit. In short, it must become yours. While this is going on, life is reduced to a few movements and a few expressed thoughts.

The Great Manu[1] taught three important rules which should never be forgotten:

1. *Speak only when you are questioned.*
2. *Remain silent if you are asked an illogical question or if you detect a disguised motive in it.*
3. *Keep silent among fools; play with them on their level.*

Never uphold your personal ideas in discussion with a saint, a wise man, a *paṇḍit*, nor with a Brahmin who knows the Vedas, nor yet with your parents.

The yogi's role is not to be a savior of souls; but by the fact of persistently and deliberately working on his own ego, he impels an inner power in us that will open our eyes to our own egos.

When one has consciously set out on the path of search, there is no turning back. It is as though one were intoxicated. But the impetus of the start is often slowed down by all the heavy and useless burdens we carry with us.

In an episode of the *Avadhūta*[2] the crow tells a story:

I was flying with a piece of meat in my beak. Twenty crows were chasing me and quarrelling, trying to grab it. I had to fly high and fool them. I was weary. Suddenly, I dropped the piece of meat and saw the twenty crows in a great hurry and with loud cawings gliding down after it and fighting over it. Then I shook my wings. How wonderful it felt not to have anything to carry. All the sky belonged to me!

Every spiritual discipline is a detailed work. After a period of conscious efforts, there is always a period of temporary retreat, of 'cave life,' to attain mastery over the disorderly movements of prakriti, which defends itself and attacks in a sly way. We should not talk about the force of prakriti. It remains a secret.

During this period three rules should be followed:

1. *Be humble so as to disarm that which resists.*
2. *Accept everything.*
3. *Be intimate with no one.*

If these three rules are respected, the 'abstract sound' propelling the effort will remain pure.

The couch grass that has encroached a field causes great havoc. Likewise, in man, an objective vision, even if fragmentary, works on him and cannot be uprooted. Once one has learned to see, one can no longer live like a blind man. Every question, whatever it is, carries its own answer and reveals the prison of him who asks it. The Master touches the sensitive point where the freedom he reveals and the disciple's obscurities confront one another. One could also say that, at the point where the liberty of the disciple who is progressing comes up against the discipline demanded by the Guru, then that discipline appears like a prison.

An unusual quality of courage is needed to follow the advice, 'Rely only on yourself!' This is the same as saying, 'Isolate and cultivate the direct experience you are living until it becomes a part of yourself. Do not reveal it until you are able to connect it with something known and precise.'

The difficulty arises from the fact that one is surrounded by other disciples, each of whom remains enclosed in concern for his own personal discipline. Everyone is working by himself. The same holds true for the gods. In every temple, each god is seated on his own lotus flower. But collectively the gods are the permanent supports of a definite effort, whereas in their individual efforts disciples have only a momentary stability.

If you ask an old disciple or a co-disciple to help you, he will stay close to you, but if you do not follow his way, he will exclude you from his thoughts. At any moment you risk feeling rejected by the group of disciples. To pass from one level of understanding to another is equivalent to a surgical operation. Many lack the courage to get over the obstacles before them and in order not to see them, they 'ossify' their base, which gives them a rock of certainty to hang on to. From then on, such disciples are always talking about their sincerity as being an essential quality of yoga, whereas the man who is daring enough to follow the Law in its farthest ramifications is the one who makes the 'spiritual discovery.'

There is in man such anguish, such dissatisfaction with himself that even if he had thousands of words at his disposal, they would not suffice to express it. His pursuit of all the things by which he seeks some solace will never bring him the inner peace desired. And how could it be otherwise? Every path he follows is thorny. Disgusted by the difficulties, he abandons one path after another. Until he awakens to himself, and realizes that he is in fact the owner of his own field, he will lament but he will never acquire the plowshare and the plow with which to till it thoroughly!

While meditating, one is often tempted either to force the mind to pursue a definite line or to get rid of the influx of thoughts. However, the only correct way is to harmonize the waves of impressions with the indispensable plane of peace. The ritual of the Vaishnavites, the worshippers of Vishnu, gives valuable indications on this subject: instead of torturing the mind in order to make it pass through the eye of a needle, one must draw to oneself the full 'life of the body' and the entire 'consciousness of the body' in order to serve the Divine in a particular aspect, to receive him, to surround him and to worship him. Thus, little by little, a unity of consciousness is established, which makes use of all the levels of the being and all conscious and unconscious efforts. Then peace and impressions become one.

In spiritual discipline, movements of attraction and repulsion are normal until such time as one reaches a certain equilibrium. Four levels have to be passed through to reach the concept of the Void:

1. *Primordial ignorance.*
2. *The plane of the ego, which is the matter of prakriti with pleasure and pain in all their forms.*
3. *The 'I' that makes it possible to observe oneself.*
4. *The Void that is everything and nothing.*

Primitive man in darkness (tamas) is very close to his animal instincts, very close to the earth with a consciousness that is not awakened. For him, to have reached the plane of the ego is an achievement with which he will remain for a long time, perhaps for several successive lives, before an impulse of another order arises. For Nature allows only a very slow development. She is more inclined to favor a change of species than a change of consciousness.

One of the great Samkhya disciplines is the idea of returning to what is basically primitive in us, to the point where, for the first time, an act of conscious will has given a direction to the current of life. This discipline proposes, through methodical observation, to follow the path of thought 'backward' as well as in its normal development. Then we perceive that the only foods or substances that have permanent value are those that issue from the essence of the being, whereas everything that has come from outside has been almost obliterated. To find this point again is equivalent to seeing clearly when and how our personal destiny (*dharma*) is formed. Each time this takes place, it produces a shock which makes a step forward possible.

Spirit and matter are two different aspects of the same reality. Every creation is generated in the Void. The same is true of the resistance engendered in the equipotential field of energy. Resistance creates the sensation of a compact entity we term body or matter.

Thus, on the one hand, one can say that the body is nothing but the accomplishment of the spirit. On the other hand, one can say that spirit is like the blazing of the body when it is consuming its own energy. Life is the automatic combustion of the body. Heat is transformed into light. So one has the following parallelism:

matter—	heat—	light
body—	life—	spirit

If you conceive of reality as coming down from the spirit to the body, you are following the teaching of Samkhya. If you start with the body to rise toward the spirit, you are seekers. But if, with an ever wakeful attention, you perceive clearly the interrelation between the descending and ascending movements, you can dare to work in both ways. Then you are on the path of Tantrism. May you one day pursue a true Tantric discipline in the broadest and noblest meaning of the word.

Certainly the most authentic picture of Sŕi Ramakrishna is the one given by Swami Vivekananda, who saw in him a fully realized man. If Sŕi Ramakrishna submitted to a Tantric discipline for nine years, it was in order to escape from the imprisonment within himself caused by the notions of 'good' and 'evil' and to be able later to utilize them freely.

For those who only saw Sŕi Ramakrishna at the end of his life, it is easy to say that he was born in a state of grace and followed no yoga to show the way; hence the assertion expressed in a meeting of paṇḍits that he was born an incarnation (*avatār*). This is to ignore the entire Tantric period of his life, just as many years in the life of Christ are ignored and unknown.

The seated position (*āsana*) is for each of us the one we naturally come back to in order to find ourselves again. In this position there is no tension. The body is flexible.

'I find in myself again the form of myself, which is well known to me in every detail, for nothing is left to chance. I am seated quietly, my spinal column erect. I am looking straight ahead. Even if at first my eyes are closed, they continue to look straight ahead. I know how I sit, how I get up, how I walk, how I hold my head and place my hands.'

Each of these movements is a voluntary movement connected with the āsana that makes it possible to collect oneself in a quiet moment. Everything is related to the dignity of the inner being. In life, everyone uses the body for the role one has to play. This body is both instrument and vehicle; the first duty is to care for it. Each gesture takes place by itself in a moment of interiorization, without the intervention of the will or of thought.

There is much to be said about the secret role of the 'locks' in the body. To preserve one's force and energy during moments of interiorization, a certain automatism must be gradually acquired. This is an automatic system of detection for catching any kind of contraction, since the slightest tension is an indication of a wrong direction. In brief:

> 1. *The chin will tilt toward the chest. This movement happens of itself; it corresponds to a certain letting go of tension in the spinal column, which releases the knots in the nerves. Then the abdomen spontaneously becomes concave. These two movements are so closely connected that they are practically one, with a slight lapse of time between them.*
> 2. *Another automatic movement follows: namely, the extension of the chest, without any hardening.*
> 3. *The anus closes without any contraction, giving the energy an upward direction. The closed anus is the nadir point of a current that must be maintained. If this 'lock' is not closed, the inner body will be progressively invaded by depressive and negative emotions that have no connection with the realm of true sensation.*

When a perfect chord vibrates between Master and disciple, a continuous conversation proceeds between them without any words being uttered. This takes place even without inner dialogue. At this stage the function of speech is no longer activated because the inner organs (indriyas), which link the five sense organs to their objects, no longer play a role.

On both sides, communication then becomes pure vibration. One of the conditions of this state is to be able to think without words. So long as words or any formulation arise in thought or in prayer, it means that this vibration, which is in itself creative, is not taking place.

The constant repetition of a sacred word (mantra), at first consciously, then rapidly in a mechanical and unconscious way (*japa*), is one means of minimizing the consciousness of the ego. On the other hand, the voluntary discipline of silence, one or two fixed hours during the day, or a whole day each week, leads by stages to that inner silence which is one of the most delicate of disciplines.

The vibration of thought and of speech without words has no connection with telepathy. On a certain level this vibration exists between Master and disciple because they share the same vision.

The work of inner silence is concerned with reaching the seed-bed of thought, which is the only way to return to the initial movement of the inner organs of perception. At that moment everything around you fades away of itself. It is a strange mode of perception in which the will no longer interferes. The voluntary stopping of thought leads to direct contact with the initial point of silence where the basic note of all known harmonics resounds.

Thus we come to a very few thoughts, through which one single 'sound' says many things. For instance, *'ā'* means: come, enter, approach, hold what I give you, etc., *'djā'* means: go out, it is finished, this is not the moment, etc. Thus, between silence and a flood of words, one can live with some ten syllables in whose vibrations it is possible to understand languages one does not know.

Along this same line of ideas, it is astonishing to see how the questions put to a Master are all alike. If Sŕi Ramana Maharshi lived for so long amidst his own people without speaking, it is because his basic note responded to all the vibrations of the people around him.

Gurdjieff often speaks about the plurality of 'I's'. In substance he says, 'Bring all the "I's" to the "I" of essence, knowing in advance that in the place of essence you may find an "I" who will try to fool you!'

Likewise every master of Samkhya speaks about the plurality of 'I's'. He will say, in different ways, that at the start, the 'I' towards which all the 'I's' converge is only theoretically the Void. Through a meticulous discipline you draw close to an 'I' from which you can calmly observe yourself. From there the world is seen with all its mechanical movements; from there, for brief moments, you may have a glimpse of that 'I' which is the Void.

The next step cannot be taught by any book. It must be lived degree by degree, and lived with the Master holding one's hand. It is the slow discovery that finally there is no 'I' but only 'that which is active' in you. At that moment something can take place, but the vision is so fugitive that the least movement can destroy it. It is there, both inside and outside. We experience it and see it at the same time. We also see the mechanicity of all those things that come from nowhere and go nowhere. If we do not see this with eyes full of wonder, we then have an impression of self-extinction. But if we find ourselves in the midst of unexpected miracles, the movement of prakriti ceases for an instant, and we are totally one with an impression of life and of a spiritual radiance.

At that moment the disciple can say: 'I am seized by a real feeling of dissociation. I am not here. ... I am not there. ... Where am I? Anguish could grip me, but a readjustment is certain, I have only to wait for it. I know it will take place, I can trust it, as it is automatic! I shall find myself again facing prakriti with whom I can now play in the movement of manifestation.' In that instant, the ego will have faded.

The Void exists. Two Sanskrit terms make this clear: *pudgala-nairātmya*, the Void within the ego; and *dharma-nairātmya*, the Void of the twelve, twenty-four and forty-eight cosmic Laws. Having arrived at this point of comprehension, it is possible to see how prakriti works.

Tantric teaching demonstrates that all life is born from the Void, including the gods and goddesses and the higher and the lower Prakriti. The Void is the matrix of universal energy.

One has access to it by four stages. In his book *In Search of the Miraculous*,[3] Ouspensky speaks about the first two stages. He remained silent about the last two because he had left Gurdjieff. In all of his subsequent personal teaching, which is very important, he tells of the development of these two first stages and of his experiences with his Master. The writings of Gurdjieff,[4] on the other hand, open for us the frontiers of the two last stages. These are cleverly hidden in his mythical narrations. The four stages are: plurality of 'I's', a single 'I', no 'I', the Void.

We do not want to admit that for Prakriti, man, animal, plant or mineral are merely a reserve of humus. And she needs a great deal of it. All natural cataclysms are necessities. Only the quality of the humus matters to Prakriti. In this order of things, man plays a definite role of which he is still unconscious. Those who are becoming progressively less enslaved by nature, often have a very refined natural intelligence. This natural intelligence knows how to make full use of what is recorded by the senses as well as of recurrences of every kind.

The first question asked by man: 'Why?' brings about a considerable change. With that he becomes the enemy of Prakriti, and she defends herself. And yet, so long as he asks 'why?' he will make no progress because everything manifested in him, even in a subtle way, like the spirit, is still Prakriti, including his search and its ascending movement.

The Vedas mention a precise moment when the immobile has become the mobile, and another moment when the mobile becomes the undifferentiated.

It is not possible to approach the 'why' of the first cause since there is no logical answer to it, but the question remains as to 'how' did the first movement that ever existed occur. This penetrates into the heart of the process of creation and the cosmic Laws. The fineness of the sensation of a real immobility of the body which has reached a state without any tension, and the subtlety of the elements composing the multiple envelopes (koṣas) of the psychic body, make it possible for thought to become the seat of a passive experience. Then it may be that a certain sensation of existing is manifested, which is very similar to the life hidden in a seed, a life of full power without any apparent movement.

Even if this sensation of existing were perceived for only a fraction of a second, it would nevertheless suffice to know what took place at the instant when the 'immobile' became the 'mobile', or as expressed in more usual terms to know what took place at the instant of the first spontaneous vibration between the 'immobile' and the 'mobile'. Here one touches a clearly scientific problem in which the intervention of imagination would only be confusing.

He who truly goes through the experience of 'non-being' in a state of deep meditation feels suddenly filled by such a surge of life that, for that very reason, the question of the 'why' of things no longer exists for him. This surge of life is the imperative descent of non-being to being. It is at the same time an all-pervading sensation and a recognizable flavor. It is a certitude that wipes out every question.

One has evidence of this process in the certainty with which Sŕi Ramakrishna gave himself up to ecstasies that sometimes lasted several days. Sŕi Ramakrishna knew very well that there would come a moment when this surge of life would take place; it is the evident return to life in the layers of the body and the reappearance of known sensations, while passing through all the stages of consciousness.

No great yogi goes into contemplation or deep meditation before knowing with precision the Laws of reconnection or, in other words, the limits of this temporary flight. He need fear no surprises, knowing as he does through experience the exact relationship between all the elements at his disposal; but for the disciples around him, who look after his body, this process naturally takes on the appearance of a miracle. The disciples see what is happening only from the outside. In fact, there is here an experience of which the yogi alone knows the exact formula. It cannot be transmitted; it cannot be communicated, because it is the result of an exact connection between pure Existence (sat) and the innate essence of the man who attempts the experience.

He who, even once in his life and for a fraction of a second, has touched that point X in which the 'mobile' emerges from the 'immobile,' or, conversely, the point at which the 'mobile' becomes the 'immobile', has perceived in himself something of pure Consciousness (cit). He has perceived the undifferentiated, which is living! Alas, at the very moment he becomes aware of it, from fear of losing it, he gives it a name and form (*nāma-rūpa*) under the illusion that he will be better able to find it again. And yet, what was alive has faded away, the sensation has vanished. Symbolically, this is the moment when Shiva, seeing himself for the first time in a mirror, is overjoyed by the sight of this 'second', which he discovers and which becomes manifestation. This is the end of the divine solitude.

We feel rested after a night's sleep, and this is so even though this completely unconscious sleep is a return to the matrix of life. People in whom nothing is awakened literally fall asleep without knowing how to 'detach' something in themselves that will remain conscious. In their heavy state of tamas, they are not even aware that they are asleep.

The best way to go to sleep is to do it consciously. Patanjali has pointed out four kinds of sleep, closely related to the guṇas:

1. *Heavy sleep in the unconsciousness of tamas, which is a kind of stupor.*
2. *Sleep filled with dreams and bewildering elements coming from rajas.*
3. *Sleep in which something remains alert because a quality of consciousness doesn't entirely disappear. In this kind of sleep, the being consciously seizes something coming from sattva. Something remains like an impression of night illumined by the moon.*
4. *Conscious sleep in which one touches the mystery of truth.*

At the moment when consciousness fades away into sleep, a flash can be perceived that is exactly like the flash at the moment of awakening. These two flashes are of the same nature, of the same substance. It is said, symbolically, that this brightness lights up the head behind the forehead and is diffused throughout the head. It is represented by the moon which always adorns the forehead of Shiva.

Conscious sleep resembles the sleep of a mother who is sleeping beside her child. The child's sleep is tamasic. The mother is resting, but nevertheless her sleep has a quality of alertness on account of the presence of the baby, whereas a part of herself makes use of a conscious sleep that is fed by the forces of life.

From the pages of *In Search of the Miraculous*, the voice of Gurdjieff resounds like a call, 'Wake up!' Gurdjieff points out the way to awaken, to see the mechanicalness that keeps us in prison, to come out of the automatism of heavy matter, but he does not speak of the stage of voluntary sleep in a state of awakened consciousness, at least according to what Ouspensky tells us. From other sources, however, we are able to see the amplitude of his mastery of this plane of sleep in a state of awakened consciousness.

There is a detailed technique for attaining this 'yogic sleep,' which is no longer entirely mechanical and no longer obeys psychological laws. Nor has it anything to do with the natural sleep of a healthy man. That is why one of the first questions a Guru asks his disciple is 'How do you sleep?' and his first concern is to teach him gradually to sleep without dreaming. Another question will be 'How long do you sleep?' The answer depends on the importance attached to nocturnal vigils and meditations which are an obstacle to physiological sleep, when the silent night should be a time primarily devoted to a gradual work of conscious interiorization, followed by voluntary sleep in a state of awakened consciousness. This sleep, in a body without fatigue and without tensions (except for the minimal fatigue caused by the wear and tear of time) and in a studied posture, which is always the same,[5] becomes the field of many experiences.

Learn how to go to sleep consciously, starting from a very sensitive waking state, for the descent into voluntary sleep in a state of awakened consciousness has a counterpart. It is the awakening in awakened consciousness, which likewise demands a precise discipline.

If you know this state of awakened consciousness in sleep, then you have become like the silk thread of a necklace from which all the pearls have been unstrung, one by one, in a given order. The pearls can be restrung consciously, one by one beginning with the last, in the same rhythm with which they were unstrung. A vigilant eye follows the process. While the pearls continue to be added to one another, an X period of time will pass, and as the last pearl is added, the eyes will open. Was one really asleep or not? The answer is 'yes and no.'

Sŕi Ramakrishna often spoke about this awakened consciousness during voluntary sleep. He said, 'Enter voluntary sleep starting from the heart and not from a lower center.' To picture this experience, one must imagine a lamp lit in the heart. Concentrate on the heart and move progressively to the higher planes that you know. Then, when you are sure of yourself and it is possible for you to fill all the centers of your body in the same way, without suppressing your natural impulses such as desires, greediness and passion, try it. This method has been confirmed by many yogis.

Endnotes

1. *The person thought to be the father of the human race. He is credited with a code of laws which has retained considerable authority up to the present day.*
2. *Book XI, chapters 7-10 of the* Bhagavatapurana, *a vast treatise probably dating from the sixth century.*
3. *P. D. Ouspensky,* In Search of the Miraculous: Fragments of an Unknown Teaching *(New York: Harcourt, Brace and Co., 1949; London: Routledge & Kegan Paul, 1949).*
4. All and Everything *(New York,: Harcourt, Brace and Co., 1950; London: Routledge & Kegan Paul, 1950).*
5. *See the Buddha's posture, lying on his right side, the right arm under the head, the left foot resting on the right foot.*

Chapter 15

Observation of Oneself

In observing oneself, the first thing to do is to discover whether it is the intellect, the will, or emotions that predominate in ourselves. Even if one of the three plays the part of hero, the others nonetheless exist. To establish coordination between the three is a long, and exacting labour. Without this coordination, one of these elements will develop abnormally, and then neither the Master nor the pupil will be able to do anything about it.

To discover yourself, try to abandon your thoughts. Try to return consciously to animal life, to what is most primitive in you; at that moment, you will know what really belongs to you. Later, another experience will be to return consciously to the life of the plant. A plant produces flowers in its own good time, without any publicity. And these flowers provide food for butterflies.

In observing oneself, nothing is necessary but these voluntary 'returns' which allow us to discover what is positive and negative in us. The true work is to integrate fully these observations.

Gurdjieff distinguishes at the start between man Number 1, man Number 2, and man Number 3. In India, we speak of castes. One is necessarily born into one or the other caste and enters into a life full of natural movements in which all kinds of influences (saṁskāras) are in play. This development is entirely automatic and would remain so were it not for the shocks blindly distributed by the cosmic energy of śhakti. This energy knocks over anyone who happens to be in its way or who stands up to it. Its whim is our luck! The shocks that come from it create rebellion. These are brief moments of awakening.

Without such rebellion, man would not be conscious of his reactions; he would not begin to struggle against the unknown force that defies him. Only he who responds to the attack will, when the time comes, meet a Guru, that is, a guide, a protector; but this protector, while ensuring the desired protection, may become later on the one who will consciously direct the shocks of śhakti within his disciple.

The Tantras say, on this subject, that spiritual discipline must be followed with regularity, even if it involves necessary breaks. In any case, sudden deviations are inevitable in order to create the elements of new life. Shocks coming from one's surroundings are always a stimulant, the more so if they are provoked by the Guru himself.

It is not always possible to recognize from where shocks come, for they often have the same appearance and bring the same suffering. And it is only suffering that helps us discover a deeply embedded root that resists the shocks.

By being born into this or that caste, a man is a slave to men stronger than himself, just as every beast has to submit to stronger beasts. Through successive shocks from śhakti, man will pass through successive inner births and each time all that he knows will have to be re-learned and re-evaluated on another plane. Impressions (saṁskāras) will appear always in the same succession and according to the same recurrence, but the densities will be different. Heavy as lead at the start, they will little by little become as light as the fleecy substance of the clouds.

A living spirituality is in itself too primordial to be grasped by the intellect. Philosophers try in vain to explain in words what we feel.

In his teaching, Gurdjieff touches on two important points of this extreme positivism which must be detected, namely: the heart as the seat of the emotions; and sex, with its repercussions, which are still deeper and more overwhelming than those of the heart. We could 'be' and 'do' if we were capable of uniting the pure feelings of the heart and the pure desires of sex; in this way, we would discover the very essence of man. The ordinary Christian has the idea of paradise and of hell to help him in his evolution and, between the two, morality and the precepts of charity. But in this morality no one is able to give a place to the atomic bomb and the extermination camps, which, in prakriti, have their place. The result is a strong rejection of responsibility which does not diminish in any way the two natural and automatic movements of prakriti.

The ordinary Hindu has, for himself, a system of evaluation comparable to a stairway, making it possible at each step to recognize new values, which include light and shade. Good and evil are two aspects of the same thing. Certain steps are hard to climb because of the demands inherent in them; and they arise from cosmic Laws. Fortunately, the time factor is there to soften any too violent movement.

It would be unfortunate to remain a long time on any one step of the stairway, enjoying or tepidly satisfied with a state attained or rediscovered, for then there would follow a sluggishness which is like a slow death, a true sleep in complete unconsciousness.

The steps of the stairway represent man's possible evolution. If man is free from his movements, has he the possibility of choosing their direction? His power of choice depends on his level of consciousness, and he has to learn how to discover, at his 'point of departure,' what are his particular conditions and possibilities. All the rest belongs to the play (*līlā*) of prakriti. If nothing resists her, if nothing stands in her way, prakriti will thoroughly enjoy herself, her role being to create and to eat her own creation, if it does not rise in self-defence.

To work in order to know one's point of departure means to enter into a detailed observation of oneself. If this work is attempted by a mind that does not analyze all that it perceives, the armature of logic is broken down as well as the ability of the intelligence to create compromises. The Hindu 'swallows' things more easily; he digests them without thinking. He puts his trust in the Lord Shiva, who is continually swallowing the poison of the world so that his throat is blue from it, yet without letting this disturb his divine play.[1]

It is important that he who works toward his own evolution should discover what kind of link exists between his belief and his life as it is lived day by day. Something links the two, if it be no more than a mechanical continuity. It may be that some form of meditation will become established one day, making use at first of only ordinary coarse habits; but this meditation will finally become purer. Later on, of its own accord, it will take a different form.

A lived experience is always sustained by a living paradox:

> *'If you search for God, you will surely not find Him.*
> *If you search for power, you will never have it.'*

God prefers one who struggles against Him[2] to one who is lukewarm. We can develop in ourselves only what is already in our essence. 'If you have a power in yourself, you can make it grow—absolutely nothing else.'

According to a popular saying, 'If you worship God, He will ruin you, but if after that you still love Him, He will become the slave of your slave.' An illustration of this saying is given in the *Caṇḍi*,[3] as follows:

> *The demon Shumba felt the desire to possess śhakti, appearing as a goddess who had come down from heaven. He said to his messenger: 'I want this woman. If she does not come to me, I shall drag her to me by the hair. Go tell her so!' The messenger left and transmitted the demon's order. The goddess smiled and said to the messenger: 'I made a vow a very long time ago, before I heard of a master like yours. It was this: My husband will be none other than he who insults my pride! Tell your master to come to me and ask to marry me! I am awaiting him!'*

In every spiritual discipline the great obstacle is fear. Another obstacle, still more dangerous, is meek and passive obedience. A famous Guru said: 'I am surrounded by people who do everything I wish, who obey all my requests. They are merely real sheep! I would rather see people work from love, a love that starts a fire generating life. Unruly children are the ones who have in them the most possibilities.'

If we obey our passions—greed, anger, envy, laziness, it is because we worship them as idols well hidden in us. If we throw light on them, we cannot avoid seeing their true forms and finding them horrible. We detest them and at the same time do not wish to be separated from them.

There is an exact science for cultivating memory; conversely, there is an exact science for the cultivation of forgetting. The one is as important as the other. Every day I eat with pleasure, but do I save the skin of an orange from which I have extracted the juice? In the same way, the past has its importance, but one has to remember events as they come to mind without allowing feeling to enter in. Each day a child plays with the toys that amused him the day before, but without remembering the sensations he experienced, for he does not connect one thing with another. We must consciously return to this possibility.

You must learn to welcome consciously the most unexpected events of life, to be entirely transparent in front of them, without any motivation as to right or wrong. At that moment avoid all judgement, for you do not know what Law is in operation.

Hold back your prakriti in all the spontaneous movements that may arise in you, so that it does not flow out or become diverted toward the prakriti of others. This calls for no withdrawal on your part; but it allows you to prevent heavy matters from becoming agglutinated with other disordered heavy matters. Then you will be able to observe the movements and erratic nature of others and this will help you to catch sight of your own movements. At that point, some control can be exercised, but only of yourself. This state of transparency has a relation to what one can also call 'self-remembering,' if one clearly understands that prakriti includes the entire being in the multitude of its conscious and unconscious manifestations.

Only little by little does one become acquainted with the idea of the Void.

The best way to approach it is to watch how things take place. What we call our will is not really ours. It is simply a stirring of prakriti in us—an automatic movement.

It must not be forgotten that if the flower bud has been formed, the full bloom will follow quite naturally. Then why be impatient? All true creation occurs in silence. Open yourself more and more, or rather let Great Nature unfold herself in you. A blossoming will follow as a logical development. Our only duty is to be contained within ourselves and to be fully vigilant.

The following paradox is revealing: One must keep a firm hold on the rudder of the boat that symbolizes our life, become one with it, risk everything without ever letting go of the helm. At the same time, one must know that everything is impermanent—the boat, the sea and ourselves. Although holding fast, I give up everything in advance. I hold fast, while measuring the impermanence of everything. At that moment the play of thought ceases, there is only the 'I' that knows, in the pulsation of my blood.

Do not hurry in any of your actions; be aware of exactly what dictates them. Control your thoughts rigorously before acting; this will make you slower in starting an action and will help you to maintain carefully your integrity. You will feel an inner satisfaction if you try to have this attitude. Never make a sudden decision. As women say, 'Haste makes a bad curry!'

Pay attention to everything you do, for the smallest things are the most important. Pay attention to everything you think. This control will be established once and for all as soon as you know how to record a fact in itself. Speak to the heart but without using words. Learn to live in this discipline so as to manifest the life within you.

Those who transmit a teaching do so because they have decided to return towards the masses and to help others approach the threshold of knowledge. But one must realize that no particle of truth can be given, for we never know anything of another's thoughts. To believe it would be to create for oneself an illusion as dangerously false as that of human love. Truth can be lived only after a very long purification.

There are several disciplines of voluntary detachment.

A traditional one is that of the adepts of Vedanta, who put an end to the relation of cause and effect (karma) by plunging into detachment through the solemn vows of sannyāsa. From that time on, their discipline is constantly to discriminate between the real and the unreal. That is why, under the ochre robe, there are so many monks who, at the beginning of their asceticism, are wicked, miserly, greedy and liars. They are cleansing the inner being. This work is slow and painstaking. Throughout this asceticism and because of their robe, they are sustained by those around them, helped by the whole of a society that trusts them, by the people who ask their blessing and fear their anger.

Another traditional discipline is that in which, in everyday life, I consciously die to myself each evening, to be reborn each morning, infinitely relaxed and supple. It is life in its fullness in the immediate present. 'I am the thread of the necklace, the thread of continuity, holding the beads together.' Each bead is an experience. Each bead is perfect in itself in relation to its transmuted raw material. Who am I, if not the whole of these transmutations? To pass beyond them, I must first bring them back to a central point.

The process of externalization of any spiritual experience must be observed with care and precision. Our attention must be directed for a very long time to this, for it will reveal how the opposite process of interiorization occurs, provided the observer knows how to see what takes place in himself.

The mystery will always be that 'the All' is discovered by withdrawing into oneself, and not through the process of exteriorization. Within oneself, there is no longer any submission to an outer will, but an immersion in the principle of a higher will. The Bâül and the Sufi know this very well. One returns from this a different being, even if one cannot make the experience last. It is illuminating. That is all. Intellectually, one invents means to reach it, whereas it is rather a question of chemistry or of mutation. If you could understand that, the mutation of one element into another would passionately interest you, earth into water, water into fire, fire into air, and so forth. These words are the keys to studying what takes place in us at different densities of being.

One of the means used is voluntary detachment. The only true detachment is a spontaneous result and not an effort. It can be compared to the scales that fall by themselves from the skin of a snake; the snake does nothing. Likewise the bark of certain trees cracks and falls off when the trunk grows thicker. The same phenomenon takes place in the inner being after the digestion of an integrated experience. The experience itself disappears like a good meal. The nourishment is distributed throughout the body according to a known process, which we shall not speak of here. What applies to food applies also to a lived experience; if it is perfectly integrated, there is no more to be said about it. It is quickly forgotten, but the inner being has grown.

If I speak of God, it is because I do not know who God is, what God is. He who speaks about something is outside of that thing. The only truth is the radiation of the being in living silence. But it is easy to be mistaken, for in the 'return' to life, he who knows is as mute as a stone. The Great Manu advises us to be silent. He who questions is not conscious of his heaviness; he who is silent is conscious of the transmuting ferment that dwells within him.

He who, without wishing it, without even thinking about it, brings about a transmutation in the being of people around him, has a power attributed in the old days to the philosopher's stone. He is the ferment of an integrated experience. In the course of this process, the disciple must be patient and calm like a fisherman on the water's edge. The fisherman has cast his line; the disciple has opened his heart. What will appear comes from the depths of the water or from the depths of the heart. Neither one nor the other knows what it will be. To be ready is the only thing that counts. This waiting causes the disciple to die to those who are around him.

It is not a question of an experience which can be repeated. To try to repeat it would be committing a great mistake which could be fatal, for it would mean wilfully engaging the ego in the play of powers and cosmic forces without being prepared to control them.

The traditional Schools speak of yogic experiences: meetings and contacts (darśan) with a saint, revelation, discipline for the mind, the heart, the body, life in an ashram, and so forth. All these experiences are at our disposal. They give us our chance. They have been tried by others before us, and we can rely on them according to our individual type.

These experiences can fill a life. Nevertheless, they are only the careful tilling of naturally fertile ground, which must take place before a single true sensation is felt within and can be incarnated. This sensation is the seed of life because it is entirely pure. It creates and then disappears. Its role is ended. The child to be born is potentially the embryo in the matrix of the inner being, which will one day be 'the Man whose seat is in the cavern of the heart.' There is no mystery in this. One faces reality here.

If the spirit can become malleable matter and matter made malleable can become spirit, spiritual experience will demonstrate that it can transform the behavior of the individual. This transformation—spirit-matter and matter-spirit—is, in fact, true spiritual existentialism, the consciousness of sat. But in times of danger and depression, when the passions reign that characterize the present vital plane, the human hunger represented in the West by existentialism has degraded the perspective of pure Existence (sat).

In every spiritual discipline one progresses first with thought, then with speech. The body follows only very slowly. Then only can one speak of total surrender. To establish a discipline that engages all the functions of the body is long and difficult because the body is heavy and asleep. In the life of the world, the body is made use of first. It is educated and given all kinds of habits until its behavior is considered satisfactory.

Most people know nothing about the internal sense organs (indriyas). The internal organ of thought has nothing in common with habitual thoughts turned toward the outside. It is used very rarely. The internal organ of speech is still more rarely used. Interiorized life uses only the internal sense organs, which have a double function, that of relating us to outer life and of bringing to us impressions to be stored. To recognize the functioning of these inner organs involves very careful work on oneself.

Certain Laws must not be revealed before a long preparation has given them weight. It is solely direct experience that will bring their substance to life and demonstrate their existence. These Laws are part of the interiorized experience, of the substance of life that has been 'sucked' from the Void; it can be neither eaten nor drunk, it can only be absorbed into oneself.

Here are some fragments about it. There is a saying, 'Take a broom and sweep in front of you.' On the philosophical plane, this means:

'Separate yourself from prakriti.' Part of yourself is passive and remains calm and unmoved: the other part is active, in movement, constantly acting and reacting.

We see a dog chained to his kennel and barking, but the dog itself does not know that it barks. It is only fulfilling the function for which it is there. Animals have consciousness, but not self-consciousness. The heart of the problem that interests us is the following: 'Have an eye open on yourself, observe yourself!' In life you are, in fact, like the barking watchdog; you are always watching *others*, but you never look at yourself with the same keenness.

Another way to formulate this idea is the following: One man smokes opium, absorbed in his experience; another smokes without being intoxicated because he measures what he does. Still another remains indifferent while he smokes. He feels nothing because he functions like an automaton. He is the image of sleep in a waking state where there are even no reactions. These different planes form the major part of the teaching of Gurdjieff, as it has been reported by Ouspensky. They have been given exactly. But in his own teaching, Gurdjieff touched on many other planes as well.

In your efforts of self-observation you are often stopped at a point where you are unable to formulate concretely what appears to you as objective. If you knew how to do it, you would experience bliss and pure joy (ānanda). But as yet you have only a few rare memories of such moments which, although vivid, quickly disappear. To taste this bliss in the essence of the being would make you independent. At that point one is virtually separated from prakriti. That is why intoxication is the oldest form of worship, which is a bliss of remembrance no longer bound by time.

One must know how to pass consciously to the plane of pure sensation. To achieve this, one must learn to orient oneself between two kinds of memory (*smṛtis*): memory of an event and memory of the essence that has been recognized. One of these memories is changeable, the other permanent. Memories of the event exist only in time. As long as they remain, one is either happy or distressed, according to their nature. As soon as a sensation is associated with them, they become a limitation, that is to say, 'what is finished' or 'what is lost.'

A pure memory is never a sensation, but the delight of having touched a 'point'. Hence the importance of pure things: what lies around us, what we hear and see, what we eat and breathe. Only pure memories lead to eternal memory, in which the impressions of life (saṁskāras) are effaced. One touches here a state of deep spiritual existentialism which is the eternal present. But every time one speaks about it, one destroys something of the power that is in action, for instead of interiorizing it, one exteriorizes it. That is why a Master who has accepted the task of teaching is sacrificing himself. He acts according to a descending Law. The substance of the experience that he enables others to approach is like the fetus in a pregnant woman. The Master watches over the experience without imagining the form that it will take.

The greatest mistake we can make is to believe that we can direct our actions, whereas all we can do is to feel the repercussions and reactions to which they give rise. One attitude, however, is possible, namely, that of forgetting the action as and when it is in progress. The result will be like a blank page in which memories will no longer leave an imprint.

A Buddhist discipline suggests, 'Do not attach the passing moment to another moment,' that is to say, disconnect the moments from each other. Of what use is it to connect them? Live like the child holding a toy in his hand. He gives it with a smile to one person and refuses it to another.

If one studies the life of Shankaracharya in his mystical period, one sees that a great saint never acts according to his own will, but according to the will of others who sometimes are fools. This means to act without creating inner reaction. In this state of freedom, the true creative urge arises. You will serve better, you will participate in the life of others, and you can heartily laugh at yourself!

There exists a philosophy of forgetting; practice it! The Nyaya School teaches:

> *From a lower prakriti, aspire to reach a higher Prakriti. To attain this, free yourself from past relationships; throw away your memories, which weigh so heavily. When fed by prakriti, your memories are stale*

food. Throw them into the Ganges, which has a strong current, but not into a pond, where they would decay without being destroyed.

In the way of love (bhakti), observation of oneself remains fully conscious of the movements of human nature even when they are violent; but in the way of knowledge the observation of oneself is freed in the stage of interiorization where the essence of being is nourished only by very subtle foods (prāṇa). In this new state of consciousness, there is no longer any suffering arising from prakriti because the clear consciousness is now inhabited only by the spirit of Purusha.

Observation of oneself can only be directed by a Master who knows his disciple well and will help him to see his problems. The work of interiorization is perfectly codified by Patanjali, who in his aphorisms gives a detailed plan of work. But it remains up to the Master, who knows his student's type and sees his possibilities, to apply this discipline.

Patanjali specifies the following states:

1. *A personal discipline that leads to quietening the body.*
2. *A state of consciousness in which calm has been established but the subconscious continues to work.*
3. *The mastery of tendencies and habits that reappear one after the other at long intervals.*
4. *A victory over any tendency or habit, giving a taste of freedom that can be called illumination, even if it is partial and ephemeral.*

Follow these simple and sure rules of conduct. Be silent as to the results and pass on crumbs of knowledge only to those nourished by the same blood as yourself, who are not prone to bitter criticisms and fault finding. Avoid those who pride themselves on their strength, for it serves only the lower prakriti. You are never obliged to participate in the life of someone who is not one of your co-disciples or a spiritual son of your Guru.

With the Master, be simple. Learn to have integrity. Serve him without asking questions, in complete surrender, but without any emotion.

Patanjali gives the psychological foundations[4] resulting from the experience of centuries and suggests two formulas:

1. *Relax all the joints, which activates inner relaxation. At that moment there is a feeling of being wholly at one with the earth. From this comes the deep physical joy of having a harmonious body.*
2. *Only with a global sensation of the whole body can one begin to observe the breath, which goes outwards, whereas it is in fact the force of inner life.*

If we try to observe in this way, without giving rise to the least tension or alteration, whether in thought, or in feeling, or in the body, it is possible to follow the movement of the breath and to isolate oneself in the body as in an impregnable citadel. Seat yourself in a natural way. This will be your ideal posture (āsana). Observe your breathing while allowing it to establish its own rhythm. Discover calmly whether this rhythm is introverted or extroverted, that is, whether you naturally keep your breath inside or whether the breath stops for a moment after breathing out. Then breathe normally through both nostrils. To begin with, the breathing has no rhythm. Later a rhythm becomes established provided one does not interfere.

In the beginning, the breathing is only physical, but little by little the rhythm deepens and will go down to the body's center of gravity, making it vibrate internally. There is a rule that says, 'The mind is the master of the activities of the senses, but the breathing governs the mind.'

Endnotes

1. *The gods and the demons met together to churn the ocean and extract its nectar (*amrta*). It appeared; but hoping for something still more precious, the gods and the devils continued to churn. Then poison appeared.*
2. *In India, one who struggles against God… see p. 116.*
3. *One of the oldest Puranic texts forming part of the* Markandeyapurana.
4. *See* Commentaries on the Aphorisms of Patanjali *(Raja-Yoga).*

Chapter 16

AUTOMATISM

The Law of automatism is absolute. Even if the role of this Law is to keep the masses bound to the will of prakriti, it forces the man who is a seeker by nature to find a way out and awaken to his own being.

To achieve this several things are required:

1. *An active meditative state in all the circumstances of life, that is, to become the witness of oneself in the midst of life.*
2. *A voluntary withdrawal from the mental functions, in which, by association of ideas, most reactions arise.*
3. *A conscious self-control to curb all greed.*
4. *A woman can reach this awakening state through 'natural intelligence,' that is, through her essence, whereas a man can reach it only through voluntary sacrifice and personal discipline. There is no other way for him.*

It is said that a hundred thousand seekers will come to nothing for each one who will reach the goal, just as in Great Nature an immense surplus of seeds is required for one to bear fruit. All the wasted seeds go to make good humus for the earth. All the disciples who come to nothing make up the spiritual atmosphere of India. Hindus do not discuss either their attempts or their failures in this domain. For them all movements coming from the ego have the same value; all of them spring from distorted impulses. Hence every good action performed by one's own will still belongs to the realm of personality.

Ideas and sensations are as automatic as everything else. They can be counted and classified; their frequency can be known. They are only figures and lines forming triangles with unequal sides. One has to know about that rhythm of life.

Life rolls on like a stream carrying along much refuse in its swift current. We need not haul it ashore, but rather to let it float along and disappear.

To appreciate rightly Sŕi Ramakrishna's childhood vision of infinity on seeing white cranes flying across the sky, or the force of ecstasy that led Sŕi Ramana Maharshi to the Void, one must have felt deeply in oneself the continuous pressure that Hindu society can exert on a sensitive being, imposed upon him by the rules dictated by the caste, the family and the village, from which there is no way out.

These extremely rigid conditions cause beings ready to throw off the yoke to 'explode', just as the pressure of the earth causes one seed in a thousand to burst open within it. Each tree, indeed, is a miracle of persistent effort to survive in the midst of multiple dangers. This effort is a movement of the essence, still incoherent but already prepared to pay the price of independence.

Do not leave your souls in the hands of the temple priests, but become your own architects and lay the foundations of a solid structure in which everything will be in its place. It is by progressively studying our reactions to shocks from outside that we can measure our progress and see what remains shaky in ourselves.

The only way to recognize your real 'I' is to see your reactions in detail, one after the other. That is the surest guide for penetrating toward the inner being. The duration of a reaction clearly seen is the only moment when mind and matter, soul and body are not cut off from each other. It is a moment of your own reality.

If we knew how to expand ourselves to the utmost in time and space, nothing would be difficult and the complexities of life would disappear. Life itself would carry them, in other words the Divine Mother, or the

Void, which is the first cause of prakriti. Each one individually does what he can on his own level of understanding. This idea is the generator of all upward flight as well as of all degradation.

We can ask the question, 'Why do I exist?' One of the customary answers is that we exist because of the Law of cause and effect (karma).

India believes in successive births. This belief is acknowledged and repeated to the point where it is devoid of thought and meaning. He who lives with no trace of awakened consciousness will be reborn on the same plane of evolution, even as the tree, on its plane, is reborn as a tree. It is matter and will remain matter in the admirably organized recurrence of prakriti. Well, one can voluntarily ignore the idea of karma, in spite of all the philosophical explanations given about the relation of cause to effect, coming from former lives and influencing future lives; but what cannot be ignored are the different categories of impressions (saṁskāras) and the shocks coming from outside which are constantly reaching us. We live on these impressions as on the air we breathe and the food we absorb. We must learn to recognize these impressions, to welcome them or to reject them. An exact science is involved here, in which the influence of the mother, of the father, and then of the Guru is of the highest importance.

The man who penetrates willingly into the plane of evolution thus creates impressions related to it, which then accumulate. Because of this he enters within the evolutionary will. Then ensues a definite rhythm of births and deaths (saṁsāras) until the substances utilized are refined and purified. The level of consciousness changes at each stage, for many degrees of perception mark out the path of evolution. New words come to be used related to alchemy and physics, for it is easier to speak of a scientific event than of an inner attitude in which the subjectivity is involved and therefore alters every objective observation.

The Upanishads affirm that every soul is not reincarnated since reincarnation presupposes a conscious maturity.

Chapter 17

CONSCIOUSNESS

Even the adepts of Samkhya discuss the origin of consciousness, just as much as the philosophers do: Buddhist, Vedantist, and all others.

Truth, like life itself, is a mystery. It can be recognized, but it cannot be analyzed nor imprisoned in words. In this realm, all experiences lived must move imperceptibly from the plane of outer life to the plane of inner life to nourish that which is our essence. Then some day these experiences will find expression in their own way by a particular radiation. This radiation is also automatic; it moves from the plane of inner life to that of outer life.

To be oneself, that is to say, to live in the consciousness of one's own essence, promotes the growth of a new understanding. It is just as if delicate fingers were unfolding, one by one, the petals of a lotus.

Between the spasmodic movements of the finite and the immobility of the infinite flows a continuous stream of the force of śhakti. This is the process of becoming. It can be said that the force of śhakti is continuous, since it can be perceived as such by consciousness. But if you believe that it is unconscious, its movement will be for you only a succession of jerking dots and all things will then have a beginning and an end.

But consciousness, even at the mental level, demands continuity. It lives by duration. And duration is not a blank word. This idea is at the root of the Vedic conception of reality as pure Existence (*satyam*), the rhythm of time (*ṛtam*), and constant growth (*bṛhat*). What is most important is the link between satyam and ṛtam. This is the fundamental Law of spiritual evolution.

By being conscious of oneself it is possible to pass from the plane of personality to the plane of essence, for an observer is then present. The Upanishads and the Bhagavad Gita indicate different means, each one representing fragments of discipline:

1. *To observe oneself with a sustained look.*
2. *To stand aside, without any kind of judgement whatsoever, thus allowing the essence to grow.*
3. *A neutral look will automatically see the disorder that reigns in the inner house; then a desire for order will arise of itself.*
4. *A growing essence always gives its assent.*
5. *The essence will become 'the one that carries everything in its arms,' and prakriti will follow obediently, and finally find its own place in all functions.*
6. *The Lord in the heart will always in the end conquer prakriti.*

Between the two different levels in a being in search of himself there is always an empty space to be crossed, which provokes a chaotic movement; the more protracted the effort to cross the gap, the more violent the movement becomes.

The intermediate consciousness which opens up the way to pass from one center to another is made of very fluid matter. It is in the heart of this matter that the Guru works deeply with his plowshare. This fluid matter has no connection either with the subject or with the object, it will find its own form in the Void. It can be activated only by the Master. For a long time, the seeker himself knows nothing about it. He has no organ with which to discover it or make use of it.

In this position, the disciple's attitude is to do nothing of his own free will, for then everything would be distorted. But he must observe with lucidity, of his level of understanding, all that takes place, and learn to recognize that 'active passivity' which will become a right movement at the appropriate time. This is all that concerns him.

As regards the states through which Sŕi Ramakrishna passed in order to come back to a normal state of consciousness after a long period of samādhi, he said to himself, 'Since the ego never dies, let it at least become a good servant of the Divine Mother!' To come out of ecstasy, when he still felt impelled to go further into his experience, he used to strike himself violently on the head. He said, 'One can sing an ascending scale: *sā, ri, gā, mā, pā, dhā, ni* ... but one cannot hold the last note for long. One has to come down again!' He had an immense wish to live, to have the whole universe enter the field of his experience. He saw life in its aspect of completeness in śhakti, the life of the cosmic Laws, and he absorbed it to the very limit.

Every disciple in his quest is fully aware that the personal discipline he has accepted has a practical aim, which is the complete union of human consciousness with the highest reality. The goal is to transform the mental, vital, and even the physical nature of the being, down to the smallest cells in the body, in order to attain to the understanding of the ultimate reality (Shiva-śhakti).

The extreme relativity of consciousness must never be forgotten. Those who have a highly developed personality are less easily penetrated by a new form of consciousness.

Every morning wake up, each one of you, like a young child. At noon, stand majestically as men and women in full development. In the evening, be conscious beings ripened in strength and serenity, who having drunk deep at the fountain of life, watch the approach of death. In the middle of the night, be the Void itself, the darkness of the sky in which a moon ray still shines. In this picture, I am revealing to you the secret of the *Gayatri*[1] of the Vedas, the essence of the Sun and the Law of life.

Endnote

1. *The invocation which is pronounced every morning.*

Chapter 18

SENSATIONS

All spiritual experiences correspond to sensations in the body. They are simply a closely graded series of different sensations, beginning with that of feeling oneself as heavy as a clod of earth and passing gradually, in full consciousness, to the sensation of liquidity and then to that of the emanation of heat. The last sensation is that of a global vibration before reaching the Void. The road to be travelled is indeed very long.

Each time a step is made on the ascending ladder, a sensation of expansion in space and of complete relaxation is experienced. This sensation offers a foretaste of what the experience of pure spirit (cit) might be, in which all things are transcended. At that moment spirit and matter appear to be one. But how far one is from that! This conception comes from an ancient theory of the purification of the elements, which in the Tantras is called *bhūta-suddhi* and which has been spoken of in the Upanishads.

May your present discipline become for you, in this subtle gradation of sensations, a means for expansion and later for infiltration into everything around you, both fellow beings and things. Become aware of the deep and strong sensation of passing from one element to another. There is no other means. Use for this purpose the solitude that makes it possible to interiorize many forces. Every contraction produces heat and it is this heat that will spread. A true personal discipline (tapasyā) is nothing other than this expansion of one's self radiating warmth produced by inner concentration.

Always remember that any sensation of expansion you may experience is a radiation. Remain calm and radiate this warmth. Do not question. Ask for nothing more. Live these moments to the full. This radiation is in itself śhakti, an instant of living consciousness, that is, a direct experience that becomes established in you. Your sensation is the proof of it, a certainty you can no longer efface from your memory.

In meditation, the whole body is utilized to discover a sensation of expansion which, for a long time, represents the final aim. Work on the body is a delicate matter and has to be done according to very precise rules whereby each movement, voluntary or involuntary, is a search for calm, that is to say, for a sensation of physical consciousness.

The first objective to reach is perfect solidity of the motionless body. To arrive at that, all thoughts have to be brought back one after another to the body—to its form, its weight, its balance, etc. There must be no other thought. This state is symbolized by the matter 'earth', in the heart of which, notwithstanding its heaviness and opacity, a vibration already exists.

The directed attention will gradually be fixed upon the image of a bowl. The body is really a vessel made of heavy matter which contains an effervescent wine. Concentrated in itself, attention will penetrate the body, go down the length of the spinal column until an impression of great heaviness is felt in the center of gravity. The whole body has then become as hard as a statue with a pure form.[1]

At this point, one discovers that all the inner movements: effervescence, agitation, ideas, images—all are produced by the body. The stability of the body is a state in itself. This is why, to attain it more easily, so much importance is attached to food and hygiene.

The second stage begins when the body, in its well-established solidity, can become the matrix of energy in movement. Externally hard, the body becomes internally the very pulsation of the life that fills it. An intense vibration of energy throbs in it. This state is symbolized by purification of the element water, that is to say, by the passage from a heavier to a lighter density.

Then comes the discovery that an irradiant body of extremely fine nervous sensations is contained within the body of flesh. It is only when the body of flesh has acquired a solid form that the nerve channels (*nāḍis*) can be revealed with all the sensations of the currents of life running through them. As it is pictured in the Vedas: '… the waters of a stream can pass through a rock.'

The third stage occurs when all the currents of nervous energy flowing through the inner body become currents of light, from which little by little a sensation of fire emanates. This state is symbolized by the purification of the element fire, so much so that the temperature of the body rises as in an attack of fever.

These three stages: the state of solidity of the body, the state of the sensation of the nervous currents, the state of the sensation of currents of light, are characteristic of meditation in depth. Up to this point, the individuality remains intact, described by the words: 'one of the many.'

The fourth stage is that in which individuality is lost. This state of sensation of fire which consumes the body is a further passage from a heavier to a more subtle density. The fire that consumes the inner body consumes at the same time all sense of form, to the degree that the sensation of non-form becomes irradiant. This state is symbolized by the purification of the element air. The habitual impulse to resort to forms disappears. There remains only the state of the Void, which is at the same time a precise and global sensation of multiformity. All is clarity and calm.

Meditation is in fact laboratory work and an attack directed against prakriti in order to escape from her slavery.

There are different spiritual densities owing to which the inner being can become fluid and discover what is beyond the form of his habitual being. He can thus come in contact with beings belonging to the densities he has discovered. But any kind of emotion interrupts this process. Emotion is always an identification that prevents any movement of surface expansion and any movement of interiorization in depth, whereas one of the most subtle aspects of knowledge is the passage from one density to another.

It is true that the yogis of certain disciplines are able to feed themselves at a distance with fluid elements and with the vital elements of the air. This is no miracle; it is simply a question of expansion and of the capacity to assimilate one or another kind of food.

In prakriti there are many degrees and levels of expansion. God, the Creator, and the soul, while being the very finest parts of prakriti, are nevertheless materialities, even if they are fluid. A human being has infinite possibilities of expansion; he can even approach the objective Will, which is of an entirely different order from that of the habitual will. The objective Will can be ascertained and felt as though a hand is striking you in the face.

Those who work on themselves generally proceed by intermittent leaps after having received one or more shocks from life that have awakened them or after having been in fearful danger.

In a moment of inner calmness, one can gradually, as if coming out of a dream, learn to catch the last impression received and observe it without losing it. The effort to try is to isolate the sensation provoked by the impression received and trace that sensation back to the center where it arose. One sees what provoked it. In this attempt, the slightest discussion with oneself, or the slightest fear, curiosity, or judgment, will instantly blot out the given contents of the problem.

This observation can be verified in the course of morning dreams. A useful attempt is to wake up gently and to follow the indications just given, knowing that the whole being does not dream. One center at a time is exteriorized in dreaming; usually it is the emotional center. Only those in whom an active consciousness is already highly developed, dream with the whole of their being, but such a dream is no longer a dream; it belongs to another state of consciousness.

To penetrate into that realm of consciousness, sensation is the only guide we have, a continuous sensation which, whether it almost disappears or stays with us in a subtle way, can no longer be felt in our body. This sensation is nevertheless connected with the inner organs of perception, whose role and use are not yet known to us.

How to keep this sensation of oneself alive during sleep? The first effort to try is to go to sleep consciously, remaining aware of a very subtle sensation of the self. This sensation will persist far beyond the ordinary stage of consciousness which falls into the heaviness of sleep. This sensation is really a vibration of life of which the process is precisely known. On waking, the reverse process takes place. To animate the sensation of the self the vibration of life will unfold itself long before the body awakens.

How to connect these two moments of sensation of the self, separated by the sleep of the body? In this realm nothing can be willed. The progressive refining of the heavy matters in us will allow us to discover, one after another, the inner organs (indriyas) of perception whose functioning is indicated here.

When we try to control to some extent the impressions coming to us from outside and the sensations they create in us, it is important not to allow more than one sensation at a time to pervade us, one that is identifiable. We may then be able to detect its color, a taste, a smell and sound, and finally a certain tangibility in it. At that moment, we shall know exactly where it comes from and how to evaluate it.

The co-existence of several sensations creates, through comparisons and judgements, an interest and an attachment and a certain confusion, which are inevitable.

To learn to discriminate as objectively as possible entails an all-round work on the whole being in which nothing is left in the dark. At that moment one knows why one lives, one discovers the meaning of Life within life and one's own place in the harmony of a great Law. Each conquest means peace or enlightenment on one's own level of consciousness until that level is surpassed. No haste. The conscientious seeker goes from deep obscurity to a lesser obscurity. He speaks by negations, but these negations are positive. If the road is long, great patience is required.

What is a true spiritual discipline? It is a recognized rhythm of the harmonized body. All is there. Nothing could be more material than to use the body for acquiring a right sensation of God. Hence the many customs and the caste taboos regulating relationships between people, in order to prepare for the harmonious union of an awakened body with consciousness and with the eternal Prakriti. Through spiritual discipline the entire body becomes the receptacle of divine sensations. A well-conducted discipline makes it possible to identify and recognize at its base a unique sensation which is a sensation of the universe. What is known as meditation is the interiorization of the 'pure sensation' outside of time. It is a taste of eternity.

Discipline, that is to say, voluntary sacrifice, is the unique means to reverse the vital current which is habitually directed outward by the mind. From this come all the images which picture the disciple going against the current of vital fluid to go back up to the source, just as, on the concrete plane, thousands of pilgrims go upstream against the current of the Ganges to its source.

As a matter of fact a Master said:

> *I am contradicting myself when I speak to you of discipline, for I always insist that every one of you should emphasize and thus intensify his own motive for searching. The whole thing is to have a very definite motive of research as the pivot around which your attempt will be organized. People often come to me and say, 'I would like to meditate, for example, on a flame, a triangle, a luminous spot. What do you advise?' In this case I answer, 'Well then, meditate on your body. Try to find a right sensation of yourself!'*

A right sensation of oneself is in the very nature of incarnation, of penetration. At that moment, the spirit becomes matter and takes on a definite density in the body. Personal austerity (tapasyā) is the process by which a sensation comes alive, so that the whole body glows. This is a true sensation, that of the spirit becoming flesh.

This state in which no thought enters is experienced as an intense bodily joy (ānanda), for in the state of awakened consciousness it is a matter of a very precise global sensation, a wholeness. There we are touching the hidden secret of Buddhism.

The experience of a pure sensation in the physical body is in the realm of the nerve channels (nāḍis), which allow the vibrations perceived to penetrate into the physical body. They are extremely fine substances.

This leads us to the realm of music, to the study of auditory sensation, which is at the origin of the musical scale. The intervals with their variations of vibrations determine the notes; it is not the notes that determine the intervals. The same succession of irregular intervals occurs in everything manifested. Brahma himself creates in accordance with a rhythm that has its own vibration. An incalculable and chaotic movement underlies all cosmic order.

Between notes there are intervals of varying lengths, the particularities of which are known. Make the following experiment: concentrate on any one musical note and feel in yourself the modulation of the note and the length of its vibrations. The low notes resound at the base of the spinal column, the middle ones in the region of the heart and the high notes in the head.

Although the music and notation of the *Samaveda* have been lost, the notion has survived that the human organism as a whole represents different levels of consciousness obeying the same rules of modulation and frequency of sound. Each note is in itself a pure Sound (*nāda*) and pure Joy (ānanda) with different vibrations. Along the spinal column there are eight circuits of nerve experiences. The vibrations vary according to the movement of the sun. For that reason there are special songs for the short moment immediately preceding the dawn (*bhairava*) and for the moment of dawn itself (*bhairavi*). Chaitanya[2] used to pass from one ecstasy to another when he heard the name of God being sung. One of his companions who was always with him composed some well-known melodies based on his lamentations and pleadings with the Divine.

An orthodox swami, going through a village, paused in front of a poor mud house. Somebody was laughing, somebody was singing. The swami, being curious, went nearer and at the door held out his bowl. He saw a woman feeding her children. There were five of them: four beautiful children and a fifth. The fifth was the Child-Krishna, a statuette made of wood and plaster such as are sold in the markets.

The mother was making little balls of rice and putting them into one mouth after another. The Child-Krishna was receiving his share and this was why they were all laughing.

'What are you doing?' cried the swami. 'How do you dare to play with the Lord Krishna and give him that unclean food which goes from mouth to mouth? What sacrilege!' Frightened, the woman prostrated herself at the monk's feet. 'My lord swami,' she said, 'I did not mean to do wrong. My children are so happy to play with Śrí Krishna. He is their companion. If I have offended the Supreme, how can I be pardoned? Please help me!'

'Give me that statuette,' said the monk severely, 'I will take it to the village temple, where the Lord Krishna will be bathed and worshipped rightly and treated with respect instead of being used as a plaything. You will visit him when bringing your offerings to the priests!'

The children were upset. They were losing their friend. The mother wept for shame. She wrapped up the statuette and gave it to the swami. He carried it to the temple and told the priests what he had seen. They were outraged. But the same night the swami could not go to sleep. Suddenly the Lord Krishna appeared to him in all his glory. 'What have you done?' he said to the monk. 'I was so happy at that woman's house! I loved the devotion of her heart and her laughter, and now you have shut me up in a dark temple. Listen, I will not eat anything more nor accept any offerings whatever until you take me back to her. Her rice was cooked just right and that is the rice I want, no other!'

Sacred images (*mūrti*) of gods and goddesses have two aspects. The first is the philosophical aspect of a principle, the projection of an idea (*tattva* mūrti). By his devotion, the devotee is supposed to go beyond the image and the symbol it expresses. Then he discovers the second aspect, which is the sensation arising from the principle that gives life to the image (bhāva mūrti). This sensation is the passage of the idea in becoming life.

A Hindu will say, 'What does it mean to me, the idea of an Absolute, of the inconceivable Brahman?[3] I do not want to worship a reflection of light. What I want is to contemplate the Divine and worship him in my own way. It is not the impersonal Lord Krishna in his sublime glory who fills my heart, but rather Krishna the Child, who steals butter, plays the flute and plays all sorts of tricks.'

In this way the majestic attributes of the tattva mūrti are transformed into naïve simplicity to feed a true sentiment of the heart. The culmination of every spiritual discipline is this precise sensation in oneself of divine love. One must know how to make use of the force and grandeur of philosophy, but in the heart, know how to feed oneself on radiant beauty alone.

Endnotes

1. *Valmiki, who in this state of solidity of the body is said to have been covered with white ants.*
2. *A celebrated reformer and monk in Bengal (1485-1531). He himself was neither a poet nor a musician, but he inspired his disciples in such a way that over three centuries thousands of devotional songs were composed in Bengal.*
3. *The Absolute, the impersonal God.*

Chapter 19

EMOTIONS

An absolute rule in Samkhya is never to speak about one's emotions. To display sorrow is only to provoke an inner movement of prakriti instead of going voluntarily towards a possible transformation of the emotion.

Here are three practical rules which, when they work together, are the basis of a state in which emotion loses its destructive power:

1. *To utilize for oneself the fewest possible things, which creates a freedom of space.*
2. *To have no hope in the future, which gives consistency to the present and creates a freedom in time.*
3. *To die consciously every evening, which means a new birth each morning on awakening and an inner freedom.*

To render life objective, two fundamental attitudes are needed, namely:

1. *A centering of consciousness around the axis of the higher Will—which involves an attentive vigilance of the whole being, in its movements and functions.*
2. *In the face of prakriti, adopting consciously the attitude of a child. This attitude dissolves obstacles. The child is renewed by himself*

through elemental impressions, earth, water, fire, air, ether, the beauty of a face, the intonation of a voice, a profound look, etc.

Each one of us should say to himself:

'As long as "my" prakriti does not grasp these two ways of becoming alert in the midst of the great Prakriti, there will always be all sorts of reactions: inertia, breakdowns, fixations, or other forms of psychic suffering.

'All conscious work coming from the inner being is a direct attack on the power of "my" prakriti and also on the power of the great Prakriti. An ineluctable progression connects them. The greater the inner effort, the stronger my prakriti's defense of itself becomes and the bigger are the obstacles set up by the great Prakriti. But remember that in the Bhagavad Gita, Krishna says on the battlefield: "If I reveal to you such a secret about Prakriti do not repeat it. If you speak, you will be stoned."'

Emotions constantly make us mistake the path for the goal and vice versa. And they are not the same! If you want to climb to the top of a mountain, do not lose yourself in sentimental ramblings about its beauty. It is better to look for a clearly marked path that will take you to the top from the spot where you are standing.

If one does not give any value, positive or negative, to emotions, one is in the presence of a motor that makes use of prakriti only at its habitual speed. Water in a test tube is a form of heavy matter. As steam, the same matter, while taking up more space, is also more aerated. In the same way, a human being can suffer from emotions as heavy as stones in his heart, or else from emotions that have become more subtle, and while still existing allow light to show through.

Try to understand that a well-sustained objective attention, as well as a thorough self-observation, can destroy the process of reflection about oneself, that is to say, the emotion itself. What remains beyond emotion must be observed with the greatest care, for the purity towards which one is tending is a state difficult to describe. It is the state of pure Existence (sat).

It is unthinkable that a teacher should be impatient, for he knows that there will never be any change in prakriti, whether it happens to be rigid or pliable, even if one is vigilant or even if by sustained attention one could touch and taste a state that is the Absolute. Alas, this 'any one', according to the Bhagavad Gita, means *one* in a million!

Psychoanalysis works on the intensive aspects of emotions. They are brought out into the daylight with the object of cleaning out the subconscious, and are thus lived over again, which means that each of them is amplified. Instead of belonging only to the damaged part of the being, they invade the whole field of prakriti as weeds spread through a wheat field.

The very structure of emotion should be denied as such, for it arises only from one's subjective view of external elements. Gurdjieff, closely following the traditional technique of Buddhist analysis, denies the existence of a negative pull in the center where emotion arises, whereas he does recognize a negative pull within its movement. For this reason he tells his pupils to control negative emotions. In this way he methodically builds up one of the essential bases of inner balance which exists already in what is partly disengaged from the heavy sleep of prakriti. But this sleep, with its weight of ignorance, is an admirably organized automatism of Great Nature.

The traditional techniques pay no attention to emotion. Even the worshippers of Krishna, who make full use of emotion in their fundamental attitude of adoration, use only those sublimated elements of emotion that sustain the ideal.

Several levels have to be passed through before one can know how to minimize emotion at its very source, to recognize it, to isolate and to master it, so as finally to be able to get rid of it. The lower stage is to realize once and for all that an emotion is a debt to be paid – which is the beginning of a process that uproots it. This is the process of eradication. The second stage is to conceive of emotion as something to be abandoned or as a recognized recurrence. It is part of the automatism which becomes apparent but has no real existence. The third stage is that in which the light form of an ideal is voluntarily and methodically put in the place of the heavy form of an emotion which is oppressive.

There are many classical examples of circles around a Master in which the disciples know only the heavy form of an emotion and therefore interpret on their own level what is lived by the Master in front of them. For instance, Sŕi Ramakrishna said one day, 'Where is God? He is there!' and he pointed to his breast. Sŕi Ramakrishna was speaking from the deepest state of interiorization, but his disciples, who in their personal discipline were still at the stage of the heavy form of emotions, therefore deified the man who was speaking to them. Nevertheless, they faithfully observed the intellectual part of the process.

These three stages in regard to emotion are admirably illustrated by the story of the 'madwoman of Calcutta.' About twenty years ago in a residential section of the city, people used to see a very young and beautiful woman stopping passers-by on the sidewalk in front of her house and asking them, 'Where is Shyama Babu? Have you see him? If you tell me where he is, I will go and fetch him.' Her beloved was dead and she was still waiting for him, living from her love of him. And love had betrayed her. The passers-by played cruel tricks on her.

Then another phase began for her. She clung to young men as they were going by and said to them, 'You are my Shyama Babu, you have come back. ... Since she was not a prostitute, these men drove her away and ill-treated her, even threw stones at her.

After several years, one of her neighbors who had known her in the past noticed her sitting all day long at the foot of the sacred tree of that district. She had aged but her face was radiant with joy. She recognized her neighbor. He asked her, 'Have you found your Shyama?' 'Yes,' she replied with a lovely smile. 'Look, there he is ... and she pointed to her breast.

Renunciation (vairāgya), in a very precise sense, is the voluntary giving up of all emotions whatsoever. This notion, supported by long tradition, goes hand in hand with life. This is what Gurdjieff tries to indicate and to reconcile with Christian tradition, where there is nothing to support this attempt.

To be capable of mastering an emotion, one has first to evaluate and consider it for what it really is, the distortion of an uncontrolled and misplaced sensation.

When the intestines are out of order, one must follow a strict diet. The cure comes about by abstaining for the time being at least from certain foods. Thus the body regains vigor. Psychically, power is restored. This method is the opposite of psychoanalysis, which digs about in the ego. Samkhya places you under a cosmic force and is interested in the ego only to say: 'Why are you afraid of this or that? All these things are only movements of prakriti, aspects of the recurrences which concern men, animals, and the whole of Great Nature.' One must learn to live in the very moment that shapes and molds our prakriti, without trying to escape from it. To look at prakriti as a whole and see its agitated movement makes it possible not to identify with it. I observe what goes on. By doing this, I feel the movement in myself, but I do not linger on the fact that I was created in the same way. In this discipline the element time plays an important role, as well as patience. On the part of the Guru this patience is pure love.

Emotion does not enter into any spiritual discipline because in itself it has no steadiness. It is only a movement of Prakriti. When the mind is perfectly calm it is like the still water of a mountain lake. The slightest ripple on the surface is an emotion.

What happens to it? If Purusha allows this ripple, however slight, to intensify and become a wave, he himself will be swallowed. Blind emotion is then the master of the situation, although in fact it has no *raison d'être.*

If this emotion, while it is still only a ripple, is voluntarily interiorized, then little by little, because of its lack of consistency, it will disintegrate of itself and go back to whence it came, being nothing but a shining ray of beatitude (ānanda).

Chapter 20

KNOWLEDGE

Knowledge, even partial, is in constant contradiction with the practical facts of daily life. Even those who are at least partly aware of this are unable to move in a straight line, because they go from shock to shock in the midst of contradictions which unceasingly create reactions.

For behind every contradiction there is this irresistible something that impels us forward and that can only be approached by an extension of oneself, as a river in flood spreads its water over the land without losing sight of its bed.

To progress on the path of knowledge, you have wholly to live your truth of the moment. This truth will purify itself in your integrity. What matters most is to have a global sensation of yourself. In this way you can see what is taking place in you and know whether you are living according to your own truth. But it would be a mistake to speak about it. All you can do is to irradiate this experience.

There comes a time when a transposition must take place because a new Law is in question here. Don't interfere; otherwise all the explanations you give yourself will distort your vision. No one can bear the rigorous and absolute detachment of Purusha; that is why Prakriti has so many intermediate truths to offer. Once you have created unity in yourself, there will only be one Truth, even if it seems very far off.

Only a very few will enter the esoteric circle of knowledge, which is like an 'armor of steel,' for the divine power is intensely active there. At that time it is no longer a question of activity or non-activity, because he who lives in sensation sees God in everything: forms appear only to express an idea.

A time will come when two or three hundred families, each with two or three children, will live wholly in accordance with the science of inner life. The great mass of humanity will disappear or serve solely as a ground for those who know. What will take place will again be the phenomenon of castes. It was merely from ignorance that castes were imagined to be originally institutions of a social order. They had an esoteric meaning. In the beginning they divided people according to different modes of perception. The notion of caste has become atrophied and degraded in the course of inevitable deviations in the descending Law. This degradation is responsible for the loss of the rules that used to regulate the passage from one state of consciousness to another. The key word has been lost.

'To have eaten the mango' is an expression meaning to have tasted the fruit of knowledge. After having tasted knowledge, there is a state in which one says, 'I do not know,' for knowing no longer matters.

A strange fact is that someone who still likes discussions keeps on talking and teaching. And so much the better. On his level he is doing useful work. Vigilant observation of oneself means not sinking unconsciously into the depths that open up, but penetrating them gradually, for the inner being has become very sensitive.

It is said that the seed of knowledge has to be passed on secretly to him who is ready to receive it. After that it slowly ripens.

What becomes of those who have received this seed of Life? Some of them disappear with their treasure, and are heard of no more. But if a flame of living knowledge flares up in some particular place, the continuity of tradition will be recognized. There are well known signs. This fact is beyond man's vision. There is no logical explanation.

Some disciples create works bearing the name of the Master from whom they have received everything, with the aim of perpetuating his teaching: ashrams, esoteric schools, hospitals, universities and so on, which will constitute a way of progress for many people.

Other disciples, after a certain time, fritter away their treasure and even trample on it, for prakriti has once more got them in its grasp. They will seek and find a new Master, but the process of dissolution goes on without their being aware of it, because it is a part of their own nature.

In every discipline there are those who know and see the Divine beyond the Guru. They are exceptional, outside the ordinary ranks of man. They are the solitary ones who re-live, through fragments, the experiences of the sages (ṛṣis). The priests despise them and chase them, but should they become famous through their asceticism, their inner search and their wisdom, those same priests will build temples for them and celebrate sacrifices (*pūjās*) before them.[1]

'He who knows' supports the world by his realization. His only treasure is to see 'That.' This word represents either an abstract idea or 'He who reigns in the heart of man.'

Those who recognize the existence of cosmic Laws through which the primordial Energy expresses itself acknowledge a trinity which is: Father-Mother-Child.[2] There is a Tantric verse (*śloka*) which says:

... true emotion,
like a pure virgin,
dances with quick, light steps
in the heart of the yogi ...

All yogis say, 'This pure virgin of which one speaks here is real emotion; it should be offered to the Supreme Lord, there where he dwells above everything.' Then the heart melts. A moment of ecstasy, of abandonment; then comes the moment of a return to life. Such is the power of śhakti. From such a union a child is conceived, a child of ethereal substance. This child is like a living sleep, conscious twenty-four hours a day in the womb of pure emotion. He has been wished for.

If, in the phenomenal world, such a child is born, he (like all other children) is symbolically black (tamas-inertia) at birth. He will inevitably have to evolve and pass through the first cycle of colors that form the transition from black to red (rajas-energy). Complementary color cycles will develop from the red and pass symbolically to white (sattva-spirit). Amongst the complementary colors much importance is given to yellow because it has no trace of either black or red. In fact, yellow represents the energy of śhakti. Śhakti herself moves in the higher knowledge of Shiva who appears fully white. The whiteness of Shiva radiates. Projected against the dark blue of the transcendence of Krishna-Purusha, it appears still more luminous.

Samkhya says that at the time of birth, on whatever plane it occurs, there is always a mixture of colors requiring purification until the white becomes pure and sparkling. He who has passed through purification becomes a Master. A Master is one who plays indifferently with all the colors of the rainbow. Black remains black, red remains red, and yellow remains yellow, each color serving some definite aim of the Master.

In the Vedas the three colors black (night), red (dawn), yellow (noonday sun) appear daily in the same order and disappear in the inverse order. The recurrence is rigorous. Psychologically, these three colors are the fundamental modes of expression existing in each of us. Black symbolizes the unconscious heaviness or sleep of the inner being, which likes to persist in the midst of the prejudices that come with it. Red symbolizes impetuousness, agitation, temporary subjective awakening and sudden changes of direction. A period of agitation is always difficult but inescapable, for it is the time when prakriti moves by leaps and resists. This agitation will gradually cease by itself if, instead of feeding it and struggling against it, you utilize the force of knowledge. Yellow symbolizes a more subtle period. White is the vision of the whole in which 'doing' finds its place.[3]

A Master is able at will to use the unconscious heaviness of those around him because the inertia of nature is the ground on which Shiva performs his cosmic dance. A Master knows everything without reacting to anything, which in an ordinary man would be an attitude of stupidity. If a Master uses the agitation which is around him to create and destroy what must be destroyed, it becomes an energy guided by his wisdom, since he draws it from a Law known to him alone. This knowledge of a higher Law is white and faintly tinted. If a Master is conscious of this in his realization, he will make few mistakes. With this whiteness he has full control over the whole spectrum of colors. That is why Yama, the Lord of Death, is always represented esoterically in white, which is higher Knowledge. The buffalo on which he rides is pictured as black, which is the material force, and his śhakti in red, which is the operative force.

Gurdjieff had this lightly tinted whiteness. He never stopped playing with all the colors of life; that is why fools cry out against him. Ouspensky, who was a philosopher, tried to stay in the whiteness he had discovered; but if you are the disciple responsible for the kitchen, your duty is to prepare the food. If you refuse to do this, you will be sent away by the Master or you will leave of your own accord and your refusal will be a weight that will burden you for years and possibly even crush you. Who can understand what a Master is teaching in five directions at once? And how could it be otherwise? In the tradition, Shiva has five faces with which to look at life.

Chaitanya said, 'A man known for his wisdom in the world will find it difficult, even with all his intelligence, to understand the way of life and the actions of a man who has attained realization of the meaning of the cosmic Laws.' That is also why the *Katha Upanishad* and the Bhagavad Gita speak of the Master who says to his beloved disciple: '… No one can understand me, not even you. Be satisfied with praising me …' Indeed, only the heart can recognize the Master. In this connection, I shall tell you some characteristic stories illustrating the extreme freedom of those free beings who play with the Laws. I shall not give any names because in popular language they are always called 'Khepa' or 'Mast.'[4] Who they are, no one knows, for those who live near them have completely forgotten where they came from.

Once upon a time Khepa Baba was in Benares in the middle of a crowd of people who kept looking at him without daring to approach, for if anyone bothered him, he would brandish his stick and hurl insults. One daring woman came towards him moaning, 'Oh Maharaj, have pity on me.' 'Daughter of a whore!' Khepa Baba shouted at her. 'Come here and I will rape you in the street in front of everyone!' She fled!

Khepa Baba had a jug full of wine in front of him. He calmly drank it down to the last drop without saying a word. The people were stupefied at this impious act,[5] not understanding what was going on, but his disciples noticed that he had become white like Shiva; his body radiated light. Khepa Baba was in ecstasy.

With his immense power and his heart of pure gold, Khepa Baba spread almost insurmountable obstacles around him and created dangerous reefs, thus provoking deep disturbances in all those living near him. Who was he? What was he doing? He scrubbed off people's prejudices, he punctured the abscess of their ego, he burned the pillows of their laziness. Khepa Baba did all this in his uncouth way, for he himself was beyond good and evil. He provoked people into constantly facing themselves.

One day he ordered one of his favorite disciples to accompany him to Brindavan, which is one of the most sacred places of India, its atmosphere filled with the sweetness and charm of the Child-Krishna. Khepa Baba sat down among the beggars on the side of the dusty road, a piece of cloth spread out in front of him. Passers-by threw alms into it, small coins or a handful of rice. According to what he received, Khepa Baba murmured a word or two of blessing or emitted an obscene swearword. Back at his hut, he tied up the coins he had received in a rag and hung it on the wall. He lay down, but like a miser, kept watch over his meager treasure all night long, stick in hand. His disciples, silent and reproachful, were observing him. At last Khepa Baba swore at them, 'Are you criticizing me? Well then! Away with all of you! What keeps you here?'

'I couldn't leave,' related his favorite disciple. 'I remained standing there until daybreak, not understanding what was going on before me or in me; and when the Master got up, I followed him. I sat down behind him when he begged on the side of the road. Then the Master turned round and said to me in a serious voice, 'Take a good look; this is one aspect of the world, and I shall show you still others!'

'On another occasion,' continued the disciple, 'Khepa Baba sent me to the village market to steal a goat. He had seen it while passing and wanted that one and no other. It was an easy thing to do. But I was resisting. He insisted. I still refused. Then he shrugged his shoulders and went to sleep. I felt as though I were drunk, full of anguish. I started to vomit. Finally, covered with shame, I went out, weeping and gritting my teeth, and stole the goat. It was not until much later that I found out that all the goats of this supposed merchant belonged to Khepa Baba.' One day Khepa Baba brutally chased away this beloved disciple. 'Go away!' he shouted at him. 'You are able to fly now with your own wings!'

Among the disciples of Khepa Baba there was at Brindavan an illiterate villager, docile by nature and full of faith. With other pilgrims, he subjected himself once a year to a severe discipline which consisted of going around the whole town barefoot, making prostrations from time to time. At night the pilgrims rested but resumed their painful journey every morning at daybreak. The sun was blinding, the ground burned the soles of the feet, thirst and hunger were a constant torture. Well, one night Khepa Baba happened to be at one of the stopping places where the pilgrims were sleeping. He called that villager and asked him to prepare for him and others with him some *chāpātis*,[6] insisting that they be very thin. The villager went to light a brazier and began to knead the flour with water and salt. He made a pile of chāpātis and brought them to his Guru. 'What a fool you are!' said the Guru, and raising his stick, struck him full in the face. The villager did not stir; his eyes saw only the eyes of the Master. Then Khepa Baba caught him by the shoulder and pressed him to his bosom. He made him sit down by his side and then to eat first. This disciple became a great saint, who died before Khepa Baba.

Khepa Baba wore his matted hair rolled into a bun on the top of his head. One of his disciples, imagining that he had hidden jewels in there, decided to poison him so as to get hold of them. One night he went stealthily to the corner of the house where the meal was being prepared and put arsenic in the Guru's food. But he was caught in the act. Yelling, the other men seized him to beat him and throw him out.

'Don't chase that man out!' cried Khepa Baba.

'Then you must do it yourself,' shouted the disciples angrily.

'What has he done?'

'He tried to poison you with arsenic!'

'Ah!' exclaimed Kepha Baba, 'and you poison me daily with your quarrels.... Get away, all of you! Out of here!' The tumult subsided. The man remained.

It is difficult, indeed, to understand the actions of a man who has come to the realization in himself of the cosmic Laws; his life is lived under everyone's eyes day and night, and is absolutely untainted with egoism. Khepa Baba, with all the knots of his heart untied, let things happen naturally. What did it matter that someone wanted to kill him and others to avenge him? The Laws have always worked in the same way, in a prakriti that is always the same.

In the ashram in Assam the contrasts were equally violent. What is a Guru for, if not to tear us apart from ourselves? The co-disciples were often hungry while the Master had all he could possibly want. Those who could not bear it left. To others it all seemed natural; we were intoxicated by the Master's presence. We lived on his knowledge.

Endnotes

1. *Sri Ramana Maharshi is a striking example of this.*
2. *See page 96.*
3. *'Doing' is used in the sense of genuine action freely undertaken and fully conscious. This is very far from what is customarily called 'doing'.*
4. *The title of Khepa or Mast given to Sufis, like that of Bâül given to Hindus, means 'Fools of God.'*
5. *In India it is traditional for those who give themselves up to a spiritual search not to drink alcohol.*
6. *A kind of unleavened bread.*

Chapter 21

LIFE—DEATH

Let me carry Death in Life,
So that I may find Life in Death.[1]

These two lines from Tagore give a key to the understanding what we could call a spiritual existentialism.[2]

Life has to be lived against the background of death.

The idea of death permeating life can make us free, free from all bondage and limitations, whereas life by its own nature possesses and binds.

If in our lives we could keep in ourselves the quietness of death, we would have access to creative intelligence. On the moral plane this would be the level of objectivity.

To die consciously is simply the passage from one density to another in the full consciousness of the inner being.

I am not speaking of death in its physical aspect, the inevitable last scene of the human drama, but of death in Shiva, that is, of the transcendence that sustains the creative rhythm of life. All of us can 'construct' all sorts of things in ordinary life, but to create we must be liberated by conscious death in Shiva. Creative vision, in fact, belongs only to him who, without being stopped by the dance of life, dares to look within himself as far as the Void. Then what does he see? The beginning and the end, that is to say, the seed from which life springs and the flowers under which life's adventure ends. He sees the rainbow of the Void linking them both.

How desirable it would be to feel in oneself the great force that lies dormant behind the term *māyāvāda*.[3] Māyā in itself is neither illusion nor relativity. Alas! People do not wish to understand that these two words express the passivity, the sleep and the recurrences belonging to prakriti, whereas māyā by itself can mean free will and the freedom to create. Māyā is a life-idea in its multiple forms, just as the word 'flower' gives rise to endless forms in the mind.

To which form should one be attached? To each one and yet to all at the same time! Imagine that you are not attached to one form of another, that you are impartial, then every form will delight you, for in each one you will see the life-idea incarnated. And māyā is the exuberance of creation.

Thus India exists in various forms, some beautiful, some ugly, yet the dualistic distinctions become unreal as soon as a movement upward toward the light is recognized. Our life-impulse is evidence of the reality of this.

How true is the saying of the Buddha that the ultimate reality is the Void itself and that existence issues from non-existence. All we can try to do is to bring the idea of death to the very heart of life, for to know that everything will finally disappear into the Void is a great relief. We work with a smile and a feeling of freedom only if we know that nothing will last forever. In this knowledge we can be like children building castles of sand on the shore of time.

The self might be eternal but the body is not. It must wither away. When the body can no longer work, it goes to sleep or dies. The only consolation is that even then one can remain fully awake in the inner being. And then, only then, like the dying sun, one feels an expansion into oneness with reality behind. One has then no wish to take part in the devil's dance of the world. One should resign fully to this play between spirit and matter and not turn back. This is the carrying of death to glory in life.

All Raja-yoga is a study of death: how to accept consciously the living inertia and dare to face it. He who dies valiantly in war or in self-sacrifice touches a plane of consciousness which, at its best corresponds to the spiritual being. He who sees death approach with bitterness does not know really what sweetness is. He who sees death approach with sweetness knows as well the meaning of bitterness. This is a much higher plane of consciousness.

To follow this discipline throughout life is to harmonize the levels of the inner being in the face of existence, without identification, without thought, with the help of breathing exercises (*prāṇāyāma*)[4] when they have become familiar and natural. Then the Void is the return to the beginning, the matrix of Life.

At the moment of death, all that is matter returns to matter, all that is energy returns to primordial energy. Only those very rare beings who have worked consciously to bring their different 'I's together around the central axis and who have freed themselves from the grip of prakriti escape this dispersion. For them, real Existence (sat) continues.

He who is conscious of this process progresses slowly and without any will whatsoever, for unification around the axis is not the result of efforts but is made possible by a new 'substance' which arises when the right time comes. This substance is known exactly, and is described in different ways in the Upanishads.

At the moment of physical death or of passage to a lighter density, Purusha is perceptible in the vibration of śhakti. It is a moment of transubstantiation, a function of the spirit informed by sensation.

When you are face to face with death, do no struggle. Let yourself glide. The wave that will carry you away is cosmic. It is not comparable to any life force. It is written that 'death is the last of the sacrifices.' To reach this point, the sacrifice of life must have been made long before. Then, in the last sacrifice, there is not even a waiting for death. It is simply the 'life-death state', even beyond the experience being lived. Just as you progress through life, so you will progress through death. Do not struggle. It is with this attitude of openness that one can hear 'the call of the secret companion,' the voice of death. What follows no longer has any meaning; one enters a new field of forces. Does one know what is going to happen when arriving on earth? Why would it not be the same thing after death? There may be as many solutions in death as there are in life. One follows, it is certain, a road opened by an exact Law.

The monk's renunciation, sannyāsa, truly signifies death. It is one of the great traditional ways of India.

A theory of death and sannyāsa existed among the Vedic sages long before the advent of Buddhism. Buddhism, with its great monastic tradition, is a kind of organized sannyāsa. The Buddhist monks were nourished through the Samkhya philosophy, with its idealization of Shiva.

In short, Shiva and Buddha became the same ideal, expressed by the sound 'A-Ham,' which expresses the whole being and the whole ego, since this sound is composed of two letters—the first and the last of the Sanskrit alphabet.[5]

It is written in the Puranas that the first letter of the alphabet stands for life, and that the last stands for death. Therefore the two states, life-death, are united by the great mantra 'Hari-Hara,' which means 'to live a full life.' But no one understands it.

How many sincere monks are there on that difficult path of destruction (pralaya)? Very few. Most of them wear the ochre robe of renunciation as an emblem of what they are attempting to reach, but are not any the less attached to what they still possess. Sometime it is merely the idea itself which is represented by their robe. The real sannyāsin is the one described in the Bhagavad Gita, who goes about with no outer sign by which he can be recognized and who often wears different masks in the world.

The question 'What exists after death?' was formulated very early by the ṛṣis of the Upanishads.

Ramprasad[6] much nearer to our time, gave an answer to this question in one of his songs, which even today is on everybody's lips:

> *... Do you know, my brother,*
> *what man becomes after death?*
> *There remains but a water bubble ...*
> *Spurting from the wave, it sinks again into the foam*
> *forming but one with the immense ocean. ...*

The question 'What becomes of the soul after death?' was also asked long ago in the *Katha Upanishad*[7] and the answer given was exactly the same as that of Ramprasad.

If we accept this idea of the water bubble leaving the matrix of Great Nature and returning to its bosom, then there is neither paradise nor hell after death.

Indeed if this answer is *felt* to the point where the entire being is filled, all values, in this light, becomes true.

Death is luminous—its luminosity is similar to the luminous darkness recognized by science in the Cosmos, revealing all existing colors.

Time merges into space as life merges into the Void. If you always bear this in mind you are not afraid of the moment of dying. The luminous Void gives you such security!

One might go off at any moment. But one has a duty toward oneself and toward the Void, a very definite equation must be solved. If one says, 'I am in the Void,' it must be not only with the mind and prayers but with the whole being: the pure being and the impure being, both together.

Death and life cannot be separated. They are the bi-une aspect of Creation. The Bhagavad Gita states it: 'What has had a birth must one day die. What is dying will be reborn.'

Death is real communion with God; why are people so afraid of death? It is because they cannot drop their small ego. They hold on to it; then, seized by fright, they are unable to go further.

It is only when we can consciously bring death within life and life within death that we can laugh about anything or rather smile softly. What has really a meaning? What can we really do? Only be ourselves and create harmony in people and between them without interfering.

We have each of us to meet our karma and surrender fully to it. There is sometimes a strong pull upward with a feeling of lightness and joy, then comes a pull downward with pains and anguish, a drowsiness of the mind, a fatigue of the body, which almost faints and loses its hold. From this impure plane, we might suddenly be drawn upward because our eyes have seen the way. Then immediately we stand above our anguish. It has nothing to do with personality. It is simply as though the equilibrium had been broken.

When our personal karma has been fully accepted, then it is transformed into śhakti, into power, a power in which one feels responsible for the structure of one's being. But remember that the human śhakti is never equal to the śhakti of God; even if we can share His wisdom and His joy, we can never share His power! Man, however, is constantly trying to seize God's power. At present, many scientists and philosophers busy themselves with subjective and objective worlds, trying to transcend both of them. Their eyes are turned outward. They do not look inward, where the answer is kept secret.

The deep Samkhya position is that of Purusha enjoying His own acting. He knows and enjoys it in purity. When the human karma becomes śhakti, how does it merge into the power of God? There is a great calmness of the self, apart from seeing: it is a self-enjoyment in which one simply looks on.

In front of death one is automatically drawn inward, and one lives intensely the life of the great Silence radiating in every direction and penetrating everything, which is simply its own self. This is living in complete aloneness in the great Alone. This is the 'golden Germ of existence' which eternally is, as the Vedic seers said. This Aloneness is a mystery. It can be either ignorance or wisdom. Those who fear death are in ignorance. Those who face death with a steady gaze, even knowing that they cannot conquer it are at one with death and that is wisdom.

Remember the story of the great Sufi who, under Aurangzeb, affirmed his faith as he was about to be beheaded. He was put to death because he had declared; 'There is no God!' His followers knew that he had meant:

> *One day, I shall be put to death for having said 'There is no God.' For as long as I am in this body, how can I know God? Communion with God is only beyond life.*

Well, we are told that the Prince who had condemned him to death, said when he himself was dying; 'I know no peace. Do not take me as a model of Moslem life. I have never been able to surrender. I have been arrogant. I know nothing.'

You must train yourselves, day after day, to meet death at any moment, in any circumstance. It seems a very cold path. But renunciation has a strong and positive footing, which is love; while detachment is really the fear of being caught by love. Of course, one can say: 'I am not attached to you. I renounce you, and this is only because I love you. I don't allow you to be attached to me.' One would then miss the real 'I' and the real me. Real love means living a spiritual existence in spirit without name or form—it is pure love in the void.

If you reach that stage, then you come back again from the void, to body and to forms. It is from this Void that wine and bread, though they are matter, have become divine in the mystery of transubstantiation. Similarly Christ on the Cross, for one second, was fully human, carrying the agony of the whole world when he cried: '*Eloï, Eloï sabachthani*—My God, my God, why hast Thou forsaken me?'[8] In this complete surrender and in the long cry that followed in which he gave up the spirit, he was fully the Son of God, the Messenger.

Such Aloneness is communion with God.

Through a long illness, any one of us could also ask the question: 'Why? Is there no God for me?' The answer comes: 'Be patient.' In his last days, Sŕi Ramakrishna, dying at fifty-four from cancer of the throat, also put the same question and he gave himself the answer: 'Now I can see everything as total sat-cit-ānanda. Even this cancer in my throat is *That*.' Ignorance, falsehood, pains have their weight in sat-cit-ānanda, a totality, a completedness as expressed by Samkhya. *Sam* is the totality, that which is complete. *Khya* is what one sees, what one speaks, what one knows. If one loves God, one shall die to this body only. In love everything exists: what is great and what is small merge finally into Unity.

In the Vedic tradition, the attainment of immortality is connected with libations performed three times a day: when the sun rises, when it reaches the zenith, when it sets, depicting the babe at birth, maturity, and old age.

All three belong to the lower prakriti.

But in old age, facing death means knowing that 'I am immortal,' knowing that death has two masks: the dark one and the luminous one. In the *Katha Upanishad*, Nachiketas speaks to the 'luminous Lord of Death.' Death can never be conquered but entering into it consciously means keeping the vision of the Void and the flow of life within. It is from aloneness that death, as the luminous bridegroom, appears with the one sound 'OM' which is felt in the heart—a note in which the entire music of prakriti, symphonies and all noises of nature, towns, streets, minds, opinions and phonetics merge into one vibration, the divine 'OM.'

In an ignorant way, the body is killed by death and burnt. It becomes ashes, manure for the earth. But how many bodies do we have? Besides the physical body which is destroyed this way, there are two other bodies which can be felt and seen only by the inner being because they both have a subtle form. They are the 'pranic-body' made of life-forces and the 'mind-body,' which is sometimes turned outward with an objective view over the world and at other times turned inward with a subjective view over the inner being. When this inner vibration becomes intense, the world is completely forgotten. Then starts a continuous meditation, giving rise to intuition which, in itself, is a spiritual attainment. Intuition expands in a soft light, a light like the dawn in which 'one begins to feel that one is united with that light.' It is a state of liberation.

There are two sorts of man. One is the coward type who is easily crushed by shocks and blows. When he falls, he dies. The second is the hero type who emerges from any shock or blow, sustained by his pranic-body and his mind-body, which react. These bodies cannot be crushed even if the physical body dies.

How does the mind-body see death approaching? There is a point of time in which two parallel views of two different bodies merge. They can be compared to the homogeneous light of dawn. The light of dawn is equal everywhere. That flow of soft light is space, like a wide consciousness spreading everywhere.

Then the sun rises in its glory with innumerable rays of light all around it. With this movement of the sun, time appears in space. Sharp lines of light diverge in all directions from the center of the sun, every one of them touching a point in space, creating innumerable lines of consciousness—of people—nobody knowing anybody though attracted by the center! There is no unity, no fusion, but really a fission of light; except for the communion of a few beings, beginning to feel in themselves: 'I am everyone, I am the light.'

Moving toward that communion, two lines of light might be coming nearer and nearer to each other, both attracted by the one point—the self—in the center, which is the Great I. Love of the Great I is pure love in the Void.

But we belong to time, where alone there is death. We are expanding toward space, the homogeneous globular Void which, in its center, contains life, death and beyond that Nothing.

Endnotes

1. *From* Naivedya (Offerings to the Deity) *included in* Gitavitana.
2. *See pp. 149-51.*
3. *A theory according to which multiplicity or manifestation is unreal.*
4. Prāṇāyāma *are breathing exercises that can lead to a knowledge of the inner being.*
5. Aitareya Aranyaka *II, 3.8.*
6. *18th Century.*
7. Aitareya Aranyaka, *II, 1.15.*
8. *Matthew 27:46 and Mark 15:34.*

Part Three

FACING REALITY

Sŕi Anirvân

One cannot do,
but one can look on,
and see the One being,
and be with It.

Facing Reality

For most people, ordinary life is lived, under some blind impulsion, as in a deep sleep or in a narcotic state. Although not lacking an end of sorts, this kind of life has neither heights nor depths. Only a few wake up. Pained by the inadequacy they feel and see around themselves, yearning for a life which transcends the usual physical needs, vital urges and mental associations, they finally become absorbed in a new query. Hence begins man's journey toward the fullness of life in the secrecy of the heart and in the boundless independence of the soul.

The quest is integral in character, as is dimly evidenced in the world consciousness where it is as yet incipient, a striving to make a fully conscious life operate here and now. Obstacles come from the narrow outlook that considers reality not as a whole but as split up into matter and consciousness. In other words, the Totality[1] in which all polarities melt, has been distorted into a 'whole' divided into two parts, with the result that 'the integral Truth' has ever remained baffling and elusive.

It is man's destiny to realize Unity, which means realizing the Self, for the one is the manifestation of the other in degrees as well as in multiplicities. The journey is through the multiplicities and oppositions caused by ignorance and onward to the shores of knowledge. The world is the field of experiment for man's quest for Unity.

In his effort to march to the cosmic status of Laws, man produces all oppositions by the machinery of egoism and of intellect. For instance, the opposition of joy and sorrow is relative and primal; it exists not for the unifying 'I' but only for the narrow, bounded 'I.'

What is adequate for surface knowledge fails at the threshold of integral knowledge and must therefore be replaced by intuition, or knowledge by identity, in contrast to intellectual knowledge. So a retreat is indicated, a withdrawal from the sense objects outside the mind, into an immersion wherein the mind is transformed into the sixth sense of the mystics, in which alone the profound mysteries are revealed.

The entire universe is a pulsation of energy upheld by whom? What is of practical importance is that energy can be measured and put into service, that its pulsation occurs in the mind where it is upheld and manifests itself as dynamic play.

Why should existence be pulsated at all? The question can be ignored if it relates to matter, but not if it relates to consciousness. If existence is consciousness, waves of energy must also be conscious.

They do not however appear to be so in the waking state, now ignorantly regarded as the only measure of consciousness. A satisfactory reply might come through intuition, which can penetrate the depths of the self and realize its nature. Existence is consciousness and its pulsations are conscious pulsations, which in the depths of our being are apprehended as primordial joy. To an integral view, the universe is the joy of the pure Being crystallized through self-expression. Being is sat-cit-ānanda, a pure sensation.

This is the essential nature of man, though it is distorted by a sense of limitations, so that we do not feel limitless and wide but are cribbed, confined and restless. We move only by blind impulsions of pleasure, pain and indifference. This phase can be lived through by the practice of deliberate, all-accepting indifference, until finally each of our reactions lights up in consciousness and an immeasurable cosmic peace is attained.

An obvious gap in man's conscious striving has been filled by the ego's power projections, so that reality has become a mere repetition or reflected images with a variety of mutations and gradations. The power which belonged integrally to the mind was projected out of the self, but can now be drawn back into the self.

Indeed the ordinary mind looks on and passes judgement; it sees only errors in the world-process and gives its consent because it wants to. This entire process is ordained by an incorporated stress to create 'the many,' which then appears as truth, and ignorance as the acquiring of knowledge.

Yet we know of a truly creative higher-mind[2] which exists germinally within the ordinary mind. It is a living consciousness—a pure sensation in which the subject is the object. To know is then to be. Existence and consciousness are One—a harmonious whole.

The concepts of Purusha and Prakriti can best be explained by Samkhya: Purusha the timeless, the immobile, the Seer, the ingathered totality—and Prakriti with its dynamism of will in time. The life-urge rushes on, driven by some hidden force which pushes it from below or pulls it from above; but after reaching a certain point it subsides into quiescence, which in awareness means a fusion of the plenum and the Void. In itself, this quiescence is simple, colorless and indeterminate; it is the final abstract stage of pure Consciousness.

Its value cannot be measured; it is at once the zero and infinity. The sole qualitative value that can be ascribed to it is a feeling of relaxation and expansion and a sense of serene poise in the Void. It may mean a plenum which, like the consummation of death, may burst into glory at any point of the prakriti evolution.

The world of the spirit is just as real as the world of the senses and mysteries abound in both. The adventures of the human mind in both these realms are equally justifiable, because their ultimate aim is the creation of some abiding values that will widen consciousness—the last irreducible factor in the scale of being. What is hidden must be laid bare and made to yield to the growth of the being as a whole. Here science and religion meet on common ground: a leap into the beyond, whether aided by a flight of the imagination or by a living faith sustained by what seems to be an emerging truth, is the motive force in both. Both aim at converting knowledge into a utility that will lead to a harmonious growth of the collective life.

While science lays stress on tangible data, the spiritual quest is more concerned with an array of subjective phenomena which seem to elude the senses. In both, the mind is confronted with some indubitable facts of experience, behind which it perceives the existence of some occult force whose working it tries to grasp and manipulate. But it was not like this with the ancient Vedic seers. A purity of consciousness allowed them to see reality as a whole; and in the scale of matter, force and spirit, they could discern a process of gradual illumination occurring in some mental Being of universal extension and infinite potentiality. This is the integral Vedic vision on which rest the two worlds wherein matter is as easily spiritualized as spirit is materialized.

The sahaja is the innate, simple and blissfully free nature of man to be discovered in the inmost depths of his being—his essence—'what is born with him.' It lies in the inner temple of the heart, yet spreads over the earth and transcends the heavens. The sahaja can be realized either rationally by a simple intuition of the Void, or emotionally by a sublimation of human love. Indeed the Void and conscious love are two aspects of the same reality. And the conscious man is the ultimate Truth of existence.

A deep faith, a lucid rationalism, a crystal-clear vision are among the features of a distinctive sahaja mysticism, which has been variously described by rationalist schools as attaining light. The cardinal principle is an inwardization that takes the form of concentration. This corresponds to the plane of true knowledge as expressed in the Upanishads and to the state of absorption of the mind described by the disciples of the rationalist schools.

The basic ground of mystic life is always an interiorization leading to a deepening and broadening consciousness that contacts and assimilates reality. It means sensing the real and becoming the real and finding out finally the link of pure Existence within non-existence.

The Vedic delineation of the mystic path towards the Void has given rise to the practical science of Samkhya, with innumerable psychological details based upon a well-knit system of philosophical theory, codified by Patanjali in a set of *Aphorisms* which remain unsurpassed. But the mind must seize upon some objective data before it can work its way up among the described subjective data which form the core of every spiritual discipline.[3]

In the Void, the primordial energy is simply existing. In its very essence it is both dynamic and passive, the two distinctive forces which are always fighting within us! It is from the marriage of these two qualities embodied in the traits of Kardama and Devahuti, that Kapila, the founder of Samkhya and known as the Master of Wisdom, was born. In him there was a double nature: the power which had created his father, Kardama, out of absolutely pure mud, and that which had created his mother, Devahuti, out of subtle, divine matter. Devahuti, who was purely aspiration, was attracted by the material essence of Kardama, which she needed in order to make her descent to earth.

Because he was made of mud, Kapila was bound to live in underground caves. He had the double task of leading the human race to conceive of the Void in all things and of demonstrating that it is impossible to realize the Divine without having a body made of mud. Even the Buddha had such a body, so that one day he had to deny it.

Kapila's primordial wisdom would have remained an abstraction for us and would have vanished altogether were it not that his mother Devahuti, as has already been said,[4] devoted herself voluntarily to serving the human aspiration for the Divine.

The Void is at first an obscure conception to many, until the bi-une existence in us becomes a reality. The secret energy of the earth rises up like the sap of a tree, through the trunk of the body, to the crown of the head where it blooms. Such is the union of Kardama and Devahuti.

When in the practice of your discipline, you disappear into the Void, you are using your own energy which usually remains dormant. But there it is! It is your inner strength to be in the world but not of the world! You can say: 'Within ourselves we are one with our power of manifestation, while the spirit remains the witness.' Whenever you feel that they come together, you must remain quiet. You then feel an indescribable sensation of wisdom and that wisdom which is born into you comes from above! But always be humble and remember that your physical consciousness with its many contradictions, is a gift of Kardama, the being made of mud, while Devahuti, the strong aspiration of the soul, opens your eyes to a higher dimension. The life plane on which there is a search for a mental consciousness is already on a higher dimension, though still in the realm of duality. Further on, an aspiration towards unity shines like the light of an energy searching for a way to reach the Void. Of course it is a joy to live in the Void and to see things being done for us by our own power of manifestation.

The quality of a pure sensation develops little by little, because at every moment the Truth is new. One cannot reach it by accumulating experience, because the Truth is free, as are the Laws of life which govern events. The values created by the power of manifestation are real only insofar as they are relevant to the inner spirit. There one does not feel anything, as the Void absorbs all shocks and you see a serene sky overhead. The meaning of all existence is a peace which endures all.

Any real talk about scientific method is simply a return to a basic empiricism where you are nothing but a pure sensation devoid of coloring or stress.

Remain unshaken in your spirit. That is the Law of manifestation everywhere. And so, outwardly, life lives through death, while inwardly it is immortal.

The sky is clear. One may say it is pleasant. By what standard? Beyond pleasure and pain there is pure Existence; the Void which knows no comparison nor degree and so is immeasurable. It is as light and superficial as the appearance of things. Deep down in that superficiality there is sheer emptiness. And it is a fulfillment beyond comprehension. Time stops. And you are free.

Things will come and pass on. They do not come to stay. They are always on the move. One is neither attached nor detached from them; one simply looks on, standing in the heart of all movement without moving. The body which is the denser part of prakriti, is slow to move. So it often lags behind when the spirit in its turn is free. The body's mode of recovering from any fatigue is to induce deep rest within itself from the deeper source of the Void. It then becomes coexistent with the sky so vividly described in the *Taittiriya Upanishad*. It is then like the body of a small child newly awakened, in whom body and spirit are together in a state of universalization. The aging body will die one day; this is the mechanical Law of prakriti. But there will immediately be a resurrection of the Divine body in which 'the Word is made flesh.'

A vision is a common phenomenon in the beginning of spiritual experiences. It is a fact of inner reality which takes shape very naturally in outer symbolism. The symbols should never be analyzed by the intellect but should be absorbed and understood by the heart. The intellect often binds us to external conventions which do not allow us to see the uniqueness of the Truth underlying the symbol. This is an enactment of the eternal drama of the awakening of prakriti by the *random* touch of Purusha and of the inner illumination finding expression in the sign.

For some days, I have been brooding over the idea of the supreme Power (*mahāśakti*) being like a tiny girl. The experience is so wonderful! To go to the Baby-Christ, or Baby-Krishna or Baby-Gauri is to go down to the depths where the ideal and the real fuse in such a wonderfully simple way that it becomes most expressive when it is inexpressible! This vital symbolism is the real Tantric way of looking at things. And the Upanishads call it: 'After full knowledge, the spirit's return to childhood.' It is just the opposite, and, at the same time, the complement of what the Freudian psychologists would call infantile sexuality. In fact: it means going to the roots of matter in spirit. And in Christianity this means incarnation which is none other than sublimated idolatry.

This is life within, true life indeed, a volcanic eruption outside perfectly balanced Laws, and with joy in both creation and destruction.

A very simple but strange experience occurred the other day. A baby was crying loudly in a nearby house. Something must have been hurting it badly. And the mother was crooning over it and trying to soothe it. The baby was no doubt suffering. But the suffering was purely mechanical and thus meaningless to it. It had no mind as yet and so it was suffering passively and not creating more suffering through the agency of the mind. But the mother?

Her anxiety is a creation of the mind which grows as the days pass by and she cannot throw it off. And her suffering is durably greater than that of her child. The child's mind is so light—it is one with Purusha and not with prakriti. Why has the mother forgotten the art of suffering mechanically, as she did when she was a child? Therefore life has become a curse to her!

When spirit and matter come together there is a movement of energy between the two; there must arise some suffering because of maladjustments. But why bring the mind into it? Why turn an unreal mechanical suffering into a mentally created one? Why not always remain a child in one's heart?

Suffering there is and must be. But make it a dead mechanical thing, only a movement of prakriti! No mind and no suffering! And this is Samkhya appearing in the garb of Zen! Perhaps this is why Indian theater always turns a tragic drama into a comic one!

A fine comedy is staged by prakriti. It is quite natural that all things die, even noble thoughts. But after their death, we solemnly and ritually turn them into mummies and raise pyramids over them. The seed of life escapes our notice. It takes root in the soil and silently spreads a carpet of green grass around these colossal structures of man-made truths, of which the archeologists are so proud. Everyone of us will die, but the bare Truth in us will live. It will appear in a new garb. Always a new garb is woven by prakriti to cover the austere nudity of Truth, which has been pictured as the unclad Shiva roaming in the cremation ground.

Here is life and here is death, and both go together to make Truth. Many walk along this path, but only a few will reach the goal. Those who drop beside the way will turn into good manure. So nothing will be lost, and there is no regret when the heart is full carrying within itself the whole universe. 'Move on like the refreshing wind of the spring and make young leaves sprout,' as Shankara has said.

When a work is an expression of inner life, it always moves smoothly. It is like a running stream. If difficulties are thrown in its way, it will simply move round them and then flow again freely and serenely.

When facing difficulties, identify yourselves with the power of śhakti which is working behind every movement. You can work carefully at the level of your understanding. And you can take life as it offers itself to us. It is a joyful inner experience to accept it as well as everything it brings us; but the moment comes when we must know how to sever even the bonds that bind us to one another.

We should remain fully in prakriti and yet above her, seeing in ourselves the unfolding of the great drama of life, whose glorious end is already known to us. The curtain descends, and we stand gathering the whole troupe of dramatic personae within us. It is, as the Buddhists say, the turning of the wheel of destiny which never stops. The wheel is always moving. It will be moving on and on till the end of time. To reveal it to the gaze of others, to follow it with our eyes, our heart, our deathless spirit and to feel it with every atom of our being, that is immortality!

In this tremendous experience, all philosophies created by men are nothing but verbalism, like a pile of dead leaves. The 'I' vanishes like mist before light. But there again, the mind is thirsty for Truth. What is Truth? A precise sensation of the 'I-subject' completely dissociated from the 'I-object.' I am detached from my existence, from all that is matter, energy and mind. But even at that stage, the 'I-subject' is still what tastes the state of pure Consciousness. And where is the heart of the cosmic Laws, the heart of the life Principle? The mystery remains insoluble, the face of Truth is still hidden by a veil!

The idea of bringing back spiritual communism with a Vedic resurgence is quite laudable. It means a spiritual existentialism which is just a natural corroboration of living within ourselves.

But the moment we begin to live outside ourselves we are divided and separated from others by our physical, vital and mental reactions. In between the two attitudes, there is of course a land of 'spiritual romance' where the unattainable appears to be easily attained, but it leaves no mark of any kind!

The Vedas speak of spiritual existentialism as being the domain of śhakti, who is inscrutable in her mystery and is ever elusive. Yet she does all and everything. She is the pure sattva of Samkhya. If a few sincere hearts would unite in this pure sattva, they could form the core of a powerful spiritual center, which could live and progress for a long time. It will sooner or later degenerate into a church or an ashram, following then the natural Law of the running down of matter. But the idea will resurrect and will rise again from its grave.

'Spiritual existentialism' is a good expression. The idea behind it may actually be a community feeling on the economic and political level. But political ideologies are bound to starve if they are not supported by a feeling of communion with the spirit that embraces the whole of existence—matter, life, mind and spirit. This is the real Holy Communion: in Christianity you call it 'God, the Son, and the Holy Ghost.' In terms of Samkhya, it is 'the holy communion of Purusha and Prakriti;' in Tantrism, 'Shiva-śhakti;' in Vedanta, 'Brahma-Māyā;' and you cannot separate the two.

For they permeate each other as in the metaphor of 'two houses caught by the same fire,' or just as in the case of a couple locked in a love embrace where 'each is both.' This idea appears in Indian temple sculpture innumerable times. The mystics have called it sahaja. We often call it the Void, which is not a negation but a living and positive idea in which the mystery of existence seems like a commingling of black and white. The black is matter and the white is spirit.[5] They enter into each other and between the two poles of matter and spirit, or earth and heaven in the Vedas, infinite shades of coexistence occur in different degrees of densities.

Density is an important word in the philosophy of the Void which is expressed in Samkhya as the three guṇas. It is simply a philosophical expression of the natural phenomena of light becoming darkness and vice versa. You cannot separate them. The illumination of the highest realization of a seeker imperceptibly contains the dark matrix of nature, just as that dark matrix contains in itself luminous possibilities of spiritual evolution. To realize the two movements simultaneously in a single flash of awareness is to realize the Void of the life within.

Then all densities disappear and spirit and matter become one, being really the bi-une aspects of one total reality. The most subtle density of natural manifestation is the 'ego' (the 'I-ness'), which is so elusive that it is extremely difficult to eradicate it. The point of fusion between black and white is missed when the ego automatically divides the whole experience into subject and object. But when, in a spiritual experience, the two are fused, the self appears as the Void, embracing all. There is a feeling of boundless expansion (ākāśa), which covers all things and yet allows them to maintain their distinct individualities, and which are again an infinite number of points, each containing the matrix of another universe. This is Prakriti's attribute as a creative and executive force. It can be likened to an acorn which, with its innumerable tiny seeds, contains a whole oak-forest!

If someone could realize this not only in feeling but in bodily sensation, he could project a community living a real spiritual existentialism which would endure and prosper. It is a great task and requires the power of a super-human being. But it is worthwhile for a man or woman to undertake it.

I can feel that some of you are on the brink of the Void! With a little push you would fall into it locked in a close embrace. You would be transformed into a fusion of fire and ether at the same time. The ether would expand into infinite space and the fire would condense into a luminous point becoming the matrix of matter. But you have to remember that it is not a question of fission between the two, but of a fusion in which each partakes of the nature of both. And again you can be helped in your conception of this inmost communion by the metaphor of 'one fire consuming two houses,' in which the flames intermingle as a couple in love do. A Bâül mystic of Bengal described it thus: 'When I loved him, I did not know that he was a man and I a woman. Our hearts were simply ground into one paste in which two elements mingled.'

It is fascinating to discover how the higher centers—mental and emotional, work in conjunction with the lower ones, including sex. They can be physically felt in the nervous system, in which the group of five elements are carefully and methodically arranged. This gives the clue to the transformation or, as the Christian mystics call it, 'transubstantiation' of Christ's body. It shows vividly in what way the body of the Christ became the Church. And, regarding a still earlier period, it explains the dharma and the *sangha* (the universal spiritual principles and community life) of the Buddhists. You must remember here that the mystic Samkhya (and not the academic Samkhya of the third century, which broke away from the parent stock) openly teaches about the five material principles as arranged according to a scheme of different densities.

These things can be felt and projected like bright stars in the sky, as if on an illumined photographic plate. You have to be fully aware of these bright spots, not in an objective way as the ego does, but in the subjective way which is a direct seeing-feeling, not of the ego but of the self that is simply the Void. It is what a mystic will know from within, when from the center of the heart the cosmic periphery and 'a beyond' are felt. Then this beyond or transcendence becomes a positive experience and absorbs into itself all the negative modes of mental experiences. In a supreme awareness the Void is possessed without any mental fumbling.

What a mystery is this ego! If it does not move, nothing is alive; if it moves, it is subjective; if it looks around it is separated from others. Only in the instant when it is both 'this and that' do we know the density which is ours: weight, name, color, form. The deeper we go into ourselves, the more vulnerable we become until a reversal takes place like a strong gust of wind, which almost bowls us over into the Void.

There is something particular to be noticed about the Indo-European languages. They use three numbers to describe anything: singular, dual and plural. Many of the Indian languages also preserve this trait. The plural is of course descriptive of the plurality of the universe. In every phase of existence, whether material or spiritual, we encounter the 'many'. They crowd and jostle together and then group themselves in pairs; the result is that duality appears in a scheme of polarity, as light and darkness, pleasure and pain, matter and energy, body and mind, and so on. These dual opposites are surmounted by a spiritual principle which tries to express itself everywhere in a sort of monism that applies from whatever angle you look at things. So we come to the concepts of one matter, one life, one mind, one human being, one nationality, one world, one God, and so on. This universalization of any one of the apparently plural entities can be understood only when, in your awareness of them, you identify yourself with their essence.

The total awareness of the identification of the 'many,' in Samkhya, has been called Purusha. The supreme Purusha can be expressed not only as the complete fusion of all the polarities and multiplicities, but also as the bi-une Principle of the unified Purusha-Prakriti. And you can find the intrinsic duality of Purusha and Prakriti clearly shown, for example, as men and women go about in their daily life and multiply themselves in innumerable pairs of boys and girls.

Well, we are in a quandary when we emphasize only the multiple individualities. Then we quarrel. When we come to the duality, we already have a glimpse of Truth. Further on, fusion gives us the true vision of Unity.

And the whole is excellently symbolized by the picture of the two dolphins.

Furthermore, as regards language, we must be exceedingly careful from the very outset about the following: we must beware of the images produced by the words we use habitually. The ancient Samkhya masters call it mental construction (*vikalpa*), which is a hindrance to the realization of the essence of things.

For instance, when we speak of the root of a thing, meaning its essential nature, we evoke the picture of a tree but we are emphasizing only the bottom and forgetting what is at the top. In fact, what is under the ground is only at a par with what is at the top and shoots up to the sky. The root, trunk, branches, foliages, flowers and fruits all make up the tree, surrounded by infinite space. And when we want to understand what a tree is essentially, we must come to the seed which contains the tree in a shell without differentiating the various parts. The seed is at the center of the infinity that we have named the Void, without attaching any particular label or feature to it.

One must first have a good idea of this nameless and featureless infinity, which is best symbolized by the sky (ākāśa) assuming different densities, such as air, fire, water and earth, according to the old nomenclature. They can be expressed in modern terms, which you will find hinted at in old texts, as non-being or Void, and life-force (both being without any form); light or the matrix of all forms; water or the life-substance to which all matter has to be reduced; earth or the solid matter which is a cluster of innumerable particles forming an organization, for example, our bodies consisting of innumerable cells all of which have a distinct composition and function but which are cooperating to form a vehicle for the spirit. The spirit in its turn is formless and featureless—a Void.

Here we clearly see the three distinct qualities of density (guṇas) at play. At the top is sattva (meaning in Sanskrit 'being-ness' or essential nature); it is the pure aspect of Prakriti upholding Purusha, which is pure Consciousness or Awareness. Below is rajas, or the life-energy manifesting the command of Purusha over prakriti. Lastly there is tamas, or the inertia making up the body of Purusha.

In the scheme of the five spiritual elements, ether, air, fire, water and earth, sattva is represented by the sky and rajas by the air and life-energy. Light represents a double principle including formlessness. In meditation we can see with our inner eye the formless Godhead and also, just like the pagans, gods and goddesses emanating from darkness. The element below light is water which is the condensed form of life arising from gross matter. Last of all is the earth or matter itself. So all beings are an organization of spirit, energy and matter in their different aspects.

Now to realize the Void or pure spirit, you have to enter into the domain of mystic sensations behind the elemental sensations. Smell is a primitive sensation common to all with which life starts. It is either good, bad, soft or pungent, etc. Its mystic quality is a fragrance which arouses an ecstatic condition in you, hence the incense burning in temples. The common sensory taste is sweet, bitter, etc. Its mystic counterpart is flavor. The vision of mystic light is usual for all spiritual aspirants. On the ordinary level it is beauty. The mystic quality of touch is revealed in the love-touch. And the mystic quality of sound is revealed through music, which plays such an important role in all religions.

We have to train our ordinary sensations to rise, to expand and also to dive into mystic sensations. Then we will see and feel that all existences are shot through and through by spirit and energy which evolve matter out of their ethereal bodies. Remember that reality is neither one nor many; it is bi-une producing many, the love embrace of Purusha and Prakriti giving birth to the many children of the same bi-une beings. And then the two dolphins will splash energy in the Void in their frolicsome play!

As one rises in the ascending scale of rarefaction when passing through the different gradations of the five elements, one notices how an intense light between the eyebrows expands into the Void of pure Existence, which holds the unlimited universe in its ambit and remains calm and serene, full of the peace, joy and love that are the essence of all beings. There the Creator and the created are one. One is then the very stuff of reality.

The Samkhya that has been described is not book knowledge. In fact, it is at the core of all religions including even that of the primitive people. The main outlines are clearly described but not in an academic way.

If someone tries to understand not by the intelligence of the mind alone, but also with the intuition of the heart, it will not be very difficult for him or her to get at the central theme. Spiritual experiences rest upon mysticism and mysticism is not anything mysterious. It is simply the assertion of truths which we have covered up with mentally constructed words. It requires a fervor, an elasticity of the intellect, a simplicity of adolescence which sees the Truth directly without being blocked by prejudices. Reduce everything to sensations and then try to get at the sublimity of the expression of the pure Existence which underlies all sensations.

I told you earlier that the simple sensations of hearing, touch, vision, taste and smell have a touch of mysticism in them when they are experienced as music, love, beauty, flavor and fragrance. They have been minutely described by the works on yoga based on Patanjali. And he is only an exponent of a very ancient teaching which is transmitted in the Vedas and the Upanishads and still lives in Tantrism, Buddhist sahaja, and the experiences narrated by the illiterate Bâüls and Sants[6] not only in Bengal, but also in the extreme South of India. If you read between the lines, you will find that Christ's teachings are mostly in the fashion of the Bâüls. I look upon him as a genuine Bâül whose words have captured the hearts of the simple people all over the world. Samkhya is also a way of mysticism and mysticism is nothing if it is not a sublimation of sensations. It will not do only to think about God, but you have to 'think-feel' about Him!

Approaching a new dimension really means a total immersion into the Void. You must deeply ponder over this and get its secret clear and deep in your consciousness. There is a process involved which might take a whole lifetime. I give you here some hints:

Analyze a very simple proposition. You look at a child and say, 'What a fine child!' It is a matter-of-fact statement. This belongs to the stage of sensation. The child is outside of you and you are looking objectively at him and have only an impression of what he is like.

If your sense of beauty changes into love, you will come to love the child and exclaim, 'What a darling!' This is the second stage where an element of emotion enters into you.

If this stage is deeply intensified, you are approaching the third stage and feel as if the child were your own; it becomes really like your own, a child born from your womb as it were. You are then fully identified. The child and you interact upon each other. This is the last stage in the development of a pure sensation.

In the first stage, you simply observe like a scientist. In the second, you are a poet and in the third, a mystic.

A scientist looks at a thing and thinks; but if his heart is moved, he wants to understand the meaning of its working. By doing so he adds something more to what his senses discover. He is approaching a new order of Laws. A poet becomes a mystic when he identifies himself fully with what he sees. In this total identification, space and time come together as in Purusha-Prakriti (or Shiva-śhakti) and are fused on a mystical plane of consciousness.

Einstein's space-time continuum is on the objective plane, and so in the first stage of observation. The poet and the philosopher, by adding the element of feeling to it, discover the bi-une reality existing within Purusha-Prakriti, which you might also understand as Shiva-śhakti.

In the third stage Purusha-Prakriti interact and are in communion with each other till they are fused into One, which is simply the Void. Here space is fused with time and vice versa. We can say that the dolphins then stop playing and melt into each other, forming the matrix of Creation,[7] or that the feared black goddess Kali, representing time, reduces the whole universe into a pulp and swallows it! In other words, the bi-une reality of Purusha-Prakriti melts into the Void.

You can look at an atom through a microscope and infer new forces in it. But can you become the atom? No.

You can know intuitively what an atom is by deep concentration and meditation and by inwardly living and becoming within yourselves the Void. This is what the mystics have done throughout all ages and climes and have reported their findings in a cryptic language peculiar to them. What they have found subjectively by contemplation, in particular the many Laws of the universe, as set forth in the Vedas and in the many secret Scriptures of olden times, we are now trying to find 'objectively' through science.

To approach a new dimension remains the target of a deep search. Once, in a vision, I saw a pyramid of which I could barely make out the point of the apex, because the lines as seen from afar, did not meet. I wished to climb it.

It took years and years until I climbed it. The pyramid had no top but only a small plateau on which to stand for a short while.

He who climbs this symbolic pyramid is the son of man. But there, in the humility of the mystery, in the barely perceptible expansion of the fifth dimension which shines, everything is turned upside down. The son of man can only say: Who am I? I am this and 'That' also. In the dying son of man, a son of God is conceived.

One cannot remain for long at the summit. He who comes down from it knows the space that the wise men have perceived. He also knows that the many years of search in his life were instantly obliterated. Nothing remains but a reflection of immensity, the All and the Nothing, the perfect Void.

Endnotes

1. *The Void.*
2. *Which is the super-mind in Śri Aurobindo's philosophy.*
3. *In medieval India (15th-16th century) there was a confluence of the mystic currents of the three great living religions of Buddhism, Hinduism and Islam. This explains why some of their most significant terms can be considered as interchangeable.*
4. *See p. 77.*
5. *The opposition white-black always means Purusha-prakriti (spirit-matter).*
6. *Large groups of wanderers, well-known in India.*
7. *Bhagavatam.*

Part Four

RAMBLING THOUGHTS

Sŕi Anirvân

Many times, in the evening, we would sit around him
speaking about the Void.
Sometimes there was a deep silence between us.
The air was full of serenity—
life filling the space.
Sometimes he laughed, full of humor,
sometimes he was very serious,
speaking about himself.
Time was flowing in eternity.

—Calcutta 1972–1978

Rambling Thoughts

1

When I first came to the Hills, I had a Nepali servant. You can't imagine how conscientious he was! If he was two minutes late in the morning, he refused to take a full day's pay. 'If you are two minutes late in the morning, go two minutes later in the evening,' I suggested, and that seemed to settle things in his mind.

I used to ask him to share my food at lunchtime. At first he did not want to accept. I gave him whatever I was having and asked him: 'Well, how does it taste?' 'Oh! it tastes sweet,' he answered, however bad the cooking was. If it was good, he repeated: 'Oh! it tastes sweet.'

Then I thought: 'Well, for that boy, the food is neither good nor bad, it is simply sweet. What is Brahman? He is neither good nor bad; he is above everything, he is peace, he is sweet.' This simple boy was filled with grace when saying: 'Oh! it tastes sweet.' I never saw him angry, or in a bad mood of any kind. He was always ready to smile. He was simply blooming in God's light.

You see, his mind was not constantly searching for things to understand and to explain. It does not help much.

You must attain to this simplicity, to this primitiveness in which there are simply densities of various degrees between darkness, blurred vision and clarity and then light. All that has been said and written about the approach to self-observation is only minor work, only the first steps to discovering what inner knowledge really is. Knowledge is simply finding unity in the many. This is what an animal cannot do. It is the privilege of the human being alone. On whatever level of society and whatever level of civilization, man has this property of being able to arrange things around an idea. And that becomes knowledge. As soon as it enters into his being, he finds himself above everything and at the same time inside everything.

What is misleading about knowledge is that you don't see the whole, you see only a part and you think that this part is the whole. Seen from above, the part belongs to the whole and the whole belongs to the part.

Take the relationship between a mother and a child. There can be no mother without a child, nor a child without a mother. But the relation is that the mother contains the child, the whole of the child, while the child only knows part of the mother. In order to know his mother as his father knew her, he has to grow up. The mother is at mid-point. She looks down upon the child, and then looks up to the father and says: 'This child belongs to me, but I belong to you.'

To have a clear vision of this situation, to see what is the part and what is the whole, is liberation or pure existence. In a small way, the circle is closed.

2

Rise every morning as if you were born again, breaking completely with the past. Retain your youth and adolescence within you. Do you remember yourself when you were just sixteen, when the portals of mystery were just opening before your wondering eyes? Is that one lost? Can you find him again? Do you know him? Does he know what *is* born with him?

All is there, all around us. We have simply to understand what goes on. That is all. We are then at peace with everything.

If you see life as it is, you captivate the hearts of all those around you; that is the eternal adolescence which is represented by the young boy Krishna and Radha, the girl. Similarly Śrī Ramakrishna called his young wife 'Shodashi,' meaning the 'eternal girl of sixteen.' He deposited whatever he had achieved in the palm of her hand, saying to her: 'I give everything to you.' What did that girl know? Nothing! She just loved.

3

Do you remember the naughty small parrots at Lohaghat? They were so lovely to look at! They would squander all the fruit of a tree in no time. They cackled between themselves: 'We are jungle beings! Who does the fruit belong to? God has created the trees for us, as well as the fruit. They belong to us alone! We are not attached to this or that tree. You, human beings, think that everything belongs to you. You spread a net over some of the trees. Never mind, we will fly to other trees and come back later. You can do nothing to stop us!'

Do you remember the English lady, our neighbor, who asked you to watch over her orchard and not to let the village women come and pick her apples. And these simple village women were saying to themselves: 'God made the earth, God made the trees, so God is giving us the apples!' And you asked me what you should do: 'Should I guard the apples? I can't. I feel as if cut clean in two, my body here, my mind there.' So I watched the game going on, your dealing with primitive feelings and, within you, a sense of logic valuable only for the part and not for the whole.

Also in Lohaghat, near the house, there was a spring running through a ravine full of tall ferns. So much water and no flowers! I had never raised flowers, so I decided one day to sow many of them and follow the wonder of their growth. So I left my books and watched over the flowers morning, noon and night, trying to guard them against every possible accident that might threaten them, and there were many. They grew fast with bright colors. They required much of my attention and time: plowing, manuring, watering, weeding, grafting, shading, as well as love and protection.

They bloomed extravagantly and looked finally like a Persian carpet. One morning, before sunrise, I cut them all and made bouquets of them. Then I carefully turned over the earth and went back to my books. This and That. The world of flowers had filled me forever. I only retain the habit of keeping one flower in a tiny vase in front of Tara, the goddess of the Void.

To play the game of life is one thing, to know that one is playing, it is quite another thing. The Bâûl's role is to remain above the habitual level of thought.

Never fail to watch the game! If you have a witness-consciousness, you can be aware of what is going on in the players and in the onlookers and laugh at the same time.

Life being made up of many and varied episodes, gradually you are molded by what takes place. Imagine that an enormous blacksmith with a huge hammer—call him God—is looking at us. He throws some of us into the fire and when we are red hot, he gives shape to what was shapeless! While we are still red hot he dips us into the water. So raw material becomes fine steel and that is 'inner discipline!' At one end the steel is condensed, at the other one, rarefied and we become a really useful tool.

4

Well the Creator made a great mistake at the very outset by creating the human being neither fully animal nor fully human! As we are constituted with three twists in the spinal column, we have to consider that we have also twists in our thinking! Our spinal column is not straight like the stem of a lotus that rises from mud to heaven. Were it but straight, our consciousness would be different and would easily follow a straight line!

For this reason many Indian yogis affirm that if you can teach people to sit cross-legged, straight, still and stiff, looking inside right along the spinal column, then, when the physical pain has stopped, a strange light in the mind will occur.

In the West, you speak of solar plexus, thymus, pineal and other glands which are really the *cakras* along the spine as represented by the different lotuses. What is real is that this strange light which is stored at one end of the spinal column can move to the other pole of the being. This is again expressed in the theory of the Logos in the Bible: '… in the beginning was the Word', the fact of existence. One can create a complicated science for the mind about this process; one can discuss the possibility of proving that such light exists and this has been done by attaching electrodes to the skull and recording the movements of the brain. There is a lot of dabbling along that line, using fragments of ancient teachings to read aloud and people are delighted to listen.

We see that people, especially young people, are ready now to plunge into a dense forest of different teachings, in search of something they feel they lack. They are looking for knowledge, for self-knowledge.

Inner growth needs time. At first the mere idea of it will make them softer. Instead of being dispersed, their energy will turn around an axis. It will help them to establish a new relationship with themselves and with others. This is the basis for all community living. 'I myself am alive and, at the same time, I respect your right to live. I have the right to live, and therefore so do you.' With such words, their field of communication will expand, but if they continue to think in the ordinary cruel way, nothing will change.

We have to create a coordination between all these feelings. Gandhi spoke of *ahiṁsā*, of non-violence: 'At the cost of your life don't be violent to others.' Then the question arises: If someone is unjustly violent toward another person, have I any right to object? Have I any right to give him a good thrashing and make him stop his violence? Where do I stand? This question is dealt with in the Bhagavad Gita. Well, yes, we do have the right to object but under this condition: that we ourselves do not get upset or ruffled; that we remain calm and don't lose ourselves. The whole pattern of social behavior implies the attitude of a surgeon who is called to lance a boil. He knows he is inflicting pain on a patient, but he does it, with a calm mind, not to hurt but to relieve suffering. This aim can be attained only if we act knowing that harmony is to be found in just two ways: first in a mother's heart, and then in the calmness of a father's look. Do you have these two? Here we are back in Samkhya, facing the principles of Prakriti and Purusha. We are returning to the idea of self-knowledge.

First of all you have to discover, within yourself, whether you are predominantly a man or woman. Among the males, in the body of a man, a woman may in reality be living. Śrī Ramakrishna pointed it out. He said: 'What is in me is not really male, it is female; a woman has melted into me. But what is in Swami Vivekananda[1] is fully male!' This factor of predominance you will find throughout the whole of creation. Of these two attitudes, one appears to be rigid, staring into nudity, into the Void, ready to face the mystery of death; the other is just moonlight at play, serene and soft.

Each Upanishad expresses it in a different way:

'This play of the many,
let it subside,
just as at eventide
everyone subsides into sleep.'

Every night, I hear the noises subside. The whole city of Calcutta appears to me like an infant sleeping; it fills my heart with peace. 'I am That. I am that I am.' This is self-realization or knowledge of the self.

One day, this knowledge is going to save the world. People who possess this knowledge will grow in number, first independently, here one, there another; then they will become coordinated. Then there may be a flood, or something similar, and they will have to separate and start again. This will go on, say for millions of years, until gradually they reach some steadiness.

But one single soul can have the total vision of this and know what may appear in fifteen million years or so. It exists in me already! Then I smile. I am an artist, I am a poet, I am a philosopher, I am God the philosopher, God the artist—God in everything!

Now let us speak of self-knowledge starting from the fundamental mistake the Creator made! Actually the human being is built to go on all fours, his spine parallel to the earth and not erect. How can we try to correct this position?

This is where the yogic discipline says: 'Just sit straight. Close your eyes and try to feel the spinal column as straight. Forget that it is not straight. Imagine that it is straight!' Gradually you will feel a lightness and also that heat is being generated. Your temperature rises. If on a winter night you sit erect outside in the cold, even if you shiver and whine like a puppy, you will feel heat being produced within you. That is an old Tibetan teaching. They undertook by sitting straight to produce sufficient body heat to dry a sheet soaked in ice-cold water. It is said that Milarepa, in one sitting, was able to dry four wet blankets. A strange thing!

For us, more simply, to sit straight, still and rigid, eyes closed, is to be living truly within. Deep concentration takes place. What appears to you as a speck or a point of light becomes a globe. Go deeper, then you begin to feel three things at the same time: a vast calmness, a deep vital energy and an illumination. The three together. Taken separately, they are the three guṇas or the three densities working in your inner being which keep you enslaved. Together and coordinated they mean freedom and liberation.

To sit straight is to think straight. It is a severe discipline, that of self-knowledge. You must sit straight, die straight, with no crookedness and no bending. This speck of knowledge means a lot; a whole life is needed to strive after and attain it.

That is quite enough! Then you are open, waiting for eternity. Eternity is a non-negative concept, it is a positive one. We all want a glimpse of eternity. We can merge into it. Then we know that it exists, that it is the only thing that makes you capable of loving, of enduring things, of becoming pliable with yourself, with others, with every being, to live in every being, even in an ant, in a worm, in a tree. The same soul, the same God. 'The soul in me is the soul in everything.'

What can exist except life? Only life exists! Inside it is life, outside it is life. And that life is energy. Feel it deep, very deep within yourself. You will then find that things will come to you all together, spontaneously. It is not by thinking but rather by not thinking.

All this you know, deep in yourself. If you know it consciously, you become a starting-point. Perhaps you are only a repetition. I say repetition, but repetitions will come and go until everything is clear. You will even hear people shout: 'These are all faked things; we don't want them anymore. We want new ideas, new things.' But do you not see that the same things are endlessly repeated? You, me, all of us are nothing but repetitions!

5

Now comes the time to speak of self-disciplines. We shall speak of making the memory light, and of fasting. In the *Chandogya Upanishad*, it is said:

> *If you make pure what you take into yourself, whether as food or thought, then your essence becomes pure and you reach pure memory, universal memory—the only thing that has to be remembered.*

To progress you must definitely follow these disciplines. Once you reach universal memory all ties are dropped.

Those moments of purity are like beams of light which appear to you as tiny dots of light. Many people have seen some of them during their life-time. Only they don't know how to connect them, deluded as they are by the Scriptures and different teachings.

To see them one day as a continuous line of light, one must first think of every dot of light as independent one from the other, but at the same time see that each dot is self-repeating. The dots of light are all of the same nature—they are light.

Here come the facts known to science about the queen bee, which can serve as a parable. On a very clear and sunlit morning, the queen bee comes out of her hive. Immediately, all around her, there is something like a signal going through the many hives. All the workers swarm out, and also the drones, flying high in her direction. Between the drones there is a race, but finally only one clutches the queen bee, clings to her. Then he zooms higher and higher. But soon his limbs drop off and fall, one by one, like the petals of a flower in full bloom. By that one contact, the queen bee becomes productive for the whole of her life and lays millions upon millions of eggs. In the Tantras, she is named Devi on that account. She is also called Śhakti, a wonder of light and power. She is at the same time queen bee, drone and worker. She is self-generating and self-repeating. She is a pattern of the universe. Would you call it one or would you call it many? You can't say!

Similarly the dots of light by repeating themselves will come to form a line of light. Just look at them longingly, with a strong inner desire. But no clinging, no forcing! Simply look, without attachment and they will go on coming! They will form a line and separate again, come again and separate again. They will be playing with you!

Inasmuch as you can become a witness to their play, you are free, and you catch sight of the real thing. Nothing faked, nothing imaginary but ultimately only what is real.

It is not really a difficult discipline, but we lack the simplicity of a child that is required in order to approach it. But somehow, once you fall in love with it, you can't do without it because it gives you a creative power within yourself.

Another self-discipline is fasting, which is much harder. If you pursue the idea of reaching an ideal you come to the technique of fasting. The point is to be self-sufficient, not to take in anything, to feel indivisible—I am what I am—and use nothing from the many. And so for a while the body becomes a cannibal and uses up the stored energy; it gets hungry, famished and feeds upon itself. If it is strong enough, it goes beyond that, perhaps crosses the normal limit of a long fast. By fasting you know that you have received a given amount of energy. You can use it up knowing that you can replenish it with food and thus it will apparently remain a constant. But in this, you are mistaken! If you actually go, say for three days, without food, just to feel what hunger is like, it will open another dimension in your thoughts, perhaps unknown to you until then.

After pursuing this line of investigation for a while, you know what fasting means for you. You must be consciously aware of it. You discover that your consciousness acts just like a barometer. Without food, it goes down and down. And then a darkness comes. With food, it goes up and up, and light comes and you see. You see *there* and you see *here*. The vision is always there, even when you close your eyes. On the higher plane, it is the omniscience of God; on the lower plane, which is ours, it is the Law of sympathy. I feel for my child, I feel for my friend, I feel for a lame man. It is simply putting oneself in the position of others and trying to be just like them. Then gradually that total vision will become inexpressible. There is no way to express it, it can only be felt. And then 'everything tastes sweet,' as my little Nepali servant used to say.

6

All great sages have followed an eastern discipline of fasting. It is known that the Christ observed a fast for forty days in the desert. We know nothing of his regular discipline with food. But fasting has always been regarded as a necessity in spiritual life.

Many scientific investigations have been made regarding the transformation of food in the body. We have chemical studies, charts and statistics about the amount of proteins, carbohydrates, vitamins, etc., which are needed, but next to nothing is known about the psychological effects of food: what makes you feel heavy, dull, drowsy, restless, passionate, aggressive, serene, cheerful or self-poised. When you eat you immediately feel a surge of energy in the body. The 'intake' of food means strength; but it also means sex. For better or worse nobody cares to know anything about the 'transubstantiation' which takes place.

You must now study carefully the relation in yourself between food and impulsion, food and feelings. So choose your food carefully and take only the quantity you need. Pay special attention to this last question. This discipline has to be followed meticulously.

The Buddhists and the Moslems have created artificial measures to help themselves. An established rule naturally sustains an effort by applying the mind to it. Thus the Buddhist must never eat after midday; the Moslem observes strictly a long fast, during the month of Ramzan, from sunrise to sunset. But both, at other times, can eat as much as they like. Many other more balanced disciplines could be mentioned.

Any kind of dogmatism in a spiritual program is an artificial measure, because the only valuable relation to be discovered is then falsified. The discipline of fasting is individual and can only begin when one has a clear idea of the experience to be approached. The right attitude towards the whole thing requires a thorough study of the link existing between the body and the spirit.

Many fast in order to obtain an external effect, as, for example, to influence the feelings of others. Gandhi's fasts may have appeared to be of that kind, but in reality he fasted to have the inner strength to challenge the resistance to his endeavors. Fasting to attract attention has nothing spiritual in itself. A conscious fast is for keeping the 'channel of energy' open. It is rarely followed except by those who can no longer live without a clear consciousness of inner purity. It is never advertised.

By fasting, I do not mean only the fact of not eating for a certain period, but of becoming aware of the reactions of the inner being, of controlling the impulsions when no longer sustained by the energy coming from food. Is there not a finer energy to be recognized? The inner being is aware of what goes on, feels at ease or suffers because the play of the two dolphins does not stop. It cannot stop since it is life itself.

There is some confusion about the quality of food necessary and whether it should be vegetable or animal in origin. Of course, food has much to do with the building up of the mind. But there are some naïve people who imagine: 'If I eat a cat, I risk becoming catlike!' And so they decide to become strict vegetarians when they want to follow a spiritual life. But this is obviously too simple a solution. Actually, it is one's attitude toward food which determines its spiritual nature.

I do not remember if I ever told you the strange story of a fakir who wondered a lot about this question of fasting. He was living near a desert where there was a deep dry well. One day he caught, at random, some monkeys, old and young ones and threw them all into the well.

For the first few days, he threw some food down, upon which he heard violent fighting and Sŕieking. Then he stopped throwing food. For many days, the Sŕieking and hissing when on. Then it stopped.

The fakir thought: 'They must all be dead.' Then he peered over the edge of the well. No movement. No sound.

Tied to a rope, he let himself down and saw a mass of dead bodies, partly dismembered, savagely contorted. But on a stone which was jutting slightly out of the wall, there sat a small monkey, his arms wrapped tightly around his body, his eyes wide open staring at nothing.

The fakir seized hold of it and stroking its head, took it back to his hut.

As the days went by, the monkey began to show strange miraculous powers. It could not speak, but it understood whatever the fakir said to it. It could see into the past and into the future as well. When asked a question about anyone the fakir pointed to, it would answer correctly in dumb-show, as in a silent movie.

This may only be a parable. But it illustrates the great Truth that control over the crude animal impulses helps to bring out thc spiritual energies dormant within us.

7

Fasting is hard because it involves our heavy body in its basic matter. According to tradition, this basic matter is named carbon, and it is said that the rays of the sun are imbedded in it. On the other hand, the geologists tell us that the diamond, which is the symbol of light, is nothing other than carbon. From where nobody knows, a tremendous pressure came upon it and changed the arrangement of the atoms. The carbon began to glow and became light. The whole of the Buddhist discipline speaks of the change within us from matter to light. It is called the *Path of the Diamond*. For the Christians it is the birth of Christ within the inner being. The mission of Christ is to crush the heavy matter and fashion the inner being to His own likeness which is light.

The conversion of the inner being can be described as an attempt to lift a huge stone, to make it stand on end and then fall on the other side. At first you have to put forth immense strength just to lift it. It rises very slowly. Then the moment it is erect, it requires only a light 'touch and go' and over it goes! So the toil on this side is compensated for by there being no toil at all on the other side! This illustrates the conversion of the soul from carbon to diamond! That was also the teaching of Yajnavalkya.[2] He said: 'All your thirsting for knowledge and all your efforts are simply your toiling along that path. The moment will come when this will be a 'touch and go' affair: a sudden change will take place. Then you will find everything so easy; all that you were searching for outside of yourself was there all the time!'

This is called: know thyself. Do not be afraid of the darkness of the self that you discover. It appears perhaps coal black! People become afraid. Many drop out and few reach the end. There is the problem of infinite within infinity. Words like 'so much, so many' do not exist. A very subtle point is that, when we say 'infinity' we think that it must be somewhere where there is nothing finite, and infinity is beyond that!

When you are afraid, you no longer know how to think. You wander all over the place saying: 'I give up all hope.' In the *Brihadaranyaka Upanishad*, it is said:

I surrender myself to you . . .
You open your own self to Me . . .
I have heard so many things
I don't want to hear any more.
I have seen so many things
I don't want to see any more.
I reveal Thyself, I reveal Thyself!

It is like the revelation of Christ.

Fear and harshness within us should dissolve, but alas, the personality is so strong! It gets encrusted with so many things, all exterior things. Imagine two children, a brother and a sister born within a year of each other. I have seen many such pairs. They are so loving. They quarrel and love, love and quarrel, but cannot live without each other. That is a simple beginning of life, but then you begin to teach them many false things; 'to behave correctly,' to do this and that, not through the influence of your presence, but through words, dead words taken from books, and you lose that main thing, the life-touch in knowledge!

That life-touch is the infinite patience one must have with people. This patience is a mission in itself, it is God's own gift. Then you live in infinity and nothing else matters. Remember that God is infinite, infinitely patient with you.

Here is a verse from the *Isha Upanishad*:

Beyond, there is all fullness,
Down here, it is all fullness,
And from that fullness
If you take away the fullness

Still the fullness bubbles
and spills on earth.

What a wonderful way of putting things; with what depth it was written!

Sŕi Ramakrishna liked it. He said:

> *Well, you go to draw water from the ocean of life. The pitcher will float. It won't take in the water. You have to hold it by the neck and thrust it down. At first you hear: 'Glub, glub, glub. …' it wants to reject the water: 'No, no, no, I won't, I won't.' Then it becomes filled and stops. Only then it knows: an ocean inside, an ocean outside!*

We are also made like that, with a small ocean inside and a large ocean outside. That is why we can go beyond sorrow. But how we do resist God! Like the pitcher we say: 'No, no, no.' It is by force that the Master has to put the pitcher down into the water. We don't allow the infinite ocean to come in.

Sŕi Ramakrishna also said:

> *The good Guru is a good physician; he doesn't come and say: 'Well, here is a prescription for you.' No, he brings the medicine to you and thrusts it down your throat so that you are purified from within. He does it with a harshness that is real love.*

8

The heart is the cradle of love and love is not what sex is. Even a couple in whom sex predominates will sometimes experience shining moments when they know what love is. There is a quality of feeling which is finer by far than the coarseness of sex. It is a very fine spiritual feeling. This feeling blooms first in the heart of the woman. The future mother, before procreation, or even at the very outset of the process of procreation, may be as much intoxicated as the future father. They both experience a kind of madness.

But when the child is born, and even before, when the mother feels the child moving in her womb, her heart melts. But this is rarely shared by the father. He may care so little that it means nothing to him if he runs after another woman! This is the theme of innumerable stories written in the East and in the West. The same thing everywhere!

So this is an important point for the woman to realize fully. By remaining in prakriti, she, unlike the man, has full control over her own manifestation. When the child is born, and she nurses it, well, she experiences a taste of what ecstasy actually is.

Did I tell you the story of a girl I knew? This girl was living with a very bad man. Once when I was passing through Calcutta she asked me to come to her house. I went to meet her and saw that she wore the red sign of a married woman.[3] I said: 'How is this? I didn't know that you were married!'

'I belong to this household now,' she answered.

'But you didn't let me know about it.'

'I was ashamed then, but now I am very happy!'

After a year, she bore a child. As I was passing again through Calcutta, I went to her house, but there I saw something horrible. The girl was lying half unconscious on the floor and the child beside her was dead. Both had been struck down by Asiatic cholera. She opened her eyes and said: 'Oh! have you come, Rishida? Oh! bring back my child alive to me. He has been dead for quite some time.' She was half mad with grief.

I said to her: 'No use grieving. Perhaps you will forget him and again bear a child. But if you are true to your love, then cherish his memory. Just make him your Guru and do conquer all this grief.' She listened to me, and from then on, the dead child became her little Gopal.[4] At last I went softly away from her house.

Now she is a school-mistress in a Mofussil town. Her treasure is hidden in a small box; it is an image of Gopal. And she has said to me: 'This is my little child who came back to me and I see him in so many faces around me no matter whether they are boys or girls.' So her grief was turned into an expansion of love.

Can you bring people to that stage, to pure love, to the inner center of the heart? Love illumines the heart, and above the heart there is another center located between the eyebrows from where all commands come; it is pure wisdom. If you concentrate there you first get a luminosity which is like a scorching ray which burns everything and burns all dirt out of you and makes you as pure as light.

So this is the way to find the center of the heart and to go higher to pure wisdom. From this to that, and from that to this, such is the movement of śhakti. When you go still further, you find a complete circle with its circumference nowhere. And that is the power of Brahma, or God, whatever you like to call it. You are searching for something which apparently doesn't exist, but really that alone exists. You turn your back on it and so you are harsh, cruel, selfish and greedy. You run after things like a beggar when you should sit like an emperor on your throne and let things come to you. Why should you care? From this comes the strange fact that in India a sādhu, who is a wandering monk following a strict discipline, is given a kingly title of Maharaj!

The possibility of living in that way is not for everyone. But anyone who has but a grain of faith can make a good beginning, and that faith will grow and bring him to wisdom and Truth.

If that grain of faith is faith in the Truth from which the whole universe springs, then it is sure to grow from a seed to a flower, because such is the Law. We are just beginning to understand what Truth is, and we are still groping in darkness. But if you go on insisting that *That* does not exist, what can I say? Only this: 'I have faith in you and I know that you too are not without it.' Faith is a very great thing. It is seeded in man and will one day move mountains. I can only wait.

Faith grows from your own obedience, from your own discovery. It sits quietly near you and doesn't say anything; it simply touches you. And you will forget it and whine; then you have faith in your not having faith! It appears as a constant nullity which comes again and again. But faith is very patient. It just waits and gives you a little push! This faith is life and knowledge. They are very near to one another: knowledge must be living and life must be knowing. One cannot separate the two.

And you can learn this by a very simple experience of making your mind a blank. Let it remain a blank for a time. Try to feel what blankness is like. When you face blankness and enter into it, your whole body becomes numb. Then you suddenly discover that you are nothing but so many pounds of flesh lying there, with no feeling anywhere. Everything is numb. But there, suddenly in the head, there is a light; this light grows and you feel a pain. Phew!—an acute pain! It pierces your body. A minute later, it disappears and you are quiet again. What is all this?

Was it only a possibility of sensation, in any part of the body, at any time? But through this very possibility, we come to know that a light is dormant in everybody and can suddenly awaken. Because it is so very close to us, it is important to 'remember'—as the mystics say. By this they mean not the memory of events but the memory of the eternal Truth. Then you will understand how a tiny seed expands. This is life.

If you put a pebble here on the soil, it does not expand. If you bring another pebble and still another one, the process continues and will gradually form a heap of pebbles. This will not change by itself and will remain the same for millions of years. Whereas if you put a grain of barley in moist soil, it immediately begins to suck up the moisture and swells. This is life!

But in man, a three-dimensional action starts on account of his awareness. It is this three-dimensional existence that he can learn to discover. From the outside nothing is noticeable. First there is the unconscious or sleep state, the dream state and the waking state.

From the third state, one can reach the fourth one; then the totality of states one, two, three and four means pure Existence (sat). The fifth will be a fullness, a wholeness. Where is the proof? Well, just see, you will find the proof in your own self. The Law of expansion immediately begins to work: the whole becomes like a globe and in it there is an infinite stretch of space dotted with points of light. You can count them by millions and millions. And when it grows so big that you cannot swallow it, then it bursts!

9

People are very loath and unwilling to analyze themselves; perhaps in the subconscious they have a fear that bad things will come out of it,—just as, in writing an autobiography, one is full of self-praise and won't speak of the ills that are deeply hidden. People are never honest in their diaries, but they are honest in the mosaic pattern they are composing!

Self-analysis is most important. I might say that three-fourths of Samkhya is self-analyzing. It is said: 'Always go on analyzing bits of your life.'

Of course self-analysis discloses the idea of having caused or done some wrongs—but speaking from the standpoint of Samkhya, it also means: 'I am aloof, I am analyzing myself without any judgement.' That is a very great ideal which we have to reach. And I try to explain this to those who come to me. I say: 'Look into yourself; there, deep in you, something gives you a blow. It is like a flash of light. Let it look at all the impure things which are hidden, but don't nourish them! If you have to kill them, kill them mercilessly! Don't pamper yourself!'

But I find it very hard.

Why do people pamper their own self? Here Samkhya gives a very clear answer. It is because there is a sort of 'I-ness' in them, with a white-washed ego which should no more be recognized! That 'I-ness' clad with self-pride says: 'Yes, yes, I know. …' And that ruins you!

True, when one day, in a state of inner realization, you reach the Purusha and look at yourself from there, you don't see whether you are good or whether you are bad, because no duality appears. It is only when you step down into your own being that prakriti and duality reappear.

In manifestation, one breaks into two in the realm of contradictions. But if prakriti wafts you back into the Purusha, a word can express that state, described in Sanskrit accordingly as: 'bi-unity', two being one.

10

God or 'the Word,' as the Gospel says, becomes flesh. The Vedas say: 'The Word is but a vibration in the Void.' So the Creation starts from the word: *Aum*.

You blow a conch shell, you beat a drum. Have you ever seen a snake-charmer? He holds a small revolving drum, giving two very quick beats: creation—destruction! And so long as it continues the snake dances!

Most people feel these two beats in themselves. One this way, one that way; one positive, one negative. 'How can we bring them together?' they will ask. Only a few may have heard that two beats, like two strings, can vibrate faster and faster, until finally there is only one humming!

Think also of the two dolphins always sporting together! They come together, sport and play, faster and faster. Then they melt away and there is nothing more!

There also, we can say that Purusha and Prakriti clasp each other in a tight embrace and disappear in sleep. In the depths of sleep what are Purusha and Prakriti? The Void contains both of them: This and That.

Around any word, deed, work, imagery, feeling, there is always an oscillation which makes you undecided about what to do, what to think. We doubt. Am I to go this way? But at the same time I wish to go that way. This oscillation is in the very nature of prakriti; we cannot avoid it. It is the play of Creation!

All that constant going and coming remains within you as the source from which you speak. You will find out, by and by, that you are always seeing new things, saying new things, that you are never repeating anything. But at the same time, it is always the same thing that you are speaking of but in so many different ways! Such is the mystery of Creation.

There is a simile written in Sanskrit which says: 'I have a Truth, just like a plum in the palm of my hand. Do you want a taste of it? Here, I give you a bite! A tiny bit of knowledge has as tremendous a power as a tiny drop of venom.'

What power is it? The power of Truth!

11

Yes, yoga is union, the union of the individual with the universal. It is the universal containing the individual. Likewise, a spark has a center from which it originates but it cannot contain itself within itself. It simply expands, this way and that way, in every direction—until it becomes a globe. Then polarity exists: a dark globe and a white globe existing together, intermingling, held one within the other by the same axis.

When we are successful, we are also bound to have some suffering and when we are suffering, we are also bound to enjoy some success. But gradually these impressions become very thin, and finally they melt. So one can say: nothing really exists, which also means everything exists.

At the beginning of the search, we revolt against that process, but as long as we revolt we cannot feel anything. What is it that rebels? Only the material being, the life force, the mental force, the mental constructions, all that we have been taught to think from our childhood. Nobody is let alone to grow like a tree. It is as if one tree said to another tree: 'Grow just like me!'

When this period of revolt subsides, then you understand that there is but *one* existence. There is one God, one matter, one Purusha, one Prakriti, but it takes a long time to discover these dimensions.

We must be very alert, constantly watching the tiniest movement within ourselves. The way to go is very long, but suddenly everything becomes so unimaginably quick within us that one cannot even believe it. Nothing escapes you. There is great compensation for all the trouble you have taken!

Here we have a mathematical problem to consider. In the wholeness of pure Existence, which appears to us like a globe dotted with millions of sparks of light, one here, one there, another here and further on—how many can you count? You don't know. But immediately when you become very fine—one spark among them—you feel a kinship with the others and a tremendous energy-power within you. Then all things around you evaporate into pure light and there is only one will, God's will: 'Let there be light, and there was light.'

When the supreme knowledge has been perceived, there is the wish to go on, but at the same time you see absolutely no difference between going on or coming back. The same organism is to be found here and there, always propelling towards the Cosmos. When you come back to people who understand nothing, you are gentle with them and you bear with them. I have often seen that it takes thirty years to reach a soul! Many devotees have a kind of fascination, come again and again, only to go away and come again, and not understand. Then one day, suddenly, they say: 'Oh! now I know!' And after that they disappear because their quest is finished!

Our common pilgrimage toward the beyond is endless. The Void, being the cradle of birth and death, in itself means creation. It includes complete fullness and, at the same time, total solitude. It is freedom in the true sense of the word! You are free to live, free to die, free to experience pain and pleasure. All things come to you as to a child. You are taken to a wonderland where things are shown to you.

It is like an alternating rhythm with a definite strata continually moving, continually living, in which death is freedom. The pilgrimage toward the inner being binds us to speak about death or to have it constantly in the background of our thoughts.

12

Jagannath in Puri is made of neemwood. The log of wood from which the first images were made came floating on the ocean. The priests got hold of the log and turned it into the images which are worshipped in the big Temple of Puri. They are hideous. Every twelve years, they must be renewed and the old ones burned.

Just before the end of the prescribed time, the priests and the carpenters are busy reconstructing the new images behind the main altar, hidden from the public eye. When the day of installation comes, the head priest has his eyes blindfolded seven times, according to a sacred measure from the Vedas, and is ushered into the dark room where the main image of Jagannath, which is black, representing the Void, Vishnu and the sky is kept.

In its center, there is a closed, hidden cavity. The priest opens its small door and withdraws something from it. Nobody knows what it is, not even himself. He does not see it. He only feels it. He must not speak about it. This 'something' is Brahma-the-Creator turned into something palpable called *brahmavastu*. It is said that the priest who transfers the brahmavastu, the secret heart of the old statue, into the new one must die within three years from that very day. He is generally very old, no longer in charge of the Temple. He lives in retirement, waiting patiently for his end. The newly elected priest is doomed to the same functions, as well as to die within the prescribed time. It has always been so and continues to be so.

Outside, there is a great gathering because it is the day of the 'new incarnation of the Lord,' which will not recur for the next twelve years. Twelve is the number which represents the sun, its course and the whole pattern of the universe. In Vedic times, the year was the unit of time, the seasons of life following the track of twelve months, as well as plants, flowers and fruits.

The Temple of Puri is open to all except to foreigners. There is no distinction of castes. On one special day in the year, very primitive people who live in the heart of the Orissa forests come to the Temple. They call to the god: 'Jagannath, thou art our friend, our kinsman.' They become mad, exuberant, embrace the image. The priests say: 'Well, we got "This" from you primitive people!'

When you go to Jagannath, you are always prepared to make a vow, to sacrifice something dear to the god, something that you love best of what you are accustomed to eat. You have a last taste of it, then you offer it to the god. After that, back home, it should never be eaten again.

Food is sacrificed because food is life. One needs one's daily food. At the same time, it is a close and constant reminder of one's dedication to the god.

13

The Golden Rule is: minimize your activity, dive deep within yourself; then when you are firmly established in that steadiness, start working. Your work will then be like a flowering of what comes from your depth.

All around there are things, but the values we put on them are simply fictitious. What is valuable for you is not valuable for me. Let the young have their own way. But you—you remain free. But don't show that you are free. People might kill you. They would crucify you, like they did Christ.

The people who come to you, are they free? No; and do they wish to be free? If you give them freedom, they will not understand it. You have to wait for a long time. But certainly, the awakening will some day come from within.

Gods and goddesses are the bond between religion and art. They are specimens of art, expressions in freedom but at the same time submitted to many rules dictated by tradition.

Tagore, who was a Brahmo,[5] could not bow to any image, but he wrote many hymns and created many forms of worship. In his School of Art at Shantiniketan, there was a festival of the earth, trees, water, seasons, a real worship of prakriti in a primitive way, with music, dances and acting. If you come to such primitiveness, you get Truth, because Truth is naked.

So it is a naked stone which represents Shiva, the best representation of all! Jagannath in Puri is the second best because he is hideous and only an idea. So you are not tied to a beautiful thing. It is just an aspect of Truth. In itself, Truth is neither ugly nor beautiful; it is simply what it is. In that way, throwing away all things, you come to the Void, to the nudity without form. You reach Truth and then laugh or smile, you laugh when alone and you smile with others. They won't understand you, but you understand them quite well and love them.

14

Well, I am recognized by the laymen, but very much less by the paṇḍits.[6] Freedom is a word that troubles them. They simply won't understand. They frown upon the idea of freedom. They say: 'What you express is not written in the books. Tell us what you stand for? If you are a teacher, if you have received a doctor's degree from the University, then what is it for?' Others ask: 'According to what are you teaching?'

I am teaching according to Truth!

Yes, I am teaching according to what I feel, and I find the same attitude expressed in some very ancient texts. The old teachers were quite free.

Lately, I was revising Patanjali without referring to the well known *Commentaries*. I took the *Aphorisms* one by one, and meditated upon each one. This very day, I made a strange discovery. I discovered that I have always felt as I feel now, but I did not see it because the commentators stood like a wall in front of me. I could not get past them. Only this morning I found a peculiar sutra echoing this: 'if the Purusha and Prakriti are both crystal pure, this is solitude and freedom or living alone.' What is that but a spiritual existence in which Purusha and Prakriti are one?

There Purusha is taken as an ideal eternally pure, and prakriti, as the power of Purusha, is bound to come down into matter to create. When this is done, she goes up again. In coming down she creates out of herself a darkness, the matrix in which every possibility takes the form of a seed. When the seed sprouts, a tiny plant will grow into a tree which, in sacred texts, is called 'the tree of Brahma.' In other parts of the world, the same tree is called 'the tree of life.' In India, the tree of Brahma is pictured as the *aśvattha* tree (banyan), which grows upside down with fine roots going up into the sky and heavy roots plunging down into the earth. That tree is partly in the sky and partly in the earth. That's life!

Teaching according to Truth is sometimes disturbing people in their thoughts. Well, I will tell you a story about Śri Ramakrishna. You know that the idea of rebirth is basic in Hinduism, Buddhism and Jainism. Everyone speaks of rebirth. Now somebody asked Śri Ramakrishna, while he was the guest in a friend's house: 'What is your opinion about rebirth?'

> *'I don't know,' he answered. 'Since the ṛṣis have spoken about it, it might be true.'*
>
> *'Then you don't believe in it?'*
>
> *'I don't know.'*
>
> *'Well, men will have a poor opinion of you if you do not believe in rebirth.' Then Śri Ramakrishna flared up: 'What do I care for publicity? I only speak of what I know.'*

The same question was put to Ma Anandamayee. She answered: 'It is there if you believe in it. It is not there if you don't believe in it.'

Such freedom is not bound to any dogma. Do the followers of Śri Ramakrishna, of Ma Anandamayee realize such freedom? No, they don't look up to their Master but down at their books. The books are no doubt of great help because they have been written by very great people. But whenever you speak, you spoil the thought; whenever you think, you spoil the intuition; whenever you try to be intuitive, you kill your perception.

So remain nude in the Void. Then things will come to you.

At one *Kumbha Mela*,[7] a saint was crying and praying aloud the whole day: 'Oh Father, let us all become your children!' What a great prayer! Really we are all children of light and love—but we quarrel and fight, and yet that great prayer is Christian, Hindu, Buddhist, Jain, Moslem at heart.

We discover things little by little.

And my present philosophy is that there is never an end to the quest. It is always an exploration and when I am at the end of what I thought it is not the end at all! I see a light ahead in the beyond! You come then to the theory of expansion into the universe.

Never say that there is an end. Go, go on! If you say: 'There is an end,' you become self-satisfied. Don't let yourself be closed in by churches and dogmas. Even meditation can create a dogma of its own.

One day Sŕi Ramakrishna gave a fine demonstration to 'M.'[8] of how he was breaking dogmas. They were both seated with eyes closed meditating, 'M.' on the floor, Sŕi Ramakrishna on his bed with the mosquito net down. After a few minutes, Sŕi Ramakrishna came out from behind the net and said: 'Well, I didn't like that way of meditating. Can I see God only in this way and not in another way, first closing and then opening my eyes?'

Some years ago, I heard Sŕi Aurobindo say: 'I never close my eyes in meditation.' Then I thought: 'This is another dogma. Why not meditate with closed eyes as well as with open eyes?'

All bondages, whatever they are, imprison our real nature. Then I remembered the story of a sage, Ashtavakra, who was 'bent in eight parts of his limbs.' He was a cripple. He became a cripple while he was in his mother's womb. One day his father was reciting the Vedas before his wife. The unborn child said: 'Father, you are not reciting quite correctly.' Well, the father took it very much to heart and said: 'You fool, even before being born, you come to teach me! Remain as crooked as you are now in your mother's womb!' The child was born that way, but he became a great saint. And he taught: 'This is your bondage that you are trying to get a samādhi! Wherever your mind goes there is samādhi for you.'

Well, there is samādhi thus and so, there is samādhi lying, there is samādhi sitting, there is samādhi standing, there is samādhi working. Then I understood why the Bhagavad Gita speaks of a steady wisdom. There can be a samādhi when speaking, roaming about, and doing things, as well as remaining quite. One can move, live and have one's own being in God. Such samādhi is an active contemplation.

When I got back to my ashram years ago, after I had finished my university courses, something strange came upon me and stayed with me for three days and three nights. I was as if dreaming, a 'dream-thing.' One of the elders saw that strangeness in my eyes and reported it to the Guru. He looked intently at me and said: 'You are not yourself.'

'I don't know.'

He said to somebody: 'Well, he has come back from his studies, but I think that he will be escaping me, he has such a look and moves about as if in a dream. What use shall I have of him?'

I heard about it and thought: 'Well, he does not understand me.' The same night I went to him and asked him: 'If I trust you, shall I be saved? Can you guarantee that?'

He spoke very softly to me: 'Well, my boy, as you have dedicated everything to me, so I dedicate everything to you, this ashram, this whole institution!'

Of course I melted before those words. I said: 'I shall never betray you, but I tell you that the moment I am told to do things which are not in our dedication, I won't remain in your ashram.' Twelve years passed. I loved him. He loved me but finally I was simply flooded within myself by many things that I could not follow. My Guru was trapped on all sides. He knew it. The prakriti was running down. One day, he said to me: 'I know your mind. You are working hard for me but you wish to be free.'

He blessed me and said: 'I give you full freedom. I know that you are not going to bow down to anyone. I make you free.'

But disciples who don't want to be free and they are many, what about them?

That sādhu you have met here in Calcutta, with a white beard, is now at the head of the whole ashram with its many branches in every district of Bengal. He is trapped too and suffers from his entanglement. He is reigning but not ruling any more. So, of the thousand people around him there are perhaps only a few souls who are free. Does he recognize them?

15

A question is often asked: 'Can we go beyond the veil which hides the face of Truth?' Yes, we can. But what allows us to come back remains secret.

There is a secret light, a secret music, and a secret touch, vision, audition, and a tactile sensation which resounds and vibrates. But one must be very well trained to become aware of it, otherwise it is just an outside impression. A long discipline is required to become finer and lighter, in order to be more and more sensitive to oneself. What I call eating, seeing, hearing, thinking, are all experiences that should be carefully watched. It should be done through your awareness. But so many texts, opinions and quarrels, have been piled upon this fact that it has hidden itself.

If you are daring enough to look at what is now you will discover that time means nothing. At this very moment you can leap across infinite stretches. Carry on! The long preparation gone through will bring you to a state of communion between spirit and matter, a wonderful idea which is behind the idea of consecrated food (*prasāda*) shared between God and the devotee. It will bring you to the words of Christ offering his flesh and his blood and saying, 'This is the bread you are eating, and this is the wine you are drinking. You are eating my body.'

To bring the secret back to light you must first of all realize, deep within yourself, that nobody is going to help you. You alone can make the pilgrimage towards the inner being. You must feel that you are blessed to have been chosen to do it. You walk alone and nobody will look at you. The *Katha Upanishad* says so.

We can help others just a little, in a very indirect way, by expressing such things as: don't do that, don't hurt others, don't steal, don't tell a lie. So just be conscious of that and become more and more sensitive about it. It makes the teacher very humble. All the work on self-observation is only to become sensitive, nothing else.

16

There is a kind of chemical process going on within us, without our knowing it, when our mind meets a new facet of knowledge. We think: 'I havc grasped the subject.'

Yet it creates a state of confusion in your mind when you discover that you cannot express it. It lies dormant for a long time within you, then suddenly you stumble on it and a new world opens up for you; though you are in the same darkness on other planes. For a second, it is like the face of God eluding you! You run after it. You can't catch hold of it. You get intoxicated. Then it is your turn to play hide and seek with God. It is like different colors blending and reflecting one another and forming something which passes all understanding and surpasses feeling. Yet it is there.

As for that, there is a good story. When Chaitanya traveled South, he discovered a book written several centuries earlier which recounted the life of a saint whose name was Vilwamangala.

The story runs something like this:

In his youth, he had loved a prostitute so much that when he was called to his father's funeral ceremony, he said to the priest: 'Come on, finish your job as quickly as you can; I have an engagement elsewhere!'

Hearing that, the people around him said: 'What a mad fellow, what a fool!' As soon as the ceremony ended, he rushed away and ran as far as the shore of the river he had to cross. It was a stormy night and the waves were running high. There was no ferry-man, no boat, nothing. Suddenly he saw something floating on the water. He clasped it and paddling with his feet swam across the river. Again he ran and ran until he reached the prostitute's house. There he saw a rope hanging from her balcony. He grasped it and climbed up and reached her room through the window.

'How is this,' said the woman quite surprised, 'You at this unearthly hour! What brought you here?'

'But you called me,' he said.

'Did I call you? How did you cross the river? It must be

swollen by now.'

'Yes, but there was a boat.'

She exclaimed: 'But you stink horribly. What have you done?' There were worms and maggots all over him.

He said pathetically: 'Well, I suppose the boat must have been a corpse in the river.'

'Go away, go away,' shouted the woman.

'No, I will not,' said the man, 'because you called me. You even dropped a rope for me from your balcony.

'Did I indeed? Let me see!'

They both went outside and saw not a rope hanging from the balcony but a dead snake, with its head stuck in a hole. It must have struggled hard to free itself but once its head was caught, it could not slip back. So the dead serpent had been taken for a rope!

The woman was crying. 'You are mad,' she said, 'a fool to run after a prostitute like me! With such tremendous love within you, you could have found Krishna in your heart in a moment!'

The man was shaken. 'Is it so,' he said, 'is it true?' Suddenly his eyes opened. He prostrated himself before the woman and said: 'Well, you are my Guru! You have shown me the light! I have been blind for so many years ...' and he turned away.

He really became mad, running after Krishna: 'Where is Krishna? Where is my Krishna?' For days and days, he ate next to nothing; he kept running about, pining for Krishna. Then, one day, he met a young cowherd boy of dark blue complexion who milked a cupful of milk for him.

'Where have you come from?' asked the man. 'Don't disturb me. I am searching for Krishna. I am living with Krishna in my heart.'

'But you called me, ' said the boy, 'so I came. You should drink this milk, it is for you.'

The man could not resist. He drank the milk. The boy appeared again the next day, giving him more milk, and so it went on for several days. Then suddenly it occurred to the man: 'But I am getting attached to this boy! I don't think of Krishna any more, I am constantly thinking: Will that boy come again? What am I doing?'

So he said to the boy: 'Don't come back again to me!' But the boy said: 'I must come! You have called me. Promise me not to go mad again. Live, come to grips once more with life.'

'I can't do that,' said the man. 'I must know Krishna!'

'Then why do you run after me?' asked the boy.

Somehow the man was fascinated. He said: 'Come here! Let me touch you!' And suddenly he grabbed hold of the boy from behind: 'I love you,' he said, 'You are my Krishna! You can't deceive me. You are in my heart! What can I do?'

'Let me go!' said the boy.

'I have got hold of you, I will not let you go. Can you escape from my heart?'

'Yes, I am Krishna,' said the boy revealing himself. 'I can't go from your heart, neither can you from mine! We are forever together. I am now your slave!'

Sometimes it is difficult to reach God! At the end everything becomes simple as love dawns in the heart. But then love must be without attachment. It is a reciprocal self-giving. You give to the Lord and the Lord gives to you. Through love you find the way you could not find through knowledge.

17

Our 'freedom' lies in having accepted the fact that everything is recorded somewhere and that the *present* we are living now is a kind of luminous vigilance which connects our inward life to our outer life with a feeling, which is coming from above. But it is also a feeling deeply rooted in us. It is not that I don't know anything about it: I know that although on the one hand I am free, on the other hand, I am bound by everything. And when I express it in words, it adds up to a flat contradiction!

Inwardly it is not so. I view the *same* existence through different moods. For instance, imagine that you are looking at a table. A table has usually four legs, but if you look at it from a certain angle, it appears to have only three legs. If you stand above it, it appears to have no legs at all! All these differences are only due to our shortsightedness. At a glance we cannot see the whole of existence! For we either taste mystery, mysticism, fulfillment or else despair, fear and hate. Life is shrewd in every way!

It remains our privilege to be able to transcend all things. Such transcendence does not mean negation; it means accepting all things as they are but not caring about them, not being attached to them. Then, another dimension is reached. That dimension is pure joy. It is bliss like the smile of a child. How do you explain a child's smile? It expresses the Ānanda-Brahma which is deep within you. A child can be very naughty; one moment he smiles, the next moment he makes an ugly face! In such a moment you experience life as it is!

At the close of your life, after a full existence of suffering with happy and sad days—you feel at the end that it all comes to nothing. Who am I to face God? What is it all about? Just enter into your own self and everything goes back into order!

One day I was holding a glass ball in my hand. Suddenly, I don't know why, I threw it on to a stone. It broke into many parts. I picked up two parts and saw that they fitted quite well; then I hunted for the other parts. They also fitted. 'Strange,' I thought, 'if I put these parts together, they become a perfect globe, otherwise they will be lying scattered!' This has been a great teaching in my whole life. I thought: 'I shall accept everything as parts of a whole. I shall not make them fit together according to my plan, but allow them to fit together. That might have to do with a child, with a woman, with a flower, or even a god incarnate.' Then I felt a great peace within myself. I could forgive others.

Now you might ask: 'What was that great force which made you throw the ball against a stone?' I don't know. Within myself there was a sort of dialogue going on. The ball was asking: 'Are you going to crush me into pieces? Are you then going to bring all the broken pieces together? You are very extravagant!' I was thinking: 'Am I really extravagant? Well, why not greet everybody and whatever happens with a smile? It is worth trying!'

There are some Hindi verses[9] which the sages have been repeating for a long time:

Take joy in everybody,
sit with everybody,
take the name of everybody.
Whatever is heard,
said or done,
keep to your task,
don't move an inch from it.

I well know that people are not equal to that task. They will not go the whole way with me. They get quickly tired—after two hours, two days or two years—because they don't belong to infinity. Infinity is freedom. Because I am free I can toil. But don't let them see it. They would not understand anyway.

But I am afraid that freedom cannot be reached in one lifetime. It is a long task. As you pass on, vista after vista rises before you; then in all humility you drop on your knees and say: 'I surrender, I surrender!'

There is no end before you. I can't help you more than I do. Yes, sometimes you come to me and offer me some sweet candy. I can suck it. I have pleasure in it, but that is all! Whereas death is without end, and after death, it is again without end. So from death on, a new dimension starts.

Very true! I see it like this: I have been coming up to a certain point which is nearing death. Then I see that whatever I have been doing is just like a big rehearsal. What was at the extreme bottom comes now to the top and what was at the top is now coming down. And the meeting point is the 'I.' I am the meeting point.

And that 'I', if you are speaking of death, goes down and melts into the ocean like pure water into the waves. But again this pure water is changed into vapor and rises in the form of clouds, to return like rain to the ocean. Similarly, every day before our eyes, the sun is going up and going down. The worshippers of the sun are fully identified with it. They say: 'Like the sun, I shall disappear; like the sun I shall come again, but *not the same*!'

That brings us to the revolving movements of the sun: solstice, equinox and so on. You can feel that beautiful spiral movement deep within you. Within that process, I am quiet and calm. I know I have had my share of life, with enjoyments and difficulties and that's all. Life is all in parts, but there are so many 'I's': I am this man, this woman, that flower—all these things I am! Here is a rogue, a saint, and there an incarnation of a god! So many 'I's' all around, this way, that way! Well, it means self-multiplying. When God said: 'Go, and multiply yourself,' He uttered a great creative Truth.

We are trying to multiply others and to multiply ourselves. Why do I preach? Because I want to multiply. Why do I speak? Because my dogma is 'the only Truth,' not yours! So everything becomes a hotch-potch and that is why we have such a load of news every morning in the newspapers!

18

From whence does it come that I can suddenly grasp what goes on within myself? It is a mystery.

It might be an entirely new element coming from some other plane unknown to me. Nobody can help me in this. Nobody knows anything about it! Therefore I am struck down. Our thinking always clings to something that we know, even if we feel we should be ready to meet the unknown. But it eludes me. I don't know what it is.

During a moment of concentration, all that I have accumulated drops away: book knowledge, teachings of the different schools and Masters I have met. Only what I am at that very moment exists: I am facing a naked Truth.

Here in a flash, is the difference between knowledge and Truth. It catches you up, says the *Kena Upanishad*, with a sublime feeling. It is the instant when the son of man becomes the Son of God.

But the mystery remains between the known and the unknown. Don't try to compel the unknown to translate itself into the known. It would only mean a repetition of what has already been. It would mean no progress.

In speaking of eternity, I have already told you about the linear movement going up and coming down and about the circular movement, like that of two dolphins, turning around each other. The two movements are on the same level of consciousness. How can they become only one spiral movement, like the one we see on a conch shell? When the mud on the potter's wheel revolves on a spindle, that is, when the potter has placed a stick on the center of the wheel, then the mud rises. And the potter has only to shape the mud to make a pitcher out of it.

Similarly śhakti in itself is the power that climbs up toward the Absolute. At the same time, it is also the spindle around which the inner movement of our search and the mechanical circular movement of our life, are moved. It is a mystic realization.

But be very careful! You should not keep on moving in a circle! See to it that the thread of your inner movement, like a screw, comes closer and closer and, finally, like a rocket, shoots beyond! Here Patanjali comes to our aid in speaking of the three different movements along the way of our search: 'Have a resolute will to withdraw from the mechanical movements of your life; allow no compromise with anything or with any dogma; break progressively away toward inner withdrawal. But be very patient.'

19

Everyone in his own way tries to understand the other, but it rarely happens! This is quite natural because there is such a variety of human beings. It makes you want to smile at them all as at so many children around you. You can love them all!

As they grow, they all want you to fit in with their wishes, to be like this or like that, just as I, myself, am wishing them to be like me! This is because God created man in His own image! That is God's labour! He can only create in His own image, wishing everyone to become God.

The very word 'God' includes complete freedom. God is free. His creation is a free act. God has not been compelled to create. This creation is a play of power unfolding itself in a natural way, just as the tree produces fruit.

Many come forward but only a few are really seeking, eager to know what power is. Although everyone is made in the image of God, the time is not ripe for everyone. One is perhaps only a small child within himself, another is a boy, another a grown-up man, another a god! Time is very important. You will find this mentioned repeatedly in the *Bhagavatam*, where it is said: 'The first creative impulse must be translated into time.' A beautiful image expresses it further: 'Time when flowing is called Kala,' meaning a succession of things. Yes, new things are constantly added to old things. But we don't want old things any more! We want only new things! Rabindranath Tagore once said, with a smile, 'Well, let us say that they are new, but it is only the old things coming again and again, and you think they are new! They are the oldest things returning.'

That is time: a constant succession, looked upon as changes, flowing into infinity; then all changes are simply absorbed into the Void, which is also called the Great Kala.

How does time flow into space? There is a moment when time and space become one because they are the same thing on two different levels. In a flash, time becomes space. But the constant coming out, going in, coming in, going out, is time.

When we have an intuition of what is beyond it starts with time; this intuition must be translated into pure space. It is Einstein who said that time and space are one. He used a single word 'time-space.' This means that we are in fact thinking in terms of space.

This particular house, a finished product, occupies a definite space, but how long did it take to be built up and to grow? This is where time comes in. As it is being built it passes through many processes.

What is a process? It is a succession of movements. It is a reality, but what is this reality? Is it one or many things together? Well, when we look at a tree, we see one thing, but at the same time we see the trunk, the branches, the leaves, the veins in the leaves and so on. It is the same with a house when it is built up. It is one and also many things together.

Here the philosophy of the Void comes in and says: 'Such is the Void that is beyond your understanding! You see the development of the movement and at the same time go beyond that!' This is mysticism and love. Suppose two loving people are embracing each other. In this tiniest moment, the whole universe varrishes. They feel eternity. This moment contains the eternity which is space—this eternity is either a linear movement going up, coming down, or a circular movement like that of the two dolphins turning around each other.

In our age of technology, we are concerned only with movements and the succession of movements. We have gone to the moon, we are trying to reach far away planets, one day we shall go to the sun! But in a single moment of consciousness, we can have the whole universe within us. What do you say to that? The universe is only a point of space that contains eternity. Here space and time are combined; space is consciousness, Shiva, while time is a succession of movements, śhakti. We can say that India stands for Shiva, with closed eyes, and the West for śhakti, with so many things going on. They are not two different existences, but two facets of the same power. There is an image of śhakti given in the Tantras showing Kali[10], the goddess of time, crushing the whole universe into a pulp and swallowing it. It goes into her belly, which becomes a great power with millions of regrets. Remember always that Kali is time!

Think of the tremendous śhakti you have within you. But it must be without any trace of ego. Look at a cupful of milk. The milk is homogeneous throughout. In scientific terms it would be called the colloidal state. Your power likewise must be pure and homogeneous.

If you put citric acid into milk, it breaks up into millions of tiny little particles. It has been changed into the crystalloid state. If there are traces of ego in your self, millions of dots of ego are likewise going to spread all over. What was one whole gets broken into tiny little particles—although these colloidal and crystalloid states are basically the same milk.

If you have the whole universe within you, you are the pure power of śhakti. If you see the whole universe covered with so many dots, with so many particles—which are the ego—the power of śhakti becomes the three thousand millions of Hindu gods and all the Gurus of India!

Now, let us see what the ṛṣis say in the *Atharvaveda*[11]. 'Look at all these people on earth. They are all Shiva walking on earth!' Similarly I would say: 'Every Christian walking on earth is Christ, every Mahommedan, the Prophet'—even if I am stabbed for uttering such a blasphemy! I also say: 'Everybody on earth is Brahma walking on two legs!' Nowadays in the villages, peasants will say, pointing to one of them: 'Look at this little Brahma! Look at him, he is really trapped! He has set his foot on the trap of the five elements, and now, look, he is wailing!' Maybe it is only humor, perhaps rather cruel!

20

The notion of space is always difficult to grasp. It leads us to life and also to death. I learned this when I was quite young. My father and my mother would rise very early in the morning, take their baths and sit side by side before a picture of their Guru who, later on, became also my Guru. And they would meditate for a long time. We had a small house; when the curtain was drawn back, I would stare at them from my bed. They sat motionless, so still! That stillness made me full of awe. And I thought: 'There must be something in that stillness.' So, after a while, I began to imitate them and I felt: 'Oh! so this is what they have!' It was Life connected with the life all around me.

And there is another thing related to death, which also came very naturally to me when I was a boy of ten. A few of my school friends and I used to go and bathe in the river. The river was dry in the summer. There was only a thin stream with a strong undercurrent, which people avoided when they crossed it. One day, when we were playing there, splashing in the water, I suddenly saw a whirlpool and heard the boys shouting: 'Come back, come back!' As I was swiftly carried downstream, I said to myself: 'How is this? I was with them and now I am going away from them.'

Suddenly, I remembered that there was an undercurrent somewhere, and I felt that I was caught in it. Then, where was I drifting to? Toward what? I had read in books that all rivers run into the sea. 'So, I am going to the sea.' I thought: 'And what is waiting for me there? Nothing but water. So this is death approaching. Yes, death.' I closed my eyes and thought: 'I will float on.'

I very often use these words: 'Float on'—when speaking with people. That was my first feeling of consciously floating on: 'I float on, I float on.' With closed eyes, I saw nothing. Suddenly, my head bumped against something. I had simply crossed the current and come to the opposite shore. My head had struck the steps that came down into the river. I let down my legs and felt ground under my feet. . . . 'Well, that was death and this is life!'

I told no one about what had taken place, but it surely gave me an inner illumination and a sort of security. I thought: 'Everywhere and in everything, I shall be floating on, and one day I shall come to the vast ocean.' This is the whole of life, and from this you come to understand the words written in the Scriptures: 'I am Shiva! I have conquered death. . . .'

When, later on, I heard these words uttered by worshippers of Shiva, what did they convey to me? First, a feeling and knowledge of the infinite. You have to bind the two together. Everywhere you will see that first the bud appears and then the fruit. But in the case of gourds and pumpkins, you will see that the fruit appears first, a tiny fruit and then the flower opens on its top. If God's feeling comes to you first, then His aura of knowledge is a splash of wisdom! Do you then still want books?

Who chose it to be that way? The free will of God. Why the bud first and then the fruit? Why not the fruit first and then the flower? I plucked a tiny pumpkin and dissected it with a knife. I found very tiny seeds nestling inside it, preparing for future plants. And so it goes on and on. Life runs smoothly in its own fashion. The mind alone wants to know more, and still more, of the things which separate what feeling is from what knowledge is. Let the mind rest a while. Let it sleep and quiet itself, otherwise there is no chance of consciousness. People will learn this by and by and consciously experiment with life. No hurry and no worry. It should just be like the coming to bloom of a flower.

21

The notion of matter and anti-matter is also a difficult concept to grasp though it refers to space. Formerly we knew of electrons with a negative charge, protons with a positive charge, and neutrons with no charge at all, as the constituents of an atom, which is the ultimate particle of matter as commonly understood. Now we hear about a host of mystery particles called anti-electrons, anti-protons, anti-neutrons, mesons, etc., whose existence has been proved experimentally. These mystery particles are the basis of the concept of anti-matter.

The interesting thing about the concept of anti-matter is that it destroys the commonly accepted idea of 'empty space.' It was found that apart from the ordinary electrons which rotate around the atomic nucleus, there is an incalculable number of 'extraordinary' electrons distributed throughout the so-called empty space, which for long escaped detection by any experimental observation. The empty space really is an ocean packed to capacity with extraordinary electrons, only a few of which come out in an overflow from this ocean.

This ocean surrounds us on all sides and extends to infinity in all directions. This is the ocean of anti-matter composed of electrons with a negative mass. These are formed not out of nothing, but at the expense of the energy spent in their formation, according to Einstein's laws of equivalence of mass and energy.

So, in the final analysis, the notion of mass disappears and we are left with the conclusion that matter, as well as anti-matter, is after all nothing but energy. But since we are conscious beings observing these things, there must be three ultimate principles in Nature, namely consciousness, energy, and matter conjoined with anti-matter. Regarded philosophically, they have to be taken together as forming a complete entity. These are the three qualities: sattva, rajas and tamas of Samkhya, forming a complete unity. Prakriti and Purusha joined together stand as the neutral principle, immobile above them, initiating all movements in manifestation. This is also the 'immovable mover' in Greek philosophy, and can readily be observed by an interiorization of self-consciousness through yoga.

We should note that Patanjali's Godhead[12] is none other than the 'extraordinary Purusha,' who remains unaffected by the movements of the manifestation. When a man by turning inward attains this immobility in self-consciousness, which is the duality of matter and anti-matter, he reaches directly the plane of God-awareness. This is what the Christian mystics called: the 'Flight of the alone in the Alone to the Alone.' This can be achieved only by living within oneself.

So, finally, God is the Lord of matter and anti-matter, which together make up His Energy residing in and suffusing the whole world known to us through our senses. Once this is realized, the mystic sees with open eyes, 'His Signature' in the whole pervading energy.

And that Signature is what we have called the Void.

There we touch a point referring to the two dolphins. Why do they turn around each other without stopping? Can one assume an axis around which they turn; but where does the movement come from?

There is something similar in our own body. The spinal column goes like a neon rod from the crown of the head to the place where an animal has its tail. From head to tail. Now you can imagine it as not being straight, but like a serpent within striking upward to the crown of the head with its hood. What is real is the streak of light along the spine. All along that streak of light tiny and very alive atoms are pulsating. I also discovered it in the cosmic ray in the body coming from overhead. From where does this pulsating come? One can say it is an impulse that comes from nowhere, but this mere thought gives to your body, your mind, and your soul—such wonderful poise and illumination! It is an opening up of everything in you. So you don't live by bread alone by just so many proteins and carbohydrates!

This is the teaching among the Bâüls. The Bâül says: 'What are you going to reject? You reject one thing, you throw it outside yourself, then immediately life in another form comes and feeds upon it. Are you able to reject life, the universal life? No! So purify everything. Don't say there is impurity. Don't say there is sin.' Everything is light, perceived as such only in a higher state of consciousness.

What wonderful teaching! Such people are saints, saints of God walking on earth; they are Christs.

22

It was in the dead of night. I heard these words very distinctly: 'You go to sleep. From sleep you go to death. Through death you awake to the Void.'

What was that? I heard the words. I listened to them. I followed them. I closed my eyes, tried to sleep and forget everything. Sometimes I keep awake for hours. That night I suddenly saw that sleep was coming so I remained quiet and tried to see how I was dying in my sleep. I saw that it was simply slipping into the Void nowhere, and that there was light, an illumination that was the 'presence', the eternal presence of something which I cannot describe. I call it the Void. I could also call it God, or Purusha, or Brahma, or our Father in Heaven. Then a tremendous energy possessed me. There was light in my heart. It grew. Then there was a wonderful peace, an awareness. …

I remembered, it is said in the *Katha Upanishad*, that the young boy Nachiketas, who went into the House of Death, stayed there three nights. He ate and drank nothing.

Vaivaswata, the Lord of Death, was on tour gathering victims from this world. When he came back, his servants ran to him saying: 'An honored guest has arrived. For three days, he has touched neither food nor drink. The Laws of hospitality have not been obeyed. O Lord of Death, go and wash his feet with fresh water!'

'My boy,' said Vaivaswata, 'what do you want from me?'

'I wish to go back to earth.'

'Very good! For the three nights you have been here without food or drink, I give you three wishes. You have told me the first one. What else do you wish for?'

'When I go back, I wish that my father may know me again. It is hard to recognize one who comes back after having been dead.' (This is what occurred at the resurrection of Christ. Nobody knew Him again.)

'Yes, your father will know you again. What is your last wish?'

'Tell me whether I exist here or do not exist? What is this, fantasy or reality?'

Vaivaswata was taken aback. He said: 'What a question! Even the gods don't know whether they are or are not in death. Well, back on earth, enjoy all the things of the world: men, servants and all the women you want. Just play with them all.'

The boy interrupted him: 'Yes, I shall take everything that life offers me. But now that I have seen you, I want an answer to my question. You must reply!'

'Well, well, how obstinate you are! I am going to answer your question.'

What follows is the whole of the *Katha Upanishad*. The gist of it is: just as pure water dropping into an ocean of pure water exists, so does this body, soul, and everything melting into it, become one. It is a luminous state.

Vaivaswata goes on: 'You have been a Brahmin boy on earth. You have seen your father perform sacrifices, make offerings and dedicate himself; everything thrown into the fire burns, the flames rise and flash into the intermediate world of lightning.

'Beyond that there is the state of the dazzling sun illuminating the mind, and still farther, where the light softens to moonlight, there is the state of intuition. It is filled with a mystic feeling. Beyond that you rise to the stars into a consciousness which is cosmic and infinite. Piercing through it is sat-cit-ānanda.'

The last lines of the Upanishad read as follows: 'There, there is no light, no sun, no moon, not even stars. There is no lightning, no fire. But everything shines in the dark shining of death, which illumines everything.'

If we don't meet again, don't feel that I am not. I am pure Existence. *Oṁ śānti, śānti, śānti.*

Whatever I may say from now on will simply be the same thing said in a different way. Whatever we explain is only one way among many ways. The Void is everywhere.

23

Concentration should be turned towards ourselves—turned towards the self. It is an interiorized attention upon the self which in itself is nothing.

You must forget everything. You know only one thing, that you *are*. You feel deeply that you *are*. Do you remember that phrase in the Bible: 'I am that I am?' It was quoted like this and Moses heard it in the burning bush. Later on, when he described it, he said: 'Well, I didn't, at that time, say: I am that I am.'

So you see, God-consciousness and self-consciousness—both become *one*. They form together one total reality. I feel that I am dependent upon That: *That* is the greater one, and *this* is the lesser one, but they are tied together just like clasped fingers. So I can say: 'I rise up to you and stretch out my hands' and That says to me: 'I come down to you.'

Then, just at that moment, another process starts, between I and

That. The duality remains for a long, long time. It is simply a very bad habit that we have acquired when, while awake, we begin to say: 'I have to think of God, I have to pray, I have to find Him out.' These physical words are used when we are relying on our senses. But in a state of concentration the object becomes very clear and illumined, while the 'I,' myself, remains misty. Yet, I feel that I am talking and that I am seeing. What is that 'I'? Nothing! If you pursue this line and go deeper within yourself, you will see that the subject and the object finally come together and something, without your knowing it, is deposited within you. You might think: 'I have understood what goes on. I know.' But no! You *feel* that you know nothing. At that very moment, you must let yourself go and abandon yourself fully to the mystery.

You have to be patient with yourself and repeat this experience again and again. Each time you will only get, like the touch of a brush, a patch of color! If you repeat it again, then another patch! And so on for a very long time. Finally all becomes quiet and clear within you. The Law of densities takes its course.

First you will again think: 'Oh! I know that! I have got that, all is well!' But you have to feel the different degrees of densities in your thinking. When you think with words it is with the density of the earth. Your thoughts are mechanical; you utter perhaps great words, but you are like a parrot repeating words. This kind of thinking must be thrown back into the fire of experience to make it become liquid.

There is a liquid thinking in which the words have the density of water. On the ordinary plane, this thinking jumps from here to there, from there to here without end and finally reaches nowhere. But if it is the thought of a prophet or of a poet, it goes from here to there; like water being spilt from a jar it has to go somewhere. Liquid thought spreads because it has the fluidity of water.

The notion of liquid thinking comes from the *Katha Upanishad*, in which Nachiketas put that very question to the Lord of Death: 'Am I here? Am I not here? When I leave my body, what becomes of my awareness?' And the Lord of Death answered: 'It is just as though pure water were poured into an ocean of pure water. The two come together and there is only one.' That is why the mystics everywhere in the world have spoken of the sea as the origin of life. The Vedic seers also say: 'The sky is an ocean, the heart is an ocean. ...'

It is that pure state of liquidness, of vastness, which means freedom. Water in a glass takes on a shape, though water is not confined to one form but to endless forms. Water does not remain fixed in any particular form. Do away with all forms, have that freedom, that plasticity! This quality of being I found in Śrī Ramakrishna. It thrilled me! He could identify himself with anything he liked and become it. Then immediately afterwards, he could throw it off and become another thing.

If liquid thinking is the second state, the third one is the state of luminous thinking, when you hardly utter any word but radiate your thoughts with a look or a gesture. From here on, everything is subject to the principles of radiation. In this room, light is something which gives form to everything. There is nothing in the light itself. If there is light during the day, there is darkness during the night. Light and darkness are the two dolphins sporting together. A transfiguration arises from their two bodies in movement: this line and that line together are forming a circle. It is the symbol of pure life! And beyond that is the Void which contains everything and at the same time is Nothing.

Light which is formless, and which at the same time gives form to everything, has been represented in pictures by the halo round the head of saints. The Buddhist scriptures say the Buddha had a wide halo surrounding his whole body.

When you speak to people remain turned inward. Feel from within a halo around you. Then people will come to you without even knowing it. This is the radiation principle which works in both directions: a radiation which is both outward and inward.

Then there is the fourth state: it is a touch-thinking which touches directly the heart of others. When all inhibitions are shed you go deeper within yourself. Then no word is used. The vibration of the soul resounds in the soul of others, a vibration which can be transmitted without any ostensible means, even from the other extremity of the earth. Silent prophets have used that Sound alone. The silence then becomes the

Word. Beyond this is the Logos—God as the Word. This is speaking from the Void whence the mystics say: 'Creation comes from the Void; Creation and the Word are one.'

In this way you expand into the Void. But the Void does not pin you down because it has no boundary. You fill it. The impact on you is that you feel no boundary: 'I am that I am!' It comes to that formula for which the Christ was crucified, the Sufi murdered. Only Buddha escaped that destiny, though he had many antagonists in his lifetime and still has!

24

The liquid body is the life principle. I talk, spend energy, meet people, eat, grow. It is all through this body which is lying here, suffering, blind, inert—a heavy body (tamas) infused with power (rajas).

After that comes the body of the mind (sattva), when the thoughts are more subtle.

Then comes the body of intuition (buddhi), when life plays with life, when it is no longer the body playing with the body.

When many foci of intuition come together a tremendous power is born. Then a revolution is created; it assumes a form like a new incarnation. Then the gross body, the liquid body, the mind body, are all forgotten. And the Void is beyond.

I touch it, just as I am here on solid earth which will not give way. But do I want to test it? No. I let myself live like a child, taking everything for granted and looking at everything with wide open eyes.

And that gives me freedom.

25

I have analyzed my dreams and discovered that up till now I have never dreamt that I am lying here. I am always moving about, going along here, going along there. Even though I am resting here, at the same time I am moving very fast. I remember the beautiful description of Brahma's wanderings given in the *Isha Upanishad*: 'He rests, he sits quiet and at the same time he travels far distances. He is lying on his back, though he is moving everywhere.'

The mind is a wonderful instrument when it is well tamed. Keep it always under control! Sŕi Aurobindo speaks of the mind, of the supermind, meaning to see Brahma in everything. It is the most ancient teaching which appears as new. It brings people, in the end, to the wide conception and understanding that mind and love can become one. Everywhere this deep experience is the same.

Of course, it happens that some disciples want to break away from the believers who remain attached to words and to forms. Do they find happiness in that separation? No! I say to them: 'Keep in the fold even if you are puzzled. Control the mind, keep it from running into your ego.' Do the people who have had such a deep experience meet? Yes, sometimes. They simply gaze into each other's eyes and smile. That is all. They have nothing to say except: 'You are me, I am you.'

Only after Christ was crucified did He become the Son of God. As long as he preached or meditated, he was the son of man. His real nature came out only on the Cross. His commandment is: You come after me. Follow me. Ascend the Cross till you reach the Void. Be perfect as my Father in Heaven.

26

Yes, these years of illness have been for me a time of deep inner experiences, of many, many experiences; of deep silence also, in which Kali, the eternal time, has been flowing on.

I listen to the noises around me until midnight: shouting, quarreling, market cries, and radio—then all the noises die down.

I sleep two hours. Then, awake, I simply close my eyes and remain very, very quiet. Time flows on. This is Kali, the time's spirit, the Void. I think of Kali. I have been living for many years in Calcutta but I went there only once to her temple. I saw her. I paid homage to her. I am not afraid of her.

It is just as if, in my imagination, I hear her voice. Then I say to her: 'What do you want from my life? I give you everything. Well, you have already taken my movements, my feet, my voice, and soon you will be taking my sight. If I am lying prostrate like Shiva under your feet, if you are tramping upon me, what will you take then? Your feet might get tired, you should go to sleep somehow.'

There is something wonderful—as long as I remain awake I think: 'Well, I should have been dreaming, I am creating my dreams!' I see the awakened state and the great quietness that follows. If I look into it, then I suddenly know: 'Well, I am awake!' It is all power. I am simply aware. All values which are put upon awareness mean nothing. Awareness is freedom to see without entering into anything. By that you throw away so much of the weight of life, so much ballast. You soar up! Like a balloon.

There Samkhya comes in—how? In this way: this awareness is the Purusha within me, the Shiva aware that Kali is dancing on my chest. I am simply aware of that. She dances. I don't dictate anything. I don't wish anything. I don't love or hate. I am simply aware. Then a joy comes—a wonderful serene joy. And perhaps that joy is felt by a Kali who has thrown away all her power, who then becomes a little girl with eyes twinkling merrily for joy. She becomes herself again!

Endnotes

1. *Narendra Nath Datta (1860-1902) who founded the Ramakrishna Mission at Belur, Calcutta.*
2. *A ṛṣi who lived in Mithila, 8th century B.C.*
3. *A red line on her head where the hair is parted.*
4. *The pet name of the child Krishna.*
5. *The name of a religious group with a unitarian tendency, founded in 1828 and very influential, especially in Bengal.*
6. *Learned men, knowing the sacred texts.*
7. *A great religious gathering of wandering monks and ascetics held every three years, by rotation in Hardwar, Allahabad, Ujjain and Nasik.*
8. *Mahendra Nath Gupta, one of his faithful followers.*
9. *Composed by Tulsidas.*
10. *She is the female energy of Shiva, with two characters, one mild, the other fierce.*
11. *The Fourth Veda.*
12. *Ishvari, the highest conception of a personal God.*

Part Five

LETTERS

Sŕi Anirvân

LETTERS

January 18, 1951

Don't look up to man for help. Behind every man, see the power in whose hands the man is only an instrument. No man can help or harm the divine will that you are. A smile and silence. Yes, that will be your response to everything that comes to you. Things are good or bad only to the diseased or prejudiced mind which automatically criticizes everything. They are ripples of power to one who sees and creates.

Feel that Śhakti within you—the Śhakti called "Mahishamardini,"[1] who smilingly crumples in her hands the enraged and obstinate buffalo, the demon of ignorance. Smile, but at the same time crush and transform!

March 25, 1951

Remain calm and mistress of yourself. Draw yourself in. Create from within your being. Live in the Void. Do not let life's shocks disturb you nor the questions arising from them.

Make every shock a source of intense spiritual strength that will create within you a form hard as granite, white as the snows of Haïmavatî, the consolidation of power on earth—the dream of my whole life.

April 2, 1951

If you are feeling lonely, it is because you do not yet know who you are.

You must not depend upon people or things around you. The day you really come to know your own self, you will become impersonal.

The utmost that can be predicted about you then is that you are a force or an idea.

Yes, your background is activity. Why should you not be yourself? Don't imitate others. Everyone must be guided by his own destiny (dharma). You know the secret. Let the Void be your support; lean back on the cushion in the Void.

Let the episode that troubled you be buried quickly. Whatever gets heavy and troublesome, it is best to send it down again to the bosom of Mother Earth. But this must be done quite consciously. Laying down a burden does not mean to reject it. The earth will know how to turn the deposit into good manure. Even rotten things can be turned to the best use in that way.

March 22, 1952

As time goes on, how everything appears so distant and fantastic! I remember how I used to feel like this when I was young and labored night and day for my Guru. But for whom am I laboring now? For my dream.

I don't know if I shall see it fulfilled while I am on earth. Only I feel that I am diving deeper and deeper into her bowels like a meandering root. I am thirstily sucking her sap and sending it up to flower and bloom, which perhaps I shall never see. I can only say, "A great austerity (tapasya) has come upon me."

April 20, 1952

This is how I understand your return to "life." It is in tune with the rhythm of your personal destiny (svadharma); you must be true to it. My loyalty to "Death" (Yama) will be the background against which your "life" will shine.

As for me, I have my "work" that I have to do, and there is the "dream" that I shall always be dreaming, without ever hoping to see it realized. I have felt the pulse of India and do not expect any big result. These are the days of preparing nothing more than manure. We sow only to mow down the young plants. The great seed will be cast when the soil is ready. I see the mighty tree in my dream that will exist one day. It is my God—but only a Dream-God.

I am carried in my work neither by hope nor by despondence. It is like the mighty stream of Brahmaputra moving slowly and majestically with hardly any ripple on it. I like this rhythm in which sound the words, "I am alone with the Alone." It is not joy. It is peace and a sweet, sad love beaded with sparkling tears.

April 27, 1952

… If a time of dissolution (pralaya) were to come, what would be your reaction to the "ugly" face of truth? Remember that truth is always beautiful because it gives freedom, and we must be free within to have a real taste of life.

I was looking today at a picture of Śri Ramana Maharshi. For sixty years he did nothing. He simply lived and stared into the Void. This is good! I have also been reading Śri Aurobindo's *Savitri*, a staggering pyramid of fantasies! For forty years he had been a recluse, spinning dreams around him. That is also good! I like them both. They lived in their own way—one in the nudity of Death, the other in writing *The Life Divine*—are they not the faces of the same Inexpressible? Well, we have to live, to grow, to bloom, to seed, and then to die. Let us do it with grace, like the season's flowers!

December 3, 1952

You must have received news of me by this time en route. As yet there has been no flux of visitors. The weather is not too cold.

The calm of Haimavati remains intact. Have I lost my grip on life? Perhaps not. The phrase "spiritual existentialism" we coined has become so real here. I can exactly imagine how you will feel when you come into the crowd. It will be there and yet it will not be. The soul like a little child, simply looking at things with wondering eyes—not evaluating, not passing judgment on anything, not bound by a sense of duty and yet silently active in radiating her simple joy of living; how wonderful!

Love wears a new face then; suddenly it becomes secure in the depths. I love because I exist. I possess everything because I am nothing. My love is a light that gently kisses the drooping brow of sorrow and passes on. It embraces everything but sticks to nothing.

You remember the story I told you of Devahuti, the mother of Kapila, who had known life in a womanly fullness and then known the Void in its manly grandeur and at the end of her earthly existence had chosen to change herself into a sparkling stream. That is the eternal Woman. I can't picture her a Mother today. She is the child who holds the gods on her tiny palm.

April 5, 1953

Yes, life in Haimavati has been full. It has been like a pure flame burning all dross and shooting upward, melting in the Void. The material Haimavati has died in order to be changed into a luminous idea that will never die. I shall never forget the sacrifice you made to Her, not to any institution but to the idea—an idea beyond the comprehension of the mind, but how real! The last year has been wonderful, though outwardly it was a movement of dissolution. But inwardly, what wonderful freedom and ease and power. Have you not felt that?

And now let me tell you that Almora is really a land of dissolution (pralaya). This year there has not been one drop of rain for over two months. The water shortage is terrible and we have to wait another two months until the rains come. Everything is scorched, dried up, brittle. The skin cracks as it does in winter. But how wonderful it is! I feel neither dead nor alive, but in strange communion with existence. The only thing that counts is true action. All opposites have faded away in a luminous haze which envelopes everything and swallows it up. I do not know what will remain.

May 1, 1953

Always rest within the Void and you will understand. It is understanding that counts. Really it is something like working with intelligence. Very few people do that. Actions do not matter at all. Your action benefits none but your own self. If your actions clear your vision, they are all right. If not—well, it is all illusion (Maya). Only the Void will tell you.

June 14, 1953

I am in absolute peace these days. Work is also vanishing though I work the whole day. There is no sense in working for something; you *be* the work itself. Not to *become*, it is simply *being*. A tree does not know what it is going to become, but every moment it simply *is*. Do you call that unconsciousness, stupidity? What is our consciousness but a feverish dream? When we awake—and we really awake (not simply pass from one dream to another dream, which we fondly cherish as awakening)—we no longer become, but we *are*. The whole secret of life is to pin your faith on that being, knowing that it is insensible, it is the Void.

The other day, while I was carelessly turning over the pages of my volume of *Rigveda*, I suddenly came upon a passage of Saunaka, a very old index-maker of the Vedas. He said, "There is only one God and that God is the Sun." It gave me a violent start. It was as if Saunaka was nodding his head and saying: "We all felt like that, and that produced the Vedas." And the sun said: "I have been shining for millions and millions of years. As long I shine and don't become too hot for people to live on the earth, well, you can go on weaving dreams of ashrams and Gurus, of divinization, and so on!"

Can you feel, at the bottom of your woman's heart, that you are nothing but a bit of solar energy, dead and stiffened, and yet trying to warm up into the radiance of that solar orb? And if you succeed, you will be Savitri, which literally means nothing but the solar energy.

And the sun, is he going to live for all eternity? Of course not. Every evening he goes down and I pull a chair into the yard and stare at the fading crest of Shyama Devi,[2] which looks so strangely like the heaving breast of a woman lying on her back. I see the dead earth in her. The darkness swallows everything. And then nothing remains but the Void.

Can you unite that death with life? Only then you will live! I have told you of nothing but death. You must know him (Yama) and be married to him before you go back to life—to your life. Follow the curve of life, don't struggle against it. Only know that you are secure in the Void that is beyond. And then have a good smile at life. I have always been a cipher to you because I knew that this is the only truth.

August 3, 1953

I am so happy to know that you are leaving India feeling empty and stripped of everything. That is the way to create life! You will be bringing back something other than fine, reassuring words—a pulsating life that cannot be seen or heard, but can only be felt as a vibration. Give yourself up completely. Return to the earth again, and from your self-effacement you will be giving life to thousands of sprouting seeds. Be the very spirit of the earth—the patient mother who suckles her children without uttering a word.

The unknown is before you, but the known is in you. And that which knows will master that which does not know. If you know yourself, you also know your universe, which will be molded by your understanding. May Haimavati be with you always, for it will be your strength, your Śhakti.

September 17, 1953

May your return to the West be a new birth, in every sense of the term. You have learned from life, you have learned more from death. Now let death be your Master and Lord. It is safe to walk with him along the path of life. To possess nothing, not even your thoughts, to know that everything is and simply to look at them—asking nothing, refusing nothing—that is the secret of the "no-mind." Let not life but death plant within you whatever he likes. You have simply to accept and make it fruitful with the sap of your being.

All creations are in the Void. So, there can be absolutely no frustration in any worker who has known the Void. To know this is not to quarrel, not to worry, not to hurry in getting things done. Things arrange themselves automatically around him, not according to any human plan, mind you! And the Divine has no plan at all. He is like a child playing with creation and destruction at random because he is above both. The

Vedas say, "He is death and immortality is his shadow. All is Maya." There is a complex security and freedom in the knowledge of that. But this is a truth that should not be spoken about, it must be felt.

As for me, you know I can best be of use to you if I am impersonal. You can think of me in whatever way you like, only if that leads you to your complete freedom. It it leads to the Void, then relations are true; if not—beware! If you have made all I have given you your own so that no trace of me is left in them, then you have understood. And I can be silent again, knowing I have done my part.

September 20, 1953

So! Gurdjieff has been keeping you company during your voyage?

We have lost the esoteric and the occult sense by being civilized and it has not been for our good. The upward evolution is not without difficulty. We have to reclaim what we have lost. The other day I was thinking that if evolution is true and we have passed through a vegetable stage of life, then why did we lose that power of changing inorganic matter into food? Why can we not suck our life from Mother Earth as the plants do? If we know how the plants do that, why can we not get back the technique in our own bodies? Much of occultism is thus going back to the bosom of the earth, to hunt for the lost continent of Atlantis. Yes, we have to deal with "mass" and "matter," but we have to do it in a spiritual way. A long and tiresome process, of course. But still we have to do it.

September 29, 1953

When you become one with a thing, that thing no longer exists for you and yet something may happen in you—a manifestation that is, of course, an illusion (Maya)—an inscrutable mystery. It is good to know that life is a mystery. I do not laugh at it like Gurdjieff nor do I glorify it like Sŕi Aurobindo. I simply smile.

Of course death is the greatest experience that we can have while in life. Cannot one part of you live and the other part die? Life will then be only like the twinkling of a star surrounded by a great abyss of death and darkness.

It is good to feel this darkness within you—the unmanifested which you can call Kali-the-Mother or any other name you like. Life means nothing if you know that there is death behind you, ready to absorb you again, as the great Void is absorbing every moment millions of seers, of "those who know." To know this while living, "to carry death into every movement of your life," is the consummation of life's purpose. Death is peace, death is silence, death is power. Don't laugh, don't glorify, only smile. Smile because you know.

From Shillong, April 26, 1954

A week ago I shifted to the new Haimavati at Shillong. I am gradually settling down. It is a small cottage, quite simple, where one can live as in a mountain cave. It is commanding a fine view of vast pine forests. The house is built on a piece of land belonging to the Khasias.[3] As a result, here I am living right in the heart of the dissidence which is stirring this country and I am a subject not of the Assam government but of the Khasia Parvati. So I have automatically become a rebel, which I always was by nature!

The house consists of three tiny rooms the size of the one we used as a refectory in Almora. There will be a water tap and electric light. What luxury! The place is extremely quiet. My neighbors are very poor, peaceful Khasias. Their small boy will come every day to clean the dishes with ashes. My work routine will be the same as in Almora. As you see, for a definite period, I have returned to the "cave life" I like.

May 9, 1954

In my last letter I gave you news about the new Haimavati that has grown up here. As I am writing, I am looking at the landscape through the window, a strange mixture of the soft scene of Lohaghat and the rugged beauty of Almora. I am alone, completely alone. There is a small boy now who draws water for me every day. I cook for myself and do my washing.

There are a few pupils nearby. You know them. U. sees to it that nothing interferes with my work. A. has been a wonderful help. He is copying all the manuscripts before they go off to the printer. They come twice a week to read Samkhya with me. M. comes every Wednesday to take lessons in Sanskrit. So you see it is just like what we had planned in Almora, with the difference that now I am doing all these things without the slightest idea of building up anything. I know that these students may fail me any moment. But I have to give what I have, and I give it not to the person, but to the spirit behind. Thus I serve Haimavati.

Haimavati is a living idea, whether we are referring to the place where you live in Europe or to the house in Almora. The same is true of the house in Shillong. So there the house in the Swiss Himalayas and the house in the Eastern Himalayas. Everywhere the living idea is that of the "secret cave," the temple in the heart of man in which Purusha is absorbed in himself.

I am happy to know that your work is recognized and supported. Accept any help that gives you freedom on the explicit condition that you free yourself of every hindrance that might prevent you from serving fully. If you do it consciously and silently, Purusha will uphold you. Never betray and you will be in harmony with yourself—even if things become difficult.

November 28, 1954

Continue to live the life of Haimavati and you will discover that there has been absolutely no break in the flow of Śhakti. During these last two years,[4] there was only an eddy and Śhakti now flows on as evenly as before.

Bring to your friends the spirit of Haimavati, which is the secret of India you have known, but do not stress that it is India. A mother nurses her child not with the food she eats, but with her milk, with her own life sap into which she has transformed the material food. You have passed barriers, found your freedom. Be human, which means incarnating the Divine. May the discipline of Samkhya and the spirit of the Bâül sustain your strength, your Śhakti.

December 19, 1954

Man is growing. There will come a day when we shall know true spiritual democracy, everyone standing on his own feet and hailing one another "Brother!" No Masters, no Gurus. Science, logic, democracy are all tending toward the spiritual-democratic movement. When man has learned to be spiritually free from all dogmas, learned not to lean on any staff but on his own feet, then the Vedic spirit will dawn upon him making the heaven and earth one.

There is one trait in the European mind which we here have lost for the last two thousand years—it is the love of nature as the pagan loves it, that is, for its own sake. In this trait lies one of the greatest secrets of releasing the bonds of the soul. This romanticism in a European soul is something very real which, unfortunately, is considered as something going against spirituality. The cause lies in the Semitic idea that this world is a created thing and not God himself, this latter idea being the old Vedic idea which we ourselves lost after the eleventh century, and which Rabindranath Tagore brought back to us, without himself knowing he was renewing something which was a part of our own heritage.

Always make people feel that God, soul, and Nature are one, that spiritual growth is not an intellectual process but a life process—an all-round growth. It is not the attainment of something distant but a flowering of what is within. Remove all obstacles, conventions, superstitions, and you will find that you are flooded with light which was just waiting for the windows of your heart to be opened.

Love the youthful spirit in man. Therein lies another secret. Adolescence is the flowering period of life, represented by Krishna. Our whole aim should be to make adolescence more and more conscious. You can help the beauty of a well-adjusted family life. That is true spirituality because it is worship of a life divine.

August 13, 1955

Put out strong roots into you native soil. Go ahead with the work that connects you with your search. Make it a play of Śhakti. Where there is complete detachment, there is a spontaneous flow of energy. Your way of working with a group impersonally is fine. You have caught the spirit. Feeling deeply within oneself the "real I," to live it and radiate it spontaneously—that is the law of divine work.

As far as possible, give up all outer forms in your relations with people. Of course, it is impossible not to use forms—gestures, movements, and words. But these are only preliminaries. What you are really doing is absorbing and then radiating. Always look beyond the forms and you will find prakriti—a vast ocean of energy coming in waves that take on various aspects. Absorb prakriti and remain calm. The only thing that counts is to *be*—and then let radiation take place.

February 18, 1955

I can't send you a photograph because no one has taken a picture of me lately. You can picture me as you saw me last. Perhaps I have become thinner. But the light burns bright. Only I feel more drawn inwards. A great solitude is swallowing me and I like it. People are crowding around me here from morning to evening, always asking questions, the same questions. Sometimes I go to the cinema, which is taboo for a sadhu. Am I blasphemous?

March 11, 1956

If you feel that India is calling you, of course you will come back. But you must not create circumstances. Be drawn by the stream of events. If you have courage enough to live you own inner life and at the same time let yourself be carried by the stream of life without your own will, then the whole world is yours.

You can live without any attachment anywhere you are wanted. It might be there just as well as here. You just live the life of the Bâül. He arrives somewhere, works with all his heart, and packs off as soon as he is not wanted. His inner life is all he possesses. If he joins a group, he works for it just as if he were joining in the play of children at recreation and he quietly drops away when the children are tired or simply don't want to play any more.

If you dare to conceive the movement of life like this, you are on the right side. But if you think you have something to do, that you are necessary, then you will once more be caught by the snare of Maya. Are you able to be free like the Bâüls? Not intellectually, but in activity. If so, perhaps some day you will find a "cause" to serve, just as I have found mine after I had played with things for years. And even then, you must remain free. You must not forget that this "cause" is still a play of Maya, who can devour you. The Void alone is ultimate reality.

August 24, 1956

Do not be attached to anything! Do not clutch onto anything! Only like this will life's current lead you without shock to the vast ocean of the Void. Real self-observation is exactly to find again and again the sensation of the Void in the very heart of life's struggle. This is the sensation that can illuminate death when it comes to us. Spiritual discipline implies a merciless struggle in the reality of life. Then one is conscious of what is Existence is, of which life and death are the two poles.

March 15, 1959

Simply float on. Do things as if you had nothing to do. When I am in a fix, I simply become blank and wait. Great Nature does the same.

It is best to forget everything from time to time, even for a whole day. Then things rush back in by themselves, as if they were brought by life's current. One has to learn the trick of being able to float. A stream never flows backwards.

It is good to know that you are slowly and steadily striking your roots into the soil of your country. The day will come when the principles of Samkhya will deliver the European mind from its present dreams and psychoreligious nightmares.

Last week, a young man who comes to see me every Sunday said that your book *My Life With a Brahmin Family* was on sale in one of the local bookshops in Gauhati. He stood at the counter turning page after page, thrilled by this picture of the life that is his, and almost finished the whole book. 'It was so engrossing!" was his remark. But he had no money to buy it.

May 26, 1964 (after a serious illness)

I am extremely weak. This enforced holiday was a blessing in disguise.

The experience of suffering has been wonderful. It has opened up new vistas of truth and welded all past experiences into a solid whole. So it comes to this, "All is Brahman,"[5] be it pain or joy, life or death, light or darkness." Beyond everything is the silent Void, the only objective reality, which engulfs all subjective appearances. Wonderful!

June 13, 1964

The monsoons have started. The garden is in full bloom with summer flowers. What a beauty! And in four months I am going to leave it all behind me, with a laugh. I have been quietly happy here and shall be so wherever I go. The name Haimavati remains. I leave the house in the care of a friend who nursed me so patiently during my long illness.

I feel a new life pouring into me. Not that I am looking forward to any conspicuous result—no, not that. It is simply the fullness of the Void, the pure gaze that looks through the Maya of it all, the ineffable smile of the Buddha serenity. Prakriti is wonderful! She is so prolific in her inventions and she keeps Purusha always spellbound with the novelties she ushers in from day to day. Oh, it is a joy to BE, simply to BE.

Do not get stuck! Flow on, not even caring if you reach the Ocean or not.

April 25, 1965

It is a good sign you are dissatisfied with yourself. Self-complacence would have meant death. Dissatisfaction is the stirring of the great Śhakti, which is making you feel that you have not done enough.

Take this dissatisfaction itself as a part of the great game you are playing. Don't be troubled by it. Take it easily, as you have taken so many things. And live quietly and deeply. Live as if you are not living, work as if you are not working, talk as if you are not talking, think as if you are not thinking. Then the great Śhakti lying deep within you and causing these stirrings of the heart will reveal herself. You will be taken up by her and be one with her. Then you will know what you have to know. Non-existence will then become the fountainhead of bubbling existence. Never to be satisfied is one of the main features of Samkhya discipline.

June 21, 1965

I am still in the dark about the friend who is building the new Haimavati in the former bed of the Ganges near Calcutta. He has given me lifelong freedom to use the house. According to the Scriptures, a serpent never burrows a hole; it lives in a hole made by others and leaves it when it likes. That is also what the Bâül says from the heart of his freedom.

If you come to see me, you will again have a taste of life as it was in Lohaghat. We will follow the same pattern of life again, but it will not be so quiet, as we have neighbors—all peasants, Hindus and Muslims living together like brothers, so much so that you cannot distinguish them. From the South comes the call to prayer by muezzins, from the North conches, bells and the chants of kirtans. And no breaking heads over the modes of praying to the same God.

Endnotes

1. *Name of the goddess Durga, one of the aspects of the active energy of Shiva.*
2 *The peak of the hill above Almora, below which stands Haimavati.*
3 *An independent tribe of Assam.*
4 *Since my return to Europe.*
5 *Sarvam Khalvidam Brahma.*

Part Six

Mystic Songs

Sŕi Anirvân

THE BÂÜLS OF BENGAL

The Bâüls play an indispensable role in Bengal. It would be easy to point a finger at them saying, "Madmen drunk with God," or even, "Illiterate beggars in the vain pursuit of a dream"; nevertheless, it is from them that Rabindranath Tagore derived much of his inspiration. In fact, the great poet collected the words of many of their songs and many of their touchingly simple melodies.[1] While they remain outside the orthodox traditions of India, the Bâüls nevertheless represent one of the underground currents of spiritual life which remain intensely alive. This current can be traced to a time even before that of the Vedic religions.

The name "Bâül", however, first appears in the literature of Bengal only in the fifteenth century. It seems to derive from the word "*bâtula*" (*vâtula* in Sanskrit), meaning "he who is beaten by the winds"; he, that is, who abandons himself to all his impulses. From that point to madness is only a step! But this ecstatic madness has its origin in God, and its aim also in God!

The Bâüls must not be thought of as forming a particular sect. *Sâdhakas* who follow a spiritual discipline and belong to all sorts of brotherhoods and religious groups may become Bâüls if they are so disposed. Chinese philosophy, in its closeness to nature, has perhaps the nearest approach to Bâüls in its Ch'an, Zen adepts, who so delight in paradox. The dominant note that marks the Bâüls is their complete spiritual freedom, which is an organic force without the slightest pretension. In ordinary life, thanks to their utter non-conventionality, they are typical freethinkers, who have unwittingly become a free institution. There is no outer connection between them of any kind.

They are recognizable because they generally wear long robes—though these are not distinctive of any existing religious order. They let their hair and beards grow. Since for them the Divine is formless and mythology a dead letter, they are never seen making obeisance to any image or to any human being, no matter how perfect he may be! They no longer belong to any caste.

The Bâül's philosophy is not formulated in any sacred writings. He does not depend on any tradition. Above all else he lets himself be guided by intuition.

The Bâüls' only means of expression is extemporaneous singing which voices their intimate spiritual experience. There are as many Hindu Bâüls as there are Muslim. Escaping from all orthodox forms, their lives are completely integrated in the unity that exists between teacher (Guru) and pupil (*shishya*). In fact, Muslim Gurus are known to initiate Hindus, and Hindu Gurus to initiate Muslims. This inner relationship is ordained by God.

There are monks, ascetics, and married men among the Bâüls. They go from village to village, singing, with their *ektaras*—a simple one-stringed instrument—and their small drums called *dubkis*. At certain times of the year and in certain propitious places, the Bâüls come together periodically in a big fair (*mela*) where the songs and dances continue day and night for as long as the gathering lasts. On these occasions there are no rites of worship and no oral teaching, for these mystic poets attach no importance to anything except the vibration of souls—nothing else.

The spiritual discipline of the Bâüls is centered on the cult of the man in whom God is called *Maner manush*—"He who lives in the heart." This god has only one attribute. He is all love! There is no mention of God the Creator nor of God the Destroyer.

One of the ways of reaching God is to give oneself up to a Guru who becomes the link between man and the Divine. So the Guru is highly venerated and respected, but teacher and pupil remain perfectly free on both sides with no conditions between them of loyalty or obedience, with no fixed obligation or responsibility.

The spiritual discipline of the Bâül is solely the flowering of the inner being, of the constant presence of God. There is no search for any support from outer things. Just on that account, their discipline, which begins with the body, requires that the body, which plays the role of instrument, be kept extremely pure, for the body is "the temple of God." "In this body lives the Man; if you call him, He will answer you." It is actually a technique for seeking God in oneself by using the instrument of the body that God gave us: "God made Himself man; in the perfect man who is the Guru, man is made divine, so the ideal of God can be attained in our own bodies." The cult of the Bâül, in short, is spiritualized humanism.

The spiritual attitude of the Bâül has found in Bengal a terrain well prepared to favor the growth of his philosophy's three principal ideas.

The idea of God as love has been enriched by all the adepts of bhakti-yoga and by the Vaishnavites for whom Krishna is "He who lives in the heart." The idea of the guru as the perfect man who, while still a man, has attained the highest goals, is a direct contribution of Islam. In Hinduism, in fact, the Guru is greater than all the gods, is himself divine. For the Bâül, the veneration due to the Guru (*guruvada*) is deeply rooted in the ancient history of Bengal, where it was well known long before the advent of Buddhism—that is, in the cult of the *siddhas*. What survives today of this cult of the siddhas, of Buddhism and of Islam, has been transmuted into a harmonious composite in which the Bâüls come in contact with the Absolute through ecstatic love. The idea of the body as the temple of God comes directly from the hatha cult which is the basis of hatha-yoga. The Bâüls, in fact, are acquainted with a whole science of the body called *dehatattva* (which is no more than the science of kuṇḍalinī and of the *chakras* of the hatha yogins), which is practiced by Hindus and Muslims alike.

These characteristics of the Bâüls, which in our day form the link between Hindu and Muslim, are the pure product of the ancient non-conformist schools of Buddhism which laid enormous emphasis on metaphysical aspirations: "what is the first truth?" (*shunya*), and on pure experience: "What is it born in me?" (sahaja). These ideas are still alive for the Bâüls, who speak freely and willingly of sahaja. Pure experience is the great motive of their lives. Thus the non-orthodox mysticism of medieval India forms the background for the modern Bâüls, and the saints of Northern India, such as Kabir and Dadu, were certainly Bâüls. If we go back even further, we can connect the Bâüls directly with the mysterious Vrâtya cult of the *Artharva Veda*.

Most Bâüls are illiterate and come from the poorest ranks of society, but they also include learned Brahmins who have been rejected by their caste and Muslims excommunicated by their orthodoxy. Many Sufis have also become Bâüls through fear of persecution, saying: "We escape from orthodoxy (*shariyat*) in order to follow Truth (*Haqiqat*).

These Bâüls are scattered over the entire country. Recently a Muslim Bâül even turned up in the mountains of Almora. He plucked the string of his ektara and repeated with every breath the holy Names of Rama, of Allah, of Krishna, of Buddha. When people showed some surprise, he began to sing:

All these Names are the same Name,
The only one which lives in the heart.
O my brothers, why should we quarrel?
He is everywhere, He nameless
He, is everywhere the same…

And, he added with some irony: "Now, I will tell you what is happening in the great world. …" And immediately he began to compose some sort of satirical verse scoffing at the political news of the day! "Why are you always singing?" he was asked. He replied:

Because we were born singing birds in order to sing;
We don't know how to walk on the ground
But with wings spread, in the sky, we soar…

—*Sŕi Anirvân*

Endnotes

1. *Rabindranath Tagore spoke publicly of the Bâüls for the first time in a public lecture at the University of Calcutta and in his Hibert Lectures published in* The Religion of Man.

1

Take the lamp from the Master's hands
and go down into the black abyss
awaken your senses
to the yoga of the "I" made free
for you this will be
the dawn of the supreme mystery.

Beatific visions
will fill your heart
beyond the measurable
there where the worlds dance
there where blooms the lotus of the thousand petals
in whose halo
you will know
the mystic union of delights.

Between the existent
and the non-existent
the space is love ...

—*Anonymous*

2

The lotus of the heart
  blooms far from here
mysterious
  hidden by time's ages.
It is this that has made a slave of You
and of me also, my Adored One!

This lotus blossoms
  again and again
deathless flowering,
the honey flowing from it
an intoxicating sweetness,
the bee that eats it
  can no longer fly away…
It is this that has made a slave of You
  and of me also, my Adored One!

Neither You nor I have any wish
to tear ourselves away from this embrace!
Go away if You can, my Adored One!

—*Anonymous*

3

Is my Beloved
a creaking axle
forever grinding and moaning?
Oh! speak to me of Your silence,
my Master, my Adored,
show me the path of silence
leading
to the Lotus of the Void ...

The moon and the stars
forever ride the sky
—soundlessly
in Your silence ...

—*Anonymous*

4

"Lord, show me, I beg,
how in the same man
guru and lover are but one?"

"If you live pure and sober,
experiencing divine delights,
some day, you will know it…
Lock after lock
defends the dwelling place of Darkness
in the inmost depths of being,
—and beyond.
But if the dazzling light of day
dawns in the waves of ecstasy
the luminous Darkness vanishes…"

At the threshold of the ninth dwelling
—O inconceivable mystery,
must I reveal to you
the Mother of mothers
the majestic, eternal Mother?…

—Lalan Fakir

5

O my Beloved
who in Your heart
feel all the pain of mine,
why, tell me, does my unquiet soul
aspire to Your sweet peace?
My secret soul, evenly,
slowly, pursues its aim …

But my impatient heart
is troubled,
bursts into heavy sobbing …
The soul shudders,
the bitter tears flow.
"Come, my loved one, come …"
is the seductive call!

The tide attracts the waters,
the sea, the source of rivers.
So does the heart's poison
become pure nectar …

—*Anonymous*

6

To Krishna

You and I dance
O my King
In the mad gaiety of Holi[1]
—ecstasy of our souls.

Am I alone
bitten by desire?
No! my Adored,
You also languish with it!

To give Your joy
You need my smiles;
that Your song may be known
I must be its flute!

So that my whole body may be
the cradle of Your delight,
O my Adored.
Now it is for You
to kneel before me—
come beg my love . . .

—*Anonymous*

Endnote

1. *A spring festival during which colored waters are played with.*

7

At the turn of the river
a call rang out,
the call of an unknown Voice:
"Stop, boatman!
Make your boat fast,
rest a moment..."

"No! No! I cannot stop
the current carries me away..."

In this endless voyage
what must become of me?...
The eddies tug my boat away
and my desire is in the call...
O Master, I beg You,
take the helm!

Drive out the anguish
of Your suffering Jaga
Lord...

—*Jaga, the boatman*

8

Beaten by the waves
laid low by the hard winds:
O Murshid
I take refuge in You!

In the west the storm growls
the clouds pile up in masses,
my battered boat trembles,
its masts are broken:
O Murshid
I take refuge in You!

The waves onrushing
crush the deck;
all that I treasured
like precious gems
has gone adrift:
O Murshid
I take refuge in You!

—*Anonymous*

9

Close to my house
there is a city of crystal.
There lives
my mysterious neighbor.
Never have I seen His face
for even a single moment
—His radiant face!

If my neighbor
had touched me only once
my death anguish
would have vanished . . .
But I, poor Lalan, and He,
though we live under the same sky
are separated by an immense void.
Millions of leagues,
alas, under the same sky,
separate us . . .

—*Lalan Fakir*

10

O my heart
before whom will you prostrate yourself
to whom will you say "my guru"?

He is there beside you
He is there all around you
He lives in every thing ...

The guru is the rice in your bowl
the guru is your soul's passion.

When your heart weeps
the guru is its tears ...

—*Anonymous*

11

… beneath the waters
little by little the boat is sinking
but take the risk
the last …
O boatman, drunk with joy
good fellow on your leprous boat!

Cling to the mast
sail with high prow
Courage! have no fear …

Wretched broken boat
cradle of the waves
the greedy spray caresses you
go! the eternal spell
in the bewitchment of Time!

Look, there, before you …
… the way out!

—*Sudharam Bâül*

12

In the Ocean of love
where every form weds Beauty—
I saw in a flash
Him who lives hidden in my heart . . .
a stream of burning
molten gold . . .
What joy! What desire!
I ran to meet Him
to seize Him in my arms.

Alas! I found nothing . . .

In vain, now, I search
I have scoured the thickets
Where are You?
I am anxious
I wander like a madman
Where are You?
A fire consumes me
In the depths of myself
which devours me
which will never be extinguished . . .

—*Anonymous*

13

If in my cage
 the mysterious bird
which comes whence ... I know not
going whither ... I know not
 by chance would enter
 quickly I would capture it!
I wish so much
 that I could fasten
 to one of its feet
the golden chain
 of my heart ...

—*Anonymous*

14

The one who has dived into divine love
  my heart quickly recognizes
  when he visits me!
A veil of tears shines in his eyes
the shadow of a smile lights his face
    —depth of warm tenderness
    —ecstasy of infinite love
a light is kindled in the lotus of his heart
Ah! The tide of his desires is drunk up by the sand dunes
  but overcoming all the barriers
  the river of his love has flooded everything . . .

—*Anonymous*

15

The road towards You is blocked
by so many temples and mosques!
I indeed hear Your call clearly
O my Beloved
but I cannot move forward
gurus and murshids,
bristling, guard the passage ...

What a dream—
to plunge into Your current
coolness of my blood
but flames arise
to devour the world.
Where is Your peace, O my Master?
Your message of unity
is covered with ashes ...

Heavy the chains
  that close Your door
Puranas, Koran, rosaries
robes the color of fire
sow on the dusty roads
the hard seeds of pride ...
Madan moans in pain ...

—*Madan Fakir*

16

May blessing be!
I am an cmpty vessel!

When You swim in the pond
I lean against Your breast
my head turns upon Your heart
my Beloved!

Those who are full vessels
You place upon the bank
You carry them into Your house
useful for water . . .

But I, I swim with You
I breathe to the rhythm of Your joy
Your arms of love embrace me
hold me close against You.

Drunken I give myself up
to the waves of the stream
to the waves of Your love
My Love!

—*Anonymous*

17

O my Beloved
if the fire of Your love
can burn without me
let us part!
There, at once …
… I go away!

Whirlwinds of dust
  noisy bazaars
furrows of embers burning
  hard distances of roads—
broken with fatigue, I walk …

O King of my heart
when You thirst for love
You will know how to go after me
  and find me
That is why
I have become a wanderer
on Your road
for You
—nameless!
—dust!

—*Anonymous*

18

I shall not go to Mecca nor Medina
since my Beloved
is here
in me and I in Him . . .

It would be madness to go far away
it would be madness no more to see
His face in me . . .

Neither temple nor mosque
nor puja nor bakrid,
each clod of earth
—the earth I tread
is Kashi and Mecca
each instant is the shining joy
of my Beloved . . .

—*Anonymous*

19

O! stubborn one, by your cruel impatience
by your merciless insistence,
by the fire do you really wish
to force tight buds to open,
flowers to bloom
and fill the air with their perfume?

Do you not see that the great Artisan, My Lord,
at his leisure, by his grace
since the night of time
has caused the flowers to open from the bud?

Guilty is your ambition
and your wish to force life;
truly your purpose is sterile
stubborn, gnawed by impatience …

Do you not know that the river
invites you—
silently, calm, it flows—
Give in and let yourself float
your soul filled with His melody
O stubborn one, devoured by impatience …

—*Anonymous*

20

How my heart has melted
I know not . . .
in the ecstasy of life
in the ecstasy of death
my heart is drunk with joy . . .

O Beloved
make me not languish in vain
I no longer expect anything
  from tomorrow
  nor from yesterday
Your little bells ring day and night
O miracle! I am bewildered . . .

Where is the infinite sea?
Where is the eddying river?
If you would know
the secret tide of life that makes them one,
marry your heart with your eyes.

Then in you
the eyes of your heart
will see the game of God.

—Ishân Jugi, the Weaver

21

Oh! no one has ever found
who He is
—a fool of God—
who wanders from door to door ...
—a beggar of love—
going from door to door ...

—Anonymous

22

O my spirit, rest anchored in yourself
knock not at any door.
If you go deep into yourself
you will find what you seek.

God, the true philosopher's stone
who transmutes all desires
dwells in your heart
the most beautiful of jewels.

How many pearls and diamonds
pave round about
the antechamber of your heart's pavilion!

—*Anonymous*

23

I cannot open my heart to you
  O my friend
because my lips are sealed . . .
in life's grayness
  how can I persevere
if the Beloved
  who knows all my suffering
stays so far from me?

Him who is my heart's beloved
  I would know at a glance
  But shall I ever see Him?
He passes in dreams of light
He plunges in the deeps of joy
  skillful boatman
of the high tides of divine love.

—*Anonymous*

24

Blessed am I
if the three worlds are Your flute!
I am the wind that plays on it
the breath of Your lips.
What harm, truly,
if at each note I die!
Under Your fingers my notes fall one by one
singing of good, of bad
pouring out pleasure and pain.
I am the song of dawn and of evening
and of the dead of night
but if it pleases You
I can sing also
the smiles and showers of spring.
If I am the instrument of Your song
what else could I desire?
What harm, truly,
if at each note I die?

—Ishân Jugi, the Weaver

25

In my soul
I hear a voice calling me
who is He—devoured with impatience
who caresses my two hands?
who is He—with flickering eyelids,
who seeks to take me in His arms?

My heart quivers
I cannot go forward
He who calls me is there …
His voice moves me
His song repeats without end
"Where are you going?
Oh! come, come to Me …"

In order not to hear Him
I fled …
But I walk like a blind man
—fog
in the night I walk …
Then turning back
there, in my heart,
I saw Him waiting for me
there, ready to welcome me …

—Man Mohan Bâül

26

And the Bâüls came
  they danced
  they sang

And they disappeared
  in the mist …
and the house was left empty
  empty … the house …
  in the mist …

—Song murmured by Sŕi Ramakrishna shortly before he died.

Lizelle Reymond

Lizelle Reymond was born on June 30, 1899, in Saint Imier, Switzerland, and spent her childhood in Neuchâtel. A deep spiritual foundation was laid during her childhood. She spoke of it as Christian; not as a system, but as an opening.

Following World War I, the Reymond family business was closed and reestablished in Geneva. In 1920, Lizelle Reymond obtained a central position in the young League of Nations in Geneva, becoming librarian and serving the League until the beginning of World War II in 1940. She traveled to the United States in 1928-1929, completing her training in library administration at Columbia University in New York and organizing a series of lectures aimed at making known the work of the League of Nations.

During this period, Mme. Reymond's interest in India was awakened. She was influenced by meeting the great poet Sarojini Naidu, a luminous personality close to Gandhi, and later, in Geneva, the physician and botanist Jagadish Chandra Bose and Mme. Vijaylakashmi Pandit, as delegates to the League of Nations. She also began working with Jean Herbert, known for his publications on Indian philosophy, whom she married; together they translated writings of the great masters of contemporary Hinduism, then actually unknown to the Western world.

The first journey to India was taken in 1937 with Jean Herbert, deepening and directing her interest in Indian thought. She and her husband visited different ashrams and made personal contact with masters such as Swami Ramdas, Sŕi Ramana Maharshi, Sŕi Aurobindo and Ma Ananda Moyi. Contacts were also established with people living at Ramakrishna's mission who knew the great *said*, his wife Sarada Devi, Swami Vivekananda and his disciple Nivedita. Numerous translation projects emerged from these meetings, aimed at making these teachings known in the West.

The onset of the war years interrupted these contacts, but an intense work of study and translation continued for ten years. Lizelle Reymond and Jean Herbert spent the war years secluded in Jaubergues in the south of France, living close to nature, with small farm animals and poultry, working in fields and vineyards. The daily life of Jaubergues was an authentic apprenticeship in the language of nature, an initiation into the mystery of the unity of all life. A book published in 1947, *The Game of Freedom*, bears witness to this life. Her poems also echo the understanding of Life at the heart of Great Nature in Indian texts. During this period, the works of Ramakrishna, Vivekananda, Aurobindo, Ramana Maharshi, Ma Ananda Moyi, Rabindranath Tagore and Gandhi were made available for the first time under the direction of Mme. Reymond, thus illustrating the scope and intensity of the work during the war years.

It was during this period that Lizelle Reymond met René Daumal, who collaborated actively in the translation of certain texts. Also, she was chosen to write the biography of a woman named Vivedita, originally from Ireland and already considered a saint in India. This work, *Nivedita, Daughter of India*, edited by Victor Attinger (in English, *The Dedicated: A Biography of Nivedita*, Lotus Light, 1985, 380p.) was completed in 1945. The documents, and particularly the contacts with the many people who lent their support, brought the author into intimate contact with the tradition of Ramakrishna.

After the war, Mme. Reymond was among the first to obtain a passport to the newly independent India. Her journey to India included a stop in the United States and, crossing the Pacific, to an exploration of China, leading to a contact with practitioners of tai chi, movements rooted in the ancient traditions of that country. She arrived in India at the end of 1947, in the midst of upheavals caused by the partitioning of India. This return to the source, to reunions with the great masters, took her to Madras, to Pondicherry and to Tiruvanamalai, where she had an emotional reunion with Ramana Maharshi, who had not forgotten her. She arrived at the ashram of Swami Ramdas on the coast of Malabar on the day of Gandhi's assassination, January 30, 1948. Swami Ramdas followed the way of a *sadhu*, completely outside of life, and simultaneously, the life of a patriarch, with a large community around him whose activities he organized in all aspects, making himself available to all its members. "He welcomed me as a member of his family. But what is extraordinary is his feeling of time that has not moved, the consciousness of a wink of eternity corresponding to nine years of life in the West and the war and the chaos that has severed so many ties." ("Chez Swami Ramdas." *The Blue Lotus*, 54th year, No. 6, August-September 1949).

After more than a year and a half of intense life in Calcutta, Lizelle Reymond went for a seven-month retreat at the foot of the Himalayas, near the village of Durmachala. This time of retreat and study was almost completed when she first made contact with a member of a Brahmin family from Almora. This meeting unexpectedly opened the possibility for her to pass a very crucial threshold in her understanding of the deep traditional life of India. What was proposed was extraordinary to spend some months as the guest of a family, sharing from within the heart of what could be called the *yoga* of family. Three months elapsed before this family's door opened to her, allowing a Westerner, for the first time, to live an experience that was one of India's best-guarded secrets. This profound experience, described in the exceptional book, *My Life with a Brahmin Family* (New York: Penguin Books, 1972), led to a growing feeling of being out of place, touching both thoughts and sensations, and her very way of being.

At the heart of this intense spiritual current, shaped and carried by the support of the rigorous customs of the Brahmin family, the call she felt earlier was intensified. After years of translating scholarly texts and teaching regarding various modes of search and many visits to different ashrams, a question put to her suddenly by a disciple who deeply lived his search struck her like the reverberations of a great bell: "How long are you going to go on arranging books on library shelves?" Lizelle Reymond spoke of this moment: "Under the effect of this shock, I asked myself the question: Do I have the inner stability to face the demands of my life? Do I know my place in life? What is it I know?" The living search took a definite form—in the most intimate sense of the question, "Who am I?" the day a sadhu known to the family joined them to stay for a while. He had the reputation of someone who had the simplicity of a child yet also the wisdom of a savant, translating the Vedas. His name was Sŕi Anirvân.

In the words of Lizelle Reymond, "When I saw Sŕi Anirvân for the first time, I had the impression of having touched my aim—of being in the presence of a master who would be willing to enter into the dynamics of my life and show me, step by step, how to place my feet on the rocky path." Without hesitation, the master's offer for a stay in his hermitage was accepted.

"For four days, I walked through the forest with a group of travelers in order to reach the village where, in solitude, he was writing commentaries on the Vedas. Face to face, seated on the ground, gazing into one another's eyes, we remained for over an hour without saying anything. It was a terrible test during which my whole past life was liquefied, and to the question, 'How much time do you have to work with me?', I heard myself answer, 'As long as you consider it necessary.'" "I had found the master who would take me by the hand and who, one day, would send me back to my country, the master who would negate everything that rose up in me. Six months later, after organizing my life around this aim. I joined him in his distant village in the Himalayas. The apparent indifference with which he always treated me, combined with a great solicitude, was part of the strategy of Samkhya to create an indestructible trust between us, outside of all personal relationship."

This trust was the basis of a sustained relationship lasting until Sŕi Anirvân's death in 1978. (He was born in 1896). The principal framework for this relationship was the life of a hermitage at the foot of the

Himalayas. At the beginning of 1951, Mme. Reymond was given the task of acquiring and caring for a house that could contain the life that the master initiated with a handful of disciples from different religious traditions. Life in the presence of this great master of Samkhya was characterized by the most intense questioning and the most complete mutual freedom. When she asked, "When are you going to send me away from here?" the answer was, "When you have found your place in life, you will have nothing more to do here." But one day, Sŕi Anirvân became convinced that the precise state of knowledge to which he had wanted to bring her had been attained: "Now you must return to the world and accomplish your task. This activity is your yoga. A young tiger does not stay in the forest in the shadow of one who is stronger; he needs his own territory ..." A little later, having read P. D. Ouspensky's book, *The Psychology of Man's Possible Evolution*, in one sitting (it had just become available), Sŕi Anirvân told her: "Read it very carefully. It contains the ideas that are dear to us and which have nourished you these last few years. Look for the people who are working in this direction ... this will be your task as soon as you arrive. ..." Some weeks later, toward the end of 1952, she left Haimavati, stopping first in Pondicherry. She reached Europe in August of 1953. Her companion on the trip was the writings of G. I. Gurdjieff.

Lizelle Reymond met pupils of Gurdjieff and worked with Mme. Jeanne de Salzmann as soon as she arrived in Europe. Until Mme. De Salzmann's death in 1990, Lizelle Reymond remained in close contact with her. In 1956 she was entrusted with the creation of a group in Geneva, which she led with Dr. Michel de Salzmann until the end of her life.

Simultaneously, she continued her work of deepening the heritage brought from India, writing books which testified to her experience. *My Life with a Brahmin Family* was first published in 1957 and was very successful. It was translated into German and English the following year. Her relationship with Sŕi Anirvân continued through a very rich and abundant correspondence and regular visits, in particular to Calcutta, where Sŕi Anirvân lived the last years of his life. This relationship allowed the rereading of manuscripts of works in preparation and the continuation of advice and encouragement.

Between 1958 and 1964 she organized many trips to India and China. Her interest in disciplines of the body was evident throughout her life. She had already come into contact with the practice of tai chi in 1947 in a convent for Chinese women. In the 1960s tai chi practice became a new stage of her search. She regularly attended the classes of Sophie Delza in New York, and in 1964 she offered the first classes in tai chi in Geneva and Lausanne. A similar class opened in the same year in Paris. In 1968 she met Master Dee Chao, a student of the remarkable Chen Man Ching. This was the starting point for an intense and deepening work which transformed her understanding and teaching of tai chi. In 1972 near Geneva she organized the first seminars in tai chi, which quickly attracted many Swiss, French and Belgian students. Between 1977 and 1989 master Dee Chao drew additional interest with his visits to the seminars. Lizelle Reymond devoted more than twenty years to the teaching of tai chi. Even after reaching the age of 80, she continued to explore different currents of this discipline and visit various instructors. When she could no longer continue teachine herself, she relied on dedicated students who had become capable of transmitting the meaning of this search in a vital way.

Lizelle Reymond died in 1994 at her home in Geneva.

What remains of her life and search is a heritage beyond measure: the continuing work of those men and women whom she helped to guide along "the way of life."

Glossary

The following glossary of Sanskrit words is drawn from Śri Anirvân's collection of essays, *Buddhiyoga of the Gita and Other Essays* (New Delhi, 1983). It therefore contains not only terms found in the present text, but also many other Sanskrit words that have an important place in the whole body of the Indian spiritual tradition.

a-bhaya: Fearlessness. √bhī—to fear.

abhi-kl̥pti: Comprehensive realization, √kiṛp—to make, frame.

abhi-māna: Blind will to be, erroneous conception regarding one's self, √man—to think, imagine.

adhi-ni-veśa: Soul's inertia, its fervent clinging to the status quo, instinctive avoidance of death, the worst form of delusion, √viś—to penetrate, pervade, be absorbed into, ni—deeply.

abhyāsa: Repetition, constant practice.

abhyudaya: Uplift, prosperity, aya (√i) going, ud—up.

ācārya: Teacher, guru, spritual guide, teaching ācāra or rules.

a-devāh: Men who denied the gods.

adhi-bhūtam: Phenomenal Reality as manifested in phenomenal existences.

adhi-daivatam: Reality as abiding in spirit.

adhikāra: Competence.

adhi-yajña: Relating to sacrifice.

a-dhvara gati: Straight movement. √dhvṛ—to bend, to move in a zigzag way.

adhyātma: Reality as intuited in the self, spiritual.

aditi: Virgin-Mother of gods and men. Indivisible Infinity. √di—to cut, divide.

āditya: Sun.

adṛṣṭa: Occult.

agni: The mystic Fire, the immortal principle in mortals, leading him (√ni—to lead) forward (agra).

aham-kārito bhāvaḥ: Egoistic existence. aham—I √bhū—to be.

a-hiṃsā: Non-violence. √hiṃs—to harm, injure, kill.

aiśvarya: Mastery of super-normal power. √iś,—to be master of.

aitihya: Tradition.

a-jara: Unaging. √jṛ—to wear out, grow old.

a-karma: Inaction, quiescence.

ā-kāśa: Luminous void, space. √kās—to shine, ā—pervasion, extension

akliṣṭa smṛti: Unfettered memory.

a-kṣara: The Immutable. √kṣar—to flow, wave, perish.

a-laukika: Occult.

alpa-buddhi: A person of scanty intelligence.

a-mati: Self-ruining poverty of the spirit (* This is the meaning, when the word is accented on the first syllable. When on the second, it means splendour.)

āmaya: Disease, ills.

a-mṛta: Immortality.

āmṛta-tva: Immortality.

ānanda: Bliss, quiescent joy.

an-antam: Infinity. anta—end.

anārya: Not of the Ārya.

an-āvṛtti: Freedom from repetition (re-birth).

andha-tāmisra: Blinding darkness (of ignorance).

a-ni-bādha: Unboundedness.

anna: Matter, food.

annāda: The Spirit, eater of food.

an-ṛta: Perversion of ṛta, chaos, discord.

antar-āvṛtta-tā: Cult of introversion.

aṇu: Atom, atomic.

anu-bhava: Awareness, experience. √bhū—to become, anu—along.

anu-mantā: Permitter, one who sanctions.

anu-vidhāna: A mechanical assent.

ānv-īkṣikī: Rational thinking, metaphysics. anu-√īkṣ—to see, think.

anyad antaram: The inner other.

aparā-prakṛti: The lower nature. Creative evolutionary nature of the Lord.

a-pauruṣeya-tva: Non-human (non-personal) origination, puruṣa—person.

apa-varga: renunciation leading to final beatitude. √vṛj—turn, apa—away.

āpta: Authoritative person.

ārambha-vāda: The principle of the origination of things.

artha-nitya: Eternal in spirit (meaning).

artha-vāda: Explanation of the meaning of any precept, eulogium.

ārya: Noble, cultured. √ṛ—to go.

ārya-satya: (Four) noble truths of Buddhism.

asad-graha: Obduracy of the spirit.

āsana: Disciplined posture, as in Yoga.

aśanāyā: Impulses of self-fulfilment, vital humger. √aś—to eat.

asaṇga-tva: Non-attachment.

a-sat: Non-existence, the Zero.

ashrama: One of the four stages of a brahmin's life; a guru's household

a-sta: Home.

āstika: One who believes in the existence of God and another world, etc. asti—there is or exists.

āstikya-buddhi: The buddhi of an āstika, the intuition of the existence beyond.

asura: Demon, demoniac force, opposed to deva.

āsura: Dark, demoniac hostile.

asurāh: Men of āsuriac, temperament.

āsu-tṛpaḥ: Men whose only delight (√tṛp) is in the good things of life (asu).

aśva: Horse, symbol of spiritual vigor.

aśvattha: Mystic tree with roots above and branches below representing the universe. Commonly the holy fig tree.

aśvin: Vedic twin-gods.

ati-ṣṭhā: Transcendence, existence (√sthā) beyond (ati).

ati-tiṣṭhati: Transcends.

ātman: Self. An integral dynamic whole of body-life-spirit. √at—to go.

ātmano mokṣo jagad-dhitañ ca: Self-liberation and philanthropy.

ātma-śuddhi: Self-purification.

ātma-tuṣṭi: Self-delight.

Aum (also Oṃ): The sacred syllable, the supreme mantra, the seed and source of all wisdom.

avara: Lower.

avatāra: Incarnation.

āveśa: Possession by the divine. √viś—to enter.

a-vibhakta: Un-divided.

a-vidyā: Ignorance.

a-vyakta: The unmanifest, a synonym for Prakṛti.

a-vyaya: Inexhaustible.

ayam: This (creation), manifest existence.

bahu-dhā: As many.

bala: Force.

bandha: Bondage.

bhāgavata: Follower of Viṣṇu (bhagavān)-cult.

bhakta: devotion; participant in bhakti.

bhakti: "devout sharing"; devotional worship

bhartā: Supporter. √bhṛ—to support.

bhāva: Spiritual entities, an original idea, conceptual existence, the becoming, nascent potentialities.

bhāva-loka: Plane of conceptual existence.

bhāvanā: The subtle potency of an ideational creativity.

bhoga: Enjoyment. bhuj—√to enjoy.

bhogaiśvarya: Power and enjoyment.

bhoktā maheśvara: The Supreme (mahā) Lord (iśvara) in us who enjoys.

bhūmi: Level of consciousness.

bhūta: The final phase of becoming, physical being, conscious being, tangible actualities. √bhu—to be, become.

bhūtāmā: Subtle body, individual soul, soul of all beings.

bhūta-śhakti: Material forces.

bhuvana: The world, the dynamization of existence as phenomenal appearances.

bīja: Seed-form.

bodhi: Perfect knowledge or wisdom, illumined intellect (in Buddhism and Jainism).

brahma: Expanding consciousness of the Vast, the all-pervading matrix of creation, the pure Existence-Consciousness-Bliss, the power of knowledge, the transcendent, etc. √bṛh—to expand.

brahma-karma-samādhi: A complete harmony between brahma-consciousness and its spontaneous energism.

brahma-granthi: The knot of Brahmā, *i.e.* creative material energy.

brahma-mīmāṁsā: Authoritative dissertation on spiritual knowledge.

brahmaṇas-pati: Vedic god, Lord of Vāk (Word).

brahma-vāda: The philosophy postulating brahman as the highest and all-pervading entity.

brahma-vana: Cosmos conceived as a forest.

brahma-vṛkṣa: Cosmos conceived as a tree.

brāhmī tanu: Body (tanu) fit to realize the brahma-consciousness.

brahmodya: Dissertations about brahma.

bṛhas-pati: Vedic god, lord of the Vast Word.

bṛhat: Ever-expanding Vast. √bṛh—to expand.

bṛhatī: Rhythm of bṛhat.

bṛhat jyotiḥ: Ever-expanding vastness of Light.

buddha: The enlightened one.

buddhau śaraṇam anv-iccha: Seek your refuge in buddhi.

buddhi: Intelligence, (spiritual) awakening or illumination. √budh—to kindle, to wake up, be awake, arise, know, a perception of the luminous core of being, *universalised* and illumined consciousness.

buddhi-grāhya: Seizable (√grah—to seize) by buddhi.

buddhi-guhā: the innermost hidden depths (√guh—to hide) of buddhi.

buddhi-mat: The kindler—an adjective of Agni.

buddhi-yoga: Communion with the Supreme through buddhi. √yuj—to join.

budhna: Bottom, depth, illumination, illumination of the depth.

cakra: Cycle, wheel.

cetas: Vision, consciousness. √cit—to perceive.

chandas: Rhythm.

chela: disciple of a guru.

cid āyave: (kati-dhā) At the root of life (āyu).

cit: Consciousness.

citti: Planes of perception.

cyuti: (theory of) Flux. √cyu—to move, fall, perish.

daiva: Divine.

daivam cakṣuh: The Divine Eye.

daivī sampad: Divine aptitude and achievement.

daivyā vratāṁ: Selective (√vṛ—to choose) divine laws.

dama: Self-control. √dam—to control.

daṇda: Politics.

darsána (darśan): seeing; vision of God or His representative.

daśāvarā pariṣad: Council of at least (avara) ten (daśa) members.

dehāntara-prāpti: Assumption of new bodies, re-incarnation.

deva (pl. devāh): Gods, luminous ones. √div—to shine.

deva-nid (pl. nidaḥ): Deniers of gods. √nind—to censure.

deva-śhakti: Spiritual force.

devatāti: Expansion (√tan—to spread) into god-consciousness. See sarva-tāti.

deva-vāda: Theory of God and gods.

deva-yu: Person yearning for deva.

dharma: Law, the fundamental law of being, eternal laws, law upholding life. √dhṛ—to hold, preserve, maintain.

dharma-dhātu: The basic element of creation.

dharma-mīmāṃsā: Dissertation on dharma (duty, law, sacrifice), name of Jaimini's pūrva-mīmāṃsā.

dharmāviruddhaḥ kāmaḥ: Desire in conformity with dharma.

dharmya saṃgrama: Fight for the cause of dharma, righteous battle.

dhātu-prasāda: Transparency of the substratum, purity of the basic elements (dhātu) of body-mind.

dhī: Spiritual knowledge and spiritual action.

dhīra: Steadfast, equipoised, balanced, highest type of aspirant who has ascended the plane of āditya-consciousness.

dhīti: Activity, flames of the mystic Fire.

dhṛti: The energy of tenacity. √dhṛ—to hold.

dhruvā smṛti: Timeless memory.

dhyāna: Meditation. √dhyai—to meditate, one of the constituents of Patañjali's saṃyama, belongs to the fourth level of consciousness known as ekāgra-bhūmi.

dhyāna-citta: (ninefold) States of consciousness in meditation.

dīdhiti: Flames and rays of illumination.

dīkṣā: Initiation in spiritual life. √dah—to burn.

div: The luminous expanse. √div—to shine.

divya: Divine.

divya-bhāva: Divine state.

divya karma: Divine action.

divyaṃ cakṣuḥ: The divine eye, spiritualized vision.

dravya-yajña: Sacrifice by offering material things, realization through rituals.

dṛṣṭa: Visible, sensible. √dṛś—to see.

duḥkha: Sorrow, misery.

dvandva: Dualities. (of pleasure and pain etc). dvi—two.

dveṣa: Aversion. √dviṣ—to hate.

dyu-sthāna: Plane of unitary Āditya-consciousness.

ehi-paśyika: One who comes and sees for oneself. ehi-come, paśya—see.

ekāgra-bhūmi: Fourth of the five levels of consciousness, viz. mūdha (ignorant), kṣipta (restless), vikṣipta (distracted), ekāgra (concentrated) and niruddha (restricted, absorbed).

ekāgra-tā: One-pointed-ness, concentration.

ekaṃ sat: The One Existence.

ekaṃ tat: That One, the Ineffable.

etāvad iti niścaya: Determined refusal to look beyond etāvad—thus far and no farther.

gāyatrī: A particular Vedic meter, the mantra Ṛv. III. 62.10 in that metre. See sāvitrī.

ghora karma: Workings of the grim forces of Nature.

gopi: cowherd woman; village girl, devotee of Krishna.

gotra: lineage through the male line.

guṇa: Threefold qualities of individual and cosmic nature, viz., sattva, rajas and tamas.

guru: Spiritual guide, teacher. √gur—to raise, lift up.

hetu: Cause, motive. √hi—to impel.

hetuka: Logician.

hetu śāstra: The science of dialectics.

hṛd: Heart, the luminous seat of mystic realization.

hṛdā manīṣā manasā: By heart, by intellect and emotion, by mind.

hṛdat aṣṭa: Fashioned by the heart. √takṣ—to chisel, fashion.

hṛdayyā ākūti: Yearning of the heart.

icchā: Desire.

idam jagat: This moving-world, manifest universe, √gam—to go.

idam sarvam: All this, the whole gamut of existence.

indriya: Sense-organ.

Iśāno bhūta-bhavyasya: Lord of what has been and what shall be.

Iśvara: Lord, God.

Iśvara-bhāva: Lordliness.

itihāsa-purāṇa: History, amplifying and illustrating eternal truths.

jalpa: Polemics, maze of speculation. √jalp—to prattle.

jalpi: Same as jalpa.

janma-bandha: Bondage of re-birth.

jarā: Decay, the process of aging. See ajara.

jarā-bodha: Application of Agni, who kindles (√budh) our waning energies.

jāti: Race.

jāti-dharma: Racial instinct, custom, tradition.

jijñāsā: Spirit of enquiry. √jñā—to know.

jīva: Individual soul.

jīvan-mukta: Liberated in life.

jīvan-mukti: Liberation in life.

jīva-prakṛti: Individual nature.

jīva-śhakti: energy of conscient individuation (jīva).

jñāna: Knowledge, faculty of subtle discrimation, sense-perception. √jñā—to know.

jñāna-ātmā: The individual knowledge-self.

jñāna-bhūmikā: (sevenfold) Levels of knowledge.

jñāna-kāṇḍa: The section of the Veda dealing with knowledge, i.e. upanishads.

jñānamayaṃ tapaḥ: Askesis through knowledge.

jñāna-yāña: Sacrifice and realization through knowledge.

jugupsā: Aversion, re-coiling-shrinking. √gup—to hide.

kaivalya: Perfect isolation (kevala-alone), beatitude.

kāla: Time-spirit, Death.

kāma: Desire.

kāmātmā: Desire-soul.

kāmāvacara: (sixfold) Spheres or worlds of desire (in Buddhism) also called devaloka.

kāmāyanī: Daughter of Desire (Primal Creative Urge), adjective of śraddhā.

karma: Action, cosmic energy, spiritual activity, the store of vital energy with which one starts in life. √kṛ—to do, act.

karma-bandha: The chain of unillumined actions.

karma-kāṇḍa: The section of the Veda dealing with rituals.

karma-mīmāṃsā: Dissertation on rituals, same as dharma-mīmāmsā.

karma-sampatti: Effective realization of an end.

karṣaṇa: Senseless repression. √kṛṣ-to torture.

kauśalam: Art, skill.

kavi-kratu: Seer-Will, epithet of Agni.

kāvya: Poetry, the yearning of a poetic soul. √kū—to cry out.

kleśa-vṛtti: Constricted functioning of consciousness.

kliṣṭa-smṛti: Fettered memory, an experience in time. See akliṣṭa-smṛti.

krama-mukti: Liberation by stages.

kratu: Creative will. √kṛ—to act.

krīyā: Action, spiritual activity. √kṛ—to act.

krodha: Anger.

kṣatra: Spiritual vigor, the urge to conquer new realms by self-exertion.

ksamā: Forbearance. √kṣam—to endure.

kṣānti: Same as kṣamā.

kṣātriya: A man of the warrior-caste.

kṣepa: Projection. √kṣip—to throw.

kṣetra: Field of experience.

kula: Family, caste, tribe, etc.

kula-dharma: Family-customs, primeval tribal instrinct.

līlā: The state of desireless ease and play.

linga-śarīra: Subtle body.

loka: Levels of consciousness, planes of Reality, worlds. √luc—to shine.

loka-saṃgraha: Social service, social well-being.

madhurā rati: Love between the lover and the beloved, the fifth and the highest kind of love towards the divine, the other four being śānta, dāsya, sakhya, and vātsalya.

madhv-ada: Enjoyer (√ad—to eat) of bliss (madhu—honey), getting joy in all experiences of life. See pippalāda.

mahā-karuṇā: Great Compassion.

mahān ātmā: The Great Self.

mahas: The Great Illumination. √mah connotes greatness, strength and light.

mahat: The Great Shining Principle reflecting the luminosity of the transcendental consiousness, universalization, the first evolute of Prakṛti.

mahat brahma: The matrix of the karmic energy, the cretive aspect of brahma.

mānādhīnā meya-śuddhiḥ: Clear conception (śuddi) of the object-to-be-known (meya) depends (adhīna) on the purification (śuddi) of the means of knowledge (māna).

manana: Thinking, reflection, meditation. √man—to think.

manaś: Mind.

maniṣā: Higher intelligence, synonymous with buddhi, connotes both the intellective and emotive aspects of spiritual experience, mental upsurge. √man—to think, √īs—to go, or √iṣ—to pour out, stream out, etc.

mano-maya koṣa: Mental level (sheath) of consciousness.

mano vyākaraṇātmakam: Analytic and discursive function of mind. vi-ā-√ kṛ—to analyze.

mantra: A product of spiritual mentation. √man—to think, spontaneous revelation. √man + trai—to save > that which liberates.

mantra-maheśvara: The great lord of the mantras.

mantreśvara: The lord of the mantras.

mānuṣa: (The fire) of mental illumination, one who has that, i.e. , man.

manv-antara: Universal thought-cycles, the period of transition (antara) between two Manus.

mā śucaḥ: Do not grieve. √śuc—to grieve.

mātrā-sparśa: Sense-object contact.

māyā: Divine Wisdom and creative power.

medhā: Force of penetration, intelligence.

mimāmsā: Dissertations, an intensive exercise of the mind. √man—to think, reflect, a logical development of the ancient 'oha'.

moha: Delusion.

mokṣa-bhīti: Fear of liberation.

mokṣa-dharma: The way of liberation.

mokṣa-sāstra: Scriptures on liberation.

mṛtyu: Death.

mūrti: idol; material form of God.

nāda: Thrill of joy. √nad—to vibrate + √nand—to be pleased, delighted.

nair-yoga-kṣema: Living above the hankering after having (yoga) and keeping (kṣema).

nāma-yajña: A sacrifice only in name.

nānyad astitvādaḥ: Determined refusal to look beyond, the stand (vādaḥ) that (iti) there is nothing else (na anyad asti).

nara: Man, hero, fighter, following the path of Reason ('oha').

narottama: Supreme Man.

na sat nāsat: Neither existence (sat), nor non-existence (a-sat).

nāstika: Non-believer. See āstika.

nidaḥ: (pl. of nid) Detractors. See deva-nid.

ni-didhyāsana: Profound (ni) and repeated meditation. √dhyai—to meditate.

nidra: Sleep, drowsiness of the spirit.

nidrā samādhi-sthitiḥ: Sleep as a poise of samādhi.

niḥ-śreyas: Most excellent, highest good, final beatitude, or knowledge that brings it.

ni-meṣa: Lit. closing of the eye-lid, dissolution of the world, absorption of śhakti in śiva (self).

niṇyā vacāṃāsi: Words rising from the depths. niṇya—interior, hidden, mysterious.

nir-lepa: Non-attachment. √lip—to smear, pollute.

nirodha-samskāra: Habitual ingathering of forces leading to nirodha.

nirodha-yoga: Yoga of self-control. √rudh—to restrain.

nir-ṛti: Opposite of ṛta, disorder, chaos.

nir-vāṇa: Blowing out, cessation, extinction, Void.

nitya-sattva: Immutable essentiality, also known as śuddha-sattva.

nitya-tva: Eternality.

ni-vid: Ancient formularies containing epithets or short invocations of gods, knowledge (√vid—to know) of the depth (ni), called 'embryo of śāstras,' by Aitareya Brāhmaṇa.

ni-vṛtti: Withdrawal, introvert movement, ingathering of forces.

nyag-rodha: Banyan tree. √ruh—to grow, nyak—downwards.

oha: Reason, the path of reason, later known as tarka. √ūh—to infer, reason.

oha-brāhmaṇāḥ: Men who have attained brahma-consciousness through oha.

parā gatiḥ: Supreme movement.

paraḥ puruṣaḥ: The Supreme Person.

paraḥ sanātano bhāvaḥ: Transcendent eternal existence (light).

paramā gati: The highest state.

parā prakṛti: Supreme Nature, the matrix of pure individuality.

pārārthya: Purposiveness, having an ultimate (para) purpose (artha).

para vairāgya: Supreme detachment.

parā vāk: The Supreme Word.

parjanya: Vedic god, the shower of determinate cosmic powers.

paśu: Animal, the unregenerate vital impulses in man, the empirical individual bound by avidyā (spiritual nescience).

paśyan muniḥ: Silent seer.

phala: Fruit, definite result.

pippala: Berry of the sacred fig tree symbolizing sensual pleasure.

pippalāda: One who eats (√ad—to eat) pippala, i.e., transmutes the variety of experiences into the stuff of the spirit, radiant ego. See madhvada.

pitā-putrīyaṃ saṃpradānam: Transmission (of power and knowledge) from father to son.

pra-budh: Awakening.

pra-jā: Progeny, dynamic march of life.

prajñā: Spiritual knowledge, wisdom, final illumination.

prajanaḥ kandarpaḥ: Procreative urge.

prajñā-vāda: Sophistications of reason, travesty of wisdom.

pra-kṛti: Nature, Divine Matrix, the Creative Principle, counterpart of Puruṣa, Puruṣa's dynamism of will in time.

prakṛti-sambhavāḥ guṇāḥ: Wavering modes of phenomenal existence.

pra-laya: Dissolution.

pramātṛ-pada: Levels of consciousness.

prāṇa: The Primary Vital Energy, Life √an—to breathe.

prānāyāma: to "stretch the breath out"; disciplined breathing.

pra-sāda: Transparency. See dhātu-prasāda.

prati-bodha: Awakened perception.

Prathamaḥ spandaḥ: First thrill (of creation). √spand—to vibrate.

prathamāni dharmāṇi: Primal spiritual laws.

prati-ṣṭhā: Basis.

pratyabhijñā: Recognition.

pratyāhāra: Withdrawal of senses from objects.

pra-vṛtti: Extrovert movement.

preti-īṣaṇi: Adjective of Agni (mystic fire) who impels onwards, √iṣ—to impel.

prīti: Satisfaction of the heart.

priyaḥ priyāyāḥ: As the lover (bears) with the beloved.

pūjā: worship.

puruṣa: Person, the principle of witness-consciousness (sākṣicaitanya), a universal form of being gathering in itself the past and the future, the timeless, the immobile, the seer and yet an ingathered totality, the conscious Being.

puruṣārtha: Aim of human life.

puruṣa-viśeṣa: The Universal Puruṣa.

pūrva-pakṣa: Challenge, objection.

rāga: Attachment. √rañj—to be affected, excited, delighted.

rahasyam: Esoteric meaning.

rajas: Principle of motion, activity and disharmony—one of the three constituents of prakṛti, the other two being sattva and tamas.

rājasa: Type in which rajas predominates.

rājasika: Same as rājasa, vital (nature).

rājs-dharma: Duties of a kṣatriya, of a king.

rasa: Flavor, the first part of anything, emotional content.

raso'pyasya paraṃ dṛṣṭvā nivartate: Even (apī) the relish (rasa) turns away (nivartate) from one (asya), after one has seen (dṛṣṭvā) the supreme (param).

rathī: The self or the divinity within who is the traveller in the chariot (ratha) of the body.

ṛju-nīti: Straight movement, same as adhvara-gati.

ṛṣi: The indefatigable traveller (√ṛṣ—to go) who pierces (√ṣṛ—to pierce) into the Mystery and sees (√ṛṣ—to see) the Truth, Seer.

ṛta: The universal moral order, cosmic harmony, rhythm, dynamic unfolding of Truth in rhythmic Time-order, predestined cause of becoming. √ṛ—to go.

ṛta-yu: One yearning for ṛta.

ṛtu: Season, life's seasons, the rhythm unfolding itself through life's seasons.

rūpa: shape, form.

sadā-śiva: Ever-benign Divinity.

sad-bhāva: A real idea.

sādhanā: Spiritual practice.

sādhu: holy person; saint; a monk or ascetic.

sahaja: Integral simple (perception), innate essential nature.

sahajasamādhi: Natural samādhi, pure divine consciousness in which mental consciousness ceases.

sam-ā-dhi: Concentration, both comprehensive and exclusive. √dhā—to fix, ecstasy.

sam-ā-nayana: Bringing together, assimilation.

sam-anvaya: Harmonization, synthesis.

sāma rasya: Mutual absorption, unison of Śiva and Śhakti, identical state in which all differentiation has disappeared, <sama—equal, rasa—delight.

śama-tva: Equanimity, self-poise.

sam-bodhi: Same as bodhi.

Samkhya: a school of dualist philosophy; metaphysical calculation.

sam-moha: Ignorance, illusion of mind.

sam-oha: Reason. See Oha.

sam-pra-dāya: School, tradition created by transmission of knowledge from one teacher to another, giving (√dā—to give) completely without reserve (sam-pra).

sam-pra-sāda: Light of the clear void.

sam-sārī: A moving entity. √sṛ—to move, saṃsāra—world-process.

saṃskāra: Tendency, impression from a former state of existence.

saṃ-vega: Urge.

samyak dṛṣṭi: Right vision, integral view of life.

saṃ-yama: Self-control; dhāraṇā, dhyāna and samādhi combined. √ yam—to control.

sanga: Emotive association.

sānkhya-buddhi: Path of introspective analysis.

sānkhya-yoga: Way of realization through Sāṇkhya.

saras-vān: Vedic god, consort of Sarasvatī.

sarasvatī: Vedic goddess, stream of divine consciousness, name of river.

sārathi: Charioteer, symbolizing buddhi. See rathī.

sarga-pratisarga: Creation and dissolution.

śarīra: Body, fluxional embodiment of the psychic entity. √śṛ—to disintegrate.

sarvāṇi bhūtāni: All beings, totality of the Spirit's Self-becoming.

sarva-tāti: Expansion into all-consciouness. See deva-tāti.

sarvātma-bhāva: The experience of all (sarva) becoming the self (ātmā).

śāstra: (revealed) Scripture.

śastra: Laudatory hymn. √śaṃs—to praise.

śāśvata: Eternal.

sat: Pure existence.

sat-pati: Lord of Existence.

satta-śuddhi: Purification (√śudh—to purify) of the essence, one of the daivī sampad-s.

ṣaṭ-tarka: Six rationalist schools.

sattva: Essence, consummation of mystic experience, psychic entity forming the core of personality, light and harmony—a constituent of Prakṛti.

sattvāpatti: Fourth jñāna-bhūmikā, first level of Brahma-realization. Āpatti—attainment. √pad—to go, stand fast as fixed.

sattva-prakāśa: Same as nitya-sattva, prakāśa—manisfestation, light. √kāś—to shine.

sattva-suṃśuddhi: (Same as satta-śuddhi) Purification (√śudh—to purify) of the essence, one of the daivī sampad-s.

sāttvika: Type in which sattva predominates.

satya: Truth, truth as Existence.

Savita: Vedic god, the luminous (deva) Impeller (√su—to impel), the Sun of divine impulsion.

Sāvitrī: The famous verse to Savitā, Rv. III. 62.10. See gāyatrī.

savya-sācī: Name of Arjuna, one who can wield weapons with the left (savya) hand too.

śayuḥ kati-dhā: (the spark of Fire) Lying (√śī—to lie down) in so many ways.

sāyujya: Spiritual communion. √ynj—to join.

śhakti: Potency, power of Śiva to manifest, maintain and withdraw.

śhakti-pāta: Descent of power from above.

śhakti-sañcāra: Transmission of power.

siddha: a perfected being who has achieved release.

siddhi: Attainment, realization, success.

siddhyasiddhi: Siddhi and a-siddhi, success and failure.

śītoṣṇa: Sīta and uṣṇa, cold and heat.

Śiva-Śhakti: Śiva and Śhakti, Absolute and his power, the Primal Androgyne.

Smṛti: Memory, reminiscence, the whole body of sacred tradition as 'remembered'. (√smr—to remember) by human teachers, in contradistinction to 'śruti'—revelation.

ṣoḍaśa-kala-puruṣa: Perfect Person, puruṣa of sixteen phases (kalā).

śoka: Grief. √suc—to burn.

soma: Juice of a plant (soma-latā) symbolizing Bliss, Vedic god.

spanda: Vibration, creative pulsation. √spand—to vibrate.

spḥoṭa: Bursting, expansion, Self-manifestation. √sphuṭ—to burst, blossom, blow.

śrad: Heart, the shining core within the individual which contains the luminous Void. See hṛd.

śrad-dhā: Faith, intuition of the Beyond.

śraddhā-tapas: Faith and austerity.

śrī: Fundamental harmony.

śruti: Revelation, 'Heard' (revealed) Word. √śru—to hear.

sthira-buddhi: Firmly established in buddhi, equipoised, stable-minded.

sthita-d'hi: Same as above.

sthita-prajña: Same as above.

stuti: Eulogy, prayer, an ecstatic attunement with the Superconscious.

śubhāśubha: good (śubha) and evil (a-śubha).

śuddha-sattva: Pure essentiality, also known as nitya-sattva.

sukha: Pleasure, happiness.

sukha-duḥkha: Pleasure and pain.

śukla-pakṣa: Bright half of a lunar month.

sūkta: Vedic hymn, spontaneous, superb (su) uttering (ukta).

sūkṛta-duṣkṛta: Good and bad actions, right and wrong.

śunam: The Zero.

su-ṣuptī: Sound (su), i.e., dreamless sleep. √svap—to sleep.

sūtra: Thread, a (shining) strand (of inner truth), aphorism.

Śva: The Benign Divinity, the Absolute, Transcendent Divine principle.

sva-bhāva: Individual nature, inherent nature.

sva-dhā: Self-position, self-poise, self-laws, an exclamation used in making oblations for the ancestors.

svadharma: one's own dharma; one's proper path.

svāhā: An exclamation used in making oblations to the gods, well (su)—said (āha).

sva prakṛti: (Supreme's) own nature.

svar: Light-Word, Realm of Light.

svar-jyotiḥ: The Light Beyond, Light of Svar.

svarūpa-śūnyatā: Status of the Void, experience of one's own self (svarūpa) as Void (śunyatā).

svarūpāvasthānam: Status of self-hood.

svātantrya: Freedom, self (sva)-dependence (tantra—depending on).

tama āsīt tamasā guḍham: Darkness (tamaḥ) was (āsīt) covered (guḍham) by darkness (tamasā).

tamas: Darkness, principle of inertia and delusion—one of the three constituents (guṇa) of prakṛti.

tāmasa: Type in which tamas predominates, material nature.

tāmasī dhṛti: Tenacity of tamas, blind tenacity.

tāmasika: Same as tāmasa.

tandri: Drowsiness (of the spirit). √tandr—to drowse, be lazy.

tanu-mānasa: Attenuated mind.

tapas: Energizing of consciousness, path of askesis, radiation, penance. √tap—to heat.

tapasyā: Same as tapas.

tarka: Reason, logical system.

tarkī: One who indulges in tarka, logician.

tat: That (Absolute).

taṭa-stha: Standing on a bank (tata) or borderland, indifferent.

tāṭasthya: Status of taṭastha, supreme indifference.

tejas: Fiery energy, ardor, spirit, brightness, sharpness.

titīkṣā: Calm endurance, patience. √tij—to sharpen, bear with firmness.

toka: Offspring > offspring of aspiration, touch (√tvac—to cover > tvac—skin, the sense-organ of touch) of final beatitude.

trayī: The triple sacred science, used for reciting, performing and chanting—the Vedas, embodying the spiritual realization of the seers.

turīyam: The fourth state of consciousness beyond the states of waking, dreaming and deep sleep, and stringing together all the states.

upa-draṣṭā: Witness-consciousness. √dṛś—to see.

upa-krama: Starting, setting forth. √kram—to sleep.

upa-labdhi: Awareness, understanding.

upa-nayana: A social sacrament which admits the child formally to the spiritual heritage of the commnity. √nī—to lead, upa—near, investiture of the sacred thread.

upa-ni-ṣad: Knowledge gained through close communion with the Divine (upa-√sad—to sit near), knowledge that destroys (√sad—to kill) ignorance and liberates (Śankara), Knowledge gained by sitting near the guru, the end-portion of the Veda, also called Vedānta.

upaniṣad-rahasyam: The mysterious and mystical esoteric meaning.

upa-saṃ-hāra: Winding up.

upāya: Means, the individual's self-reliant endeavor.

upekṣā: Indifference.

ūrdhva-srotas: Upstreaming spiritual power.

urvīḥ: Worlds. uru—vast.

uṣar-bhut: Nominative singular of uṣar-budh.

uṣar-budh: One who awakes (budh) with the dawn (uṣas) of spiritual consciousness.

vāc: (vāk in nom. sing.): The creative word, spiritual expression.

vācas-pati: Vedic god, divine consort of vāc. See bṛhas—pati and brahmaṇas-pati.

vairāgya: Dispassionateness, absence (vi) of attachment (rāga).

vai-tṛṣṇya: Desirelessness. tṛṣṇā—desire.

vāk: See vac, rhythm of the vast, eternal urge of self-expression.

varṇānupūrvī: Order of letters in a composition.

vārtā: Economics. < ṛtti—livelihood, profession, business.

varuṇa: Vedic god, representing void. √vṛ—to cover, encompass.

vasa brahmacaryam: Live (√vas—to live) and move about (car—to move about) in the atmosphere of the vast (brahma).

vāsas: Garment, fig. esoteric knowledge.

veda: Highest Knowledge, sacred ancient text of the Āryas. √vid—to know, to attain, to be.

vedārtha: Eternal spiritual truths, meaning of Veda.

veda-vāda: Cult of occultism—a travesty of the original spirit of Veda.

vedena: (instrumental singular of veda) With knowledge.

vena: The (eternal) lover. √ven—to long for, love.

vibhūti: Manifold (vi) self-becoming (bhū-ti), power.

vi-caranti: Move on towards the planes of intensive contemplation (vicāra), third person plural of √car.

vidyā: Knowledge, √vid—to know.

vidyā-sambandha-kṛta-vaṃśa: Line of descent (vaṃśa) brought about (kṛta) by union (sambandha) with knowledge (vidyā), spiritual descent from teacher to disciple.

vijñāna: Knowledge, buddhi, pure dream-state of consciousness, fourth sheath of being after physical, vital and mental, idea-perception.

vijñāna-ghana: Consolidated (ghana) vijñāna-consciousness.

vijñānānatya: Infinite consciousness, second of the formless planes in the Buddhistic system.

vi-karma: Wrong or unlawful action.

vi-mokṣa: Liberation.

vi-nāśa: Annihilation (√naś—to be lost), supreme attainment (√naś—to reach, attain).

vi-naśana: Name of spot where Sarasvatī disappears.

vi-pāka: Ripening, (of past energies) √pac—to ripen.

vipra: Seer-poet, trembling (√vip—to tremble) with emotion.

vi-rocana: Name of an Asura, whose glitter (√ruc—to shine) is false (vi).

vīrya: Vigor, strength, manliness. vīra—(heroic) man.

viṣāda-yoga: Yoga of dejection.

vi-sarga: Multi (vi)-potent creative urge (√sṛj—to create) of the supreme.

viṣaya: Objective field.

viṣaya-dhyāna: Preoccupation with viṣaya.

vi-ṣṛṣṭi: Self-multiplication, the spirit's outpouring of itself. √sṛj—to pour out, create.

vi-veka: Analytic (vi) discrimination (√vic—to separate, discriminate, sift).

vṛtra: Dark forces, veiling (√vṛ—to cover) the Truth, name of an Asura.

vyañjanā-śhakti: The power of suggestivity (of language).

vyathā: Wavering experiences of dualities. √vyath—to waver, tremble, > pain.

vyavasāya: Determination, resolve, vi-ava-√so—to determine, resolve.

vyavasāyātmikā (buddhi): Discriminative and definitive function of reason.

vy-ava-sthita: Pre-determined and habitual.

vyoman: Sky, security of the Vast. oman—protection (√av—to protect).

vy-utthāna: Rising to surface-consciousness (jāgrat) from samādhi. *ut-* √sthā—to rise.

ya evaṃ veda: He who (yaḥ) knows (veda) thus (evam).

yajamāna: Sacrificer (√yaj—to sacrifice), aspirant.

yajña: Sacrifice, individual and cosmic.

yajñārthaṃ karma: Action performed in the spirit of sacrifice.

yajña-tapas: Radiant energy of sacrifice.

Yama: god of the dead.

yoga: Harnessing (√yuj—to yoke) oneself in order to have communion (√yuj—to join) with the Supreme, path or means to spiritual realization.

yoga-buddhi: Cult of practical illumination.

yoga-kṣema: Acquirement and maintenance, > material welfare, prosperity.

yogī: One established in yoga.

yuktaḥ: Same as yogī, one in communion with Integral Reality.

yukta(ḥ) āsīta mat-paraḥ: Should sit in communion with Me—the Supreme Goal.

Other titles by

Lizelle Reymond

My Life with a Brahmin Family

Śhakti: A Spiritual Experience

Sŕi Anirvân

Inner Yoga: Selected Writings of Sŕi Anirvân

Buddhiyoga of the Gita and other Essays